STAFF MANAGEMENT IN LIBRARY AND INFORMATION WORK

Staff Management in Library and Information Work

Third Edition

Peter Jordan

with Noragh Jones

Gower

© Peter Jordan 1995

First edition printed in 1982
Second edition printed in 1987

Published by
Gower Publishing Limited
Gower House
Croft Road
Aldershot
Hampshire GU11 3HR
England

Gower
Old Post Road
Brookfield
Vermont 05036
USA

Reprinted 1996

Peter Jordan and Noragh Jones have asserted their right under the Copyrights, Designs and Patents Act 1988 to be identified as the authors of this work.

British Library Cataloguing-in-Publication Data
Jones, Noragh
  Staff Management in Library and
  Information Work. – 3Rev.ed
  I. Title   II. Jordan, Peter
  023

ISBN 0-566-07581-4

Library of Congress Cataloging-in-Publication Data
Jordan, Peter, 1936–
    Staff management in library and information work / Peter Jordan.–
– 3rd ed.
      p.   cm.
    Rev. ed. of: Staff management in library and information work /
  Noragh Jones, Peter Jordan.
    Includes index.
    ISBN 0-566-07581-4 : $68.95
    1. Library personnel management—Great Britain.   2. Information
  services—Great Britain—Personnel management.   I. Jones, Noragh.
  Staff management in library and information work.   II. Title.
  Z682.2.G7J67   1995
  023'.9—dc20   94-22680
                                                                      CIP

Typeset in 10 point Palatino by Manton Typesetters, 5–7 Eastfield Road, Louth, Lincolnshire and printed in Great Britain by Hartnolls Limited, Bodmin, Cornwall

Contents

Figures

Tables

Preface

Noragh Jones and I have been encouraged over the years by the reception given to the previous two editions. Both of us were aware in the early 1980s of the need for a text which would bring together up-to-date knowledge on the management of staff with practices and developments in library and information work. Working in or close to schools of library and information studies as well as with librarians, we knew how much the work was appreciated. I have lost count of the number of times I have lent my own copies to students. Noragh left library education and librarianship in 1986 and is now a writer and researcher. The third edition has therefore been my responsibility but I do owe a great deal to Noragh with whom I worked very happily on the first two editions. After the second edition we did collaborate on *Case studies in library management* which was published in 1988 and the existence of these published cases has been a major reason for omitting the work assignments appended to each chapter in previous editions. It was also known that the work was used mainly for the text and for reference purposes.

The technological, social, economic and political changes that have taken place in the last seven years have necessitated a complete rewrite of Chapter 1 as staff and the managers of staff are having to adapt to an environment rife with competition, income generation, quality issues and mind-boggling technological developments which were in their infancy a few years ago. The need to motivate staff has become more important during the last few years as staffing levels have deteriorated and demands on staff have increased. Chapter 2 has been updated with recent studies of library staff motivation. The change in title of Chapter 3 from 'Manpower planning' to 'Workforce planning' is symptomatic of the focus of attention during the last decade and recent studies supported by the Library Association and the British Library have now been included as well as the current debate on skills shortages in the 1990s.

A feature of previous editions has been the inclusion of actual documents used by libraries. I have been overwhelmed by the response to my request for examples from librarians and I cannot thank them enough. Chapters 3 and 4 have particularly benefited, with all the examples updated. New examples of staff appraisal systems are used to illustrate the enormous progress which has been made in this aspect of library staff management during the last few years. Chapter 6 has been completely rewritten to take account of these changes. The revision of Chapter 7 includes the changes made by the Library Association for achievement of its qualifications and in its continuing education programme. Chapter 8 was new in the last edition and has now been extended and reorganized to include time management, conflict management and the management of stress.

Thank you to all those libraries and organizations who have allowed documents produced by them to be used:

British Standards Institution, City University, City of Coventry, COPOL, Royal County of Berkshire, Humberside County, Royal Borough of Kensington and Chelsea, The Library Association, Library Association Publishing Ltd, Manchester Metropolitan University, Napier University, City of Newcastle upon Tyne, University of Northumbria, University of Nottingham, Richmond upon Thames, Staffordshire University, and Wandsworth.

I am also very grateful to Dr Helen Dyson and Sheila Ritchie for permission to use material on conflict management in Chapter 8, to Stuart Hannabuss for use of his appraisal analysis form, to Manchester Metropolitan University and KPMG Management Consulting for permission to quote from job evaluation documentation and to Terry Looker, Olga Gregson and Hodder and Stoughton Ltd for allowing me to use questionnaires from *Stresswise*.

My especial thanks to Nora Holt who was perfection on WordPerfect and to my friends and ex-colleagues in Manchester Metropolitan University Library.

Peter Jordan

1

The working environment

Libraries and information units have become increasingly involved in management practices, as pressures from their parent bodies (local authorities, educational institutions, industrial and professional firms) impel them to justify their services in relation to user needs as they adopt more systematic approaches to management. Since most libraries spend more than half their budgets on staff salaries there is growing concern to get the most value from this expensive resource, which means giving careful and well-informed attention to each stage in staff management.

First it is important to analyse and evaluate existing jobs and staffing structures and modify them in relation to changing needs such as automation (see Chapter 4), taking account of the balance between supply and demand for library and information workers (Chapter 3). Second it is vital to have a well thought out recruitment strategy using staff who are skilled in drawing up personnel specifications and following them through, in interviewing and other selection methods (see Chapter 5). Staff appraisal whether formal or informal reveals the success or otherwise of recruitment policies and practices but staff cannot perform well if training and development are neglected. Frequently appraisal reveals further training needs which will help them to increase their expertise and overcome weaknesses in knowledge, skills or attitudes. Staff appraisal schemes are covered in Chapter 6 and training and development in Chapter 7.

All these phases in staff management can only be put into practice successfully by people with a range of communication skills, and an understanding of motivation at work. Chapter 2 considers motivation and job satisfaction. Chapter 8 suggests strategies for developing personal and interpersonal skills, particularly through assertiveness training, analysis of personal management styles, the management of stress, time management and the development of skills which increase effectiveness in group work. It also gives guidance on how to supervise staff, which seems to cause many problems in library and information work, both for young professionals and for more senior people when promotion moves them to a job which may be over 50 per cent working with other people, rather than as isolated professionals. A basic definition, indeed, of management is 'getting things done through people' and the following questions, which are of current concern to library managers, indicate how pervasive staff management is in translating an organization's goals into reality:

1   How can we improve our performance by making more effective use of funding, materials, accommodation and staff?
2   How can we manage innovation and develop a positive approach to change?
3   How can we evaluate information services, in order to justify our work to our paymasters?
4   How can we analyse work methods and procedures to develop cost-effectiveness?
5   How can we ensure that staff development and organizational development take place in an era of low staff turnover, with the risk of professional stagnation among older staff, and frustration at lack of opportunities among younger staff?
6   How can we encourage staff at all levels to assume more responsibility, come up with ideas, initiate projects, rather than interpret their jobs as unchanging routines?

Anyone who is responsible for other staff, even one or two, is, or should be, engaged in staff management. The term 'management' is often misunderstood by librarians, who believe that only 'managers' manage, or that management is something that happens at the most senior levels. Management is in some minds seen as an undesirable activity which removes one from the 'real' professional practice of librarianship, and incarcerates one in an office, to work endlessly on new bureaucratic rules and procedures. The view taken in this book is that management skills are useful at all levels. They are just as important for a subject librarian planning an induction programme for new students, or a community librarian planning an information service for the unemployed or the housebound, as they are for senior staff planning a matrix management structure, or assessing priorities over the next five years for staff training and development. Young professionals should also be able to analyse the way they are being managed and learn from the experience.

The management cycle

The management of staff does not take place in a vacuum. It requires a clear idea of what has to be done and therefore an understanding of the cyclical nature of effective management. The starting point has to be the objectives of the library or information service which will have been derived from an analysis of its role in relation to the objectives of the organization of which it is a part and an examination of the needs of the community it is serving. In today's changing environment, in which political and economic pressures dominate, there is bound to be a good deal of heart-searching about the objectives or purposes of libraries. The public library, of course, has the most difficult job because it has tried to serve everybody, whereas the Comedia Report[1] of 1993 came to the conclusion that it should be more clearly focused. The Department of National Heritage instigated a review of public libraries in 1993. Whilst all public libraries have been influenced in one way or another by the business models of operation which will be discussed later in this chapter, some critics have argued that there is a great danger in imposing inappropriate models taken from commerce and industry on a public library service.[2]

After academic institutions funded by the Polytechnic and Colleges Funding Council became independent of local authorities as a result of the Education Reform Act 1988 they sent their strategic plans to the Council and included in those plans were mission statements incorporating the aims of the institution. Those responsible for library services were able to relate their services to the mission statements and produce their own if none existed. The Follett Report[3] recommended in 1993 that 'each institution should develop an information strategy setting out how it proposes to meet the needs of those working within it, and the place of the library in meeting those needs'. The turbulent environment identified by such management gurus as Tom Peters has meant that organizations have had to have 'clear, agreed, definitions of corporate aims' and have needed 'to identify the implications of organizational objectives in terms of information needs and information activities to meet the objectives successfully'.[4]

The popularity of various management techniques has changed over the years but all accept that there is a need to evolve processes which ensure that all managers aim for and achieve what the organization requires. Management by Objectives (MBO) was especially popular from the 1970s but there has been some disillusionment with full-blown systems and what are claimed to be more tolerable methods, such as Performance Management, have been introduced.[5]

There is often a good deal of confusion about objectives terminology. We have found it helpful to distinguish three types of objective:

1 *Aims* (also referred to as philosophy, mission, overall objectives) state the business the library and information service believes it is in, e.g. to promote the spread of knowledge, information, education and culture.
2 *Key tasks* are broad statements which sum up the main objectives of the service, e.g. to encourage and support individuals in developing and maintaining the skill of reading.
3 *Specific objectives* (also referred to as targets or goals) are concerned usually with specific services or with management and administration, e.g. to organize customer care courses for all staff during the next twelve months.

The specific objectives and the key tasks need to be compatible with the aims. In many library and information services staff will be required to decide upon specific objectives annually. The management style will dictate how decisions are made and who makes them. Chapters 2 and 8 will help readers to analyse management styles in their own institutions which may well differ among departments. In a turbulent environment staff have to change their objectives and priorities quickly and the management style should not only permit this to happen but reward enterprise.

In order to achieve objectives *activities* are needed which require resources such as time, equipment and money. There should also be some control mechanisms which monitor and evaluate how well the objectives have been achieved and enable staff to learn from the experience and to make changes where necessary.

The management cycle will therefore look something like this:

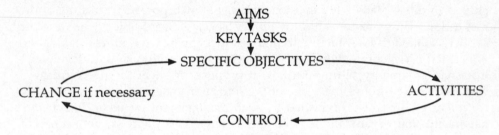

The relationship between objectives approaches and the appraisal of individuals can be readily appreciated and is further discussed in Chapter 6.

Changes in technology

The means of production in clerical and service industries have been largely automated. Libraries have become increasingly computerized in housekeeping procedures such as ordering, acquisition and circulation and in services to users such as on-line searching and CD ROMS. Interactive video will soon be common. Libraries are moving into a new phase in which it is less a case of getting used to automated systems than of making the best use of them and preparing for future developments in communication technology. By far the most exciting of these is networking including the transmission of images and the development of the 'virtual library'. Most of the preparatory work is currently being done by, or on the behalf of, academic libraries with the UK Office for Library Networking at the University of Bath playing a prominent role. Both the UK Office[6] and the Follett Committee[7] have stated what they believe to be the priorities in the next few years and both highlight the staffing implications:

> Librarians and information specialists need to explore their role as mediators of networked information on behalf of end users. The professional associations have a major responsibility in this connection.
> All levels of staff require a programme of continuing education and training.

Entrants to the profession must have curricula which are relevant to the new directions of the management of libraries and information services... The technical skills of future librarians will have to be considerably greater than they are to-day. It is important that the information handling expertise they possess is not wasted and that they play a key role in this area. Failure to recognise their special contribution would be detrimental to the whole information infrastructure.[8]

A national networked training programme for librarians and information scientists working in academic libraries should be established by the councils with funding of £1 million a year over three years.[9]

Special library and information services especially in the large commercial organizations will be only too eager to use the networks: 'Networking capability will stimulate changing work patterns which cannot be ignored by the specialist information service which now has a real opportunity to bring the library into every office'.[10]

At present public libraries have been slow to respond to the advantages of networking, so much so that Chris Batt was able to warn that 'if public libraries get marginalised because we have not responded to the great challenge of networking then it will be your fault'.[11] There is certainly some concern in the profession that access to information in the future will be restricted to an 'elite' with others joining a growing group of 'information poor' as more information becomes available only through networks.

Changes in education

Over the last decade there have been major changes in education at all levels in the UK. The Education Reform Act 1988 removed polytechnics from local government control and in 1992 they were granted university status. Also in 1992 the Polytechnics and Colleges Funding Council and the Universities Funding Council were amalgamated as the Higher Education Funding Council. The colleges of further education were also removed from local government control in 1993 and the Further Education Funding Council was set up. The result of these changes has been that the institutions are able to decide their own priorities and how they wish to be managed. These decisions have had to be made within central government guidelines and subject to the funds provided. Before incorporation the institutions did not possess funds of their own and a number of services, such as personnel, financial, and buildings and estates, were provided by the local authority. The 'new' institutions had therefore to accommodate these additional functions when reorganizing their management and committee structures.

In the early 1970s, when polytechnics' internal structures were designed, discussion and consultation were considered to be essential elements in good management, stemming from the ideas of writers such as Herzberg, Likert, and Burns and Stalker (see Chapter 2) but also influenced by contemporary political and cultural ideas. It was therefore natural that committee structures had wide representation built into them and librarians, therefore, frequently found themselves on academic boards and numerous committees. With incorporation institutions 'streamlined' their structures influenced now by ideas inherent in the Education Reform Act derived from the contemporary business world. Librarians are less likely to be members of much smaller academic boards, are unlikely to be members of senior management groups and it is more likely that they will not have a library committee. Although the sort of meetings skills discussed in Chapter 8 are still important, interpersonal skills have become even more necessary as 'formal activity has to be replaced by an increase in informal activity such as casual meetings in dining rooms and at coffee breaks and more frequent visits to departments to cultivate relationships'.[12]

Central Government has been very active in the last decade making changes which affect schools. Both the Technical and Vocational Education Initiative, set up in 1983 and extended nationally in 1987, and the General Certificate of Secondary Education, introduced in 1986 to replace the General Certificate of Education 'Ordinary' level and the Certificate of Secondary Education, emphasized new investigative ways of learning and course work as opposed to examinations. In addition the Education Reform Act brought in a National Curriculum, which was reviewed and streamlined by the Dearing Report with new curricula due to come into force in 1995. The effect of all these changes was to increase the need for a wide range of resources at a time when cuts were being made in local authority funding. The standard of library provision in schools in England is generally accepted as being poor[13] and many schools have been grateful for the enhancement of their own services by school library services, usually operated by public libraries acting as agents for their education departments. The Education Reform Act 1988 brought in local management of schools which required local education authorities to delegate certain responsibilities for financial management and the appointment and dismissal of staff to the governing bodies and permitted delegation of many of these responsibilities to head teachers. Schools have also been allowed to 'opt out' of local education authority finance and become 'grant-maintained' by central Government. Librarians, particularly those responsible for school library services, have had to develop marketing and negotiating skills to 'sell' their services to schools where, previously, centralized funds have been delegated. Peggy Heeks, who was jointly responsible for the British Library-funded research project on the management of change for school libraries which reported in 1992,[14] makes it clear that school library services have now moved into the marketplace where 'it is now obvious that the SLS which thrive will be those which are innovative and entrepreneurial in approach'.[15]

The economic and political environment

The performance of the economy has had a major influence on the amount of resources available to organizations and their library and information services. As a consequence libraries have been under constant pressure especially where increasing demands have been made upon them. The experiences of academic libraries in the last decade provide the most obvious example with increases in student numbers, reductions in the numbers of teaching staff, changes in teaching methods and increasing pressure on academic staff to carry out research. The inadequate resourcing of libraries in the UK led to the 'Save our Libraries Day' and the lobbying of Members of Parliament on 27 February 1992.

On the other hand there has been a rise in information-based and service industries as manufacturing continues to decline.

Restructuring

The response of the Government has been to push through its privatization programme, to reduce the powers of local authorities and to set in train a programme of local government reform in England, Wales and Scotland. Following the disruption and bad publicity created by the imposition of the Community Charge and its subsequent revision, staff in local government have had a particularly difficult time. It now seems that difficulties for library services will not be eased, judging by the reports of the Local Government Commission which consist of proposals for the new authorities to replace the counties largely with unitary authorities. The main concern is that a backward step is being taken in setting up more than 200 library authorities in England and Wales to replace 121.[16] A particular worry is that new, generally rural, authorities without substantial centres of population in their midst will not be able to provide access to comprehensive reference services, specialist staff, cost-effective central services, central administration and support services.[17] As well as providing an administrative headache for staff reorganizing services it is feared that some authorities will not be able to provide the career and development opportunities now available.

Whilst units in local government seem set to become reduced in size the trend in commercial organizations and academic institutions has been towards takeovers and amalgamations to produce larger units. A great deal of effort has been spent by staff in academic libraries, particularly the ex-polytechnics, in coping with amalgamations, restructuring, and the relocation of departments, so much so that it can be said that they have grown used to managing change.

Income generation – Compulsory competitive tendering – Self-service

The need to obtain funds, to save money and respond to the Government's belief in the competitive business model for public services has persuaded many librarians to give more attention to income generation. The Government's views were made known in the Green Paper issued in 1988, 'Financing our public library services: four subjects for debate'.[18] If libraries are to be successful in raising income then the necessary skills and motivation require attention. Ashcroft and Wilson's survey in 1991[19] pointed this out forcibly:

Most of their existing staff have neither the appropriate skills nor the time to acquire them and, unlike commercial enterprises, cannot generally buy them in... In addition to lack of skills there is also, in many authorities, a lack of motivation. Many junior and some middle management staff resent having to sell products. They say that if they had wanted to do this they would have chosen an occupation other than librarianship. Well-designed, but time-consuming and therefore costly training programmes, good leadership and well-structured communications have altered these attitudes in some authorities but it is recognised by senior librarians as a major constraint.

Efforts have recently been made to support income generation through sponsorship by means of a survey and a training manual.[20] The surveyors were more optimistic than Ashcroft and Wilson about the potential of library staff:

Library staff, whilst having reservations, do seem willing to try to develop sponsored initiatives but they lack professional support and training.

Although these publications were largely aimed at public libraries much of their content is of value to other librarians, particularly academic librarians who have also been under pressure to produce income. In many cases they have chosen to charge for services already provided, especially to external users, but also internally where a cost centre approach is favoured together with an internal market so that the library has to sell its services to departments. Others have gone further and developed commercial services for external users which have required them to use all the skills of an entrepreneur.[21]

The Local Government Act 1988 brought in compulsory competitive tendering for local authorities. At first many thought it was more likely to affect cleaning and catering services rather than public libraries, but the Government consultation paper 'Competing for quality'[22] published in 1991 proposed that public library support services (the tasks of acquisition, cataloguing, and processing of books and other materials) would be subject to compulsory competitive tendering. The Secretary of State, however, dropped the proposal and set up a steering committee in 1993 to investigate the feasibility of contracting out the direct delivery of all or various parts of the library service. He intends to set out a range of options for local authorities when the investigation is complete. Most libraries already contract out some of their support services but the future may well see more after the feasibility studies are carried out and, as Fred Guy sees it, 'no one lives in a CCT-free zone and that, despite rumours to the contrary, this government isn't going to forget about libraries when it comes to privatisation, CCT for libraries usually means record supply and the death of your cataloguing department'.[23]

Libraries are already used to specifying their requirements from suppliers and if contracting out did increase there would be considerable effects on staffing and staffing structures. Brent, for example, have already organized their services on a client/contractor basis.[24] Arts and libraries became a recognized business unit with its own independent bank account and full financial management responsibilities.

Libraries realized a long time ago, when they introduced open access, that costs could be reduced if users served themselves and over recent years there has been a great deal of interest in further efforts in this direction. In academic libraries user education has become an accepted part of a librarian's functions with increasing interest in providing services and guiding which users can understand readily. This has applied particularly to automated systems such as OPACS. Recently self-issue systems have been introduced to reduce the pressure on circulation counters.

Search for quality – Customer charters – Customer consultation

Quality management and total quality management have become influential concepts in recent years. TQM, strictly speaking, is about the application of the theories of the 'gurus'[25] often associated with Japanese concepts of quality and statistical measurement techniques. TQM involves focusing the efforts of all employees on a day-to-day basis towards improving and maintaining the quality of the company's products and services and its aim is to ensure complete customer satisfaction. It is argued that up to a quarter of all non-manufacturing work has to be re-done before it is correct and that staff need to see other staff as customers to whom they pass work if poor quality work is to be avoided. Techniques such as quality awareness training and quality circles are used to focus staff upon quality of production and performance. It is clear that 'people are an essential ingredient in successful quality management and therefore that good people management is equally crucial'.[26]

Achieving badges and awards has become part of the new enterprise culture. The Community Initiative Award and the Public Library Development Incentive Scheme are two examples as the culture demands that libraries cannot simply expect to receive all their funds each year but must bid for some of them and earn others through high level of performance in ranking exercises. In quality matters the British Standards Institution's BS 5750 (soon to be known as BS EN ISO 9000) is seen as a goal by some organizations. Libraries have become involved as part of organizations and others have attempted to achieve the standard on their own.[27] The standard was originally designed to cover the management processes of organizations involved in manufacturing and production and has been found to be quite difficult to interpret by service sector organizations. Plenty of advice is available on what is involved in applying for registration [27, 28] and accounts have been written by librarians who have been involved with tackling quality matters in a systematic way whether applying for registration or not.[29, 30] A Quality Forum was formed in 1993 by public librarians to discuss quality issues.

Matters of quality have been at the forefront of changes in higher education. The Higher Education Funding Council for England has set up a Quality Assessment Division and subjects are chosen for assessment each year. Institutions self-assess teaching and learning as excellent, satisfactory or unsatisfactory and submit relevant indicators. Visits are made where there is a prima facie case for excellence or where grounds for an unsatisfactory rating exist.

Library services are referred to in the documentation and librarians are being involved in the self-assessments. How satisfactory this involvement will be remains to be seen. Recent research at Manchester Metropolitan University suggests that librarians will have to fight hard for recognition.[31] Quality Audit is carried out by the Higher Education Quality Council which reviews institutions as a whole – their procedures, processes and mechanisms for academic quality assurance. Again library services are included and for a period at least they will have a higher profile because of the Funding Councils' Follett Report.[32] Each institution has its own quality assurance procedures which cover validation and review of courses, monitoring and evaluation. Frances Slack's Manchester Report and the Resources and Courses conference in July 1993 held at Manchester Metropolitan University revealed the inadequacy of libraries' involvement in these procedures nationwide.[33]

The prime minister, John Major, launched the Citizen's Charter in 1991.[34] Those parts of it which caught the public's imagination were concerned with trains running on time, cutting down on hospital waiting lists and fixed time appointments for home calls from the utilities. It also highlighted league tables of school examination results and league tables on the performance of local authorities. The Secretary of State challenged The Library Association to produce a model charter for public libraries and it was published in 1993.[35] Cambridgeshire was the first county council to launch a citizen's charter and it contained standards from the library service such as 'The widest appropriate range of fiction and non-fiction books for loan with 50 per cent of books under five years old'.[36] There is a charter for higher education produced by the Department for Education which includes the standard that 'Universities and colleges should explain the teaching and learning facilities available, including libraries, information technology and other resources'.[37] The charter displays the citizen's charter badge on the front and the crystal mark badge on the back for clarity approved by the Plain English Campaign.

Both Total Quality Management and charters are concerned with satisfying customers' needs and an important element in this is monitoring satisfaction with services. Three consequences have been an increase in the number of user surveys, greater concern for customer care and more interest in performance indicators.

Recent examples of user surveys have been those carried out at the University of Wales College of Cardiff,[38] Birmingham Public Libraries,[39] and Berkshire Library and information services.[40] The Audit Commission has been considering (1993) making results from user surveys either a voluntary or mandatory performance indicator that local authorities must publish in future years.

Customer care has become a popular concept and training effort is being expended upon it. Tina Jones has expressed the views held by many managers:

It is not just training staff to be nice to customers, looking them in the eye as you give them their goods. It includes that and more. Essentially it is helping a customer to define his or her needs, defining features as consumer benefits (in a language the customer can understand!), giving confidence in your knowledge and service by what you say, how you say it and through the presentation of yourself – making the complete interaction a pleasant one.[41]

John Hinks[42] and John Pluse[43] have also written enthusiastically about what Pluse refers to as 'the salvation of service organizations'.

The emphases on aims, quality, and customer views has led to increasing interest in finding ways to measure how well libraries are meeting their objectives. Central Government is naturally interested in indicators which can help to compare libraries with each other. Ian Winkworth[44] has written a valuable article tracing the history of performance indicator work and the current position particularly in academic libraries, whilst Catherine Cope[45] has reviewed performance indicator work in public libraries. Performance indicators for public libraries in England and Wales have been set by the Audit Commission under the Local Government Act of 1992 and for Scotland by the Commission for Local Authority Accounts in Scotland.[46]

Summary

The idea of the management cycle introduced earlier in this chapter can now be seen in the context of the present environment:

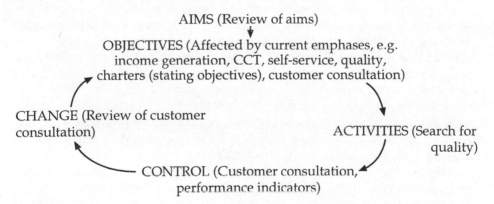

It can be seen that many of the management ideas currently in vogue fit quite well into the management cycle which is at the heart of effective management. What it requires to make it work is the sensitive application of the staff management techniques described and explained in the chapters that follow.

Legislation

It is very difficult for the non-lawyer to keep up-to-date with employment legislation and case law. Librarianship literature rarely gives it a mention so it is necessary to consult personnel management and legal literature such as Erich Suter's *Employment law checklist*,[47] the regular articles in *Personnel Management* by Olga Aikin plus the many textbooks on employment law which are regularly updated. One of the few librarianship monographs which covers legislation is Rosemary Raddon's *People and Work*.[48] Since the mid-1970s there has been a number of important Acts of Parliament whilst increasingly European Community legislation is affecting employment in the United Kingdom. The following statutes are especially important:

Trade Union and Labour Relations Act 1974, 1992
Health and Safety at Work Act 1974
Employment Protection Act 1975
Employment Protection (Consolidation) Act 1978
Sex Discrimination Acts 1975, 1986
Race Relations Act 1976
Employment Act 1978, 1980, 1982, 1988, 1989, 1990
Trade Union Reform and Employment Rights Act 1993.

It is incumbent on employers and employees to obey these laws and most organizations, of which libraries are a part, will try to ensure staff are aware of their obligations. In large organizations such as universities, colleges, local authorities and large companies the personnel department is likely to carry out this function.

When disputes between employers and employees arise which cannot be solved satisfactorily recourse can be had to the legal system. Most proceedings involving employment rights are commenced at industrial tribunals and appeals against industrial tribunal decisions are heard by the Employment Appeal Tribunal. An industrial tribunal is composed of a legally qualified president and two lay representatives, one from each side of industry, who are appointed by the Secretary of State for Employment. Proceedings are usually more informal, speedier and less expensive than claims brought in the courts. Before a case goes before an industrial tribunal a Conciliation Officer (Tribunals), who is an officer of the Advisory, Conciliation and Arbitration Service (ACAS), will try to promote a settlement without the matter going to a hearing. It has been argued that this alternative should be used more often to avoid excessive legalism.[49]

Following a decision by an industrial tribunal either side can appeal. Appeals, which have to be made within 42 days of the tribunal decision, go to the Employment Appeal Tribunal in England, Wales and Scotland. Appeal can only be made on points of law and errors of fact.

Contract of employment

There is no legal formula for a contract of employment and it can be in writing or oral. A contract of employment, like any other contract, leaves the parties free to negotiate terms and conditions that suit them. In practice most librarians do not negotiate but are engaged on terms and conditions laid down in collective agreements. Although a written contract is not obligatory there is a statutory obligation upon employers to supply a written statement not later than thirteen weeks after the beginning of the employment. The written statement must contain:

The identity of the parties.
Date the employment began and when continuity with that employer began.
Pay, methods of calculation and periods of payment.
Hours of work.
Holiday and sick pay entitlement.
Pensions.
Length of notice the employee is entitled to receive and obliged to give.
Disciplinary rules and procedures.
Title of job. There is no legal requirement to provide a job description as part of the contract and employers may regard it as prudent not to do so. It is advisable for employers to stipulate whether an employee is expected to work at more than one location. This is important if the sort of flexibility required of staff is to be achieved uncontentiously.

Disciplinary procedures

Although there is no statutory requirement for employers to have disciplinary rules the ACAS Code of Practice[50] urges this upon employers. Most librarians work for organizations which have such procedures and as managers they should ensure they are familiar with them. While very few librarians are likely to be involved with industrial tribunals many will have some involvement with internal disciplinary procedures.

Disciplinary procedures are one way in which employers can attempt to behave in a 'reasonable' way which has been a legal requirement since 1974. Most procedures are likely to include the essential features outlined in paragraph 10 of the ACAS Code:

They should:

(a) be in writing
(b) specify to whom they apply
(c) provide for matters to be dealt with quickly
(d) indicate the disciplinary actions which may be taken
(e) specify the levels of management which have the authority to take the various forms of disciplinary action, ensuring that immediate superiors do not normally have the power to dismiss without reference to senior management
(f) provide for individuals to be informed of the complaints against them and to be given an opportunity to state their case before decisions are reached

(g)   give individuals the right to be accompanied by a trade union repre-
      sentative or by a fellow employee of their choice
(h)   ensure that, except for gross misconduct, no employees are dismissed for
      a first breach of discipline
(i)   ensure that disciplinary action is not taken until the case has been care-
      fully investigated
(j)   ensure that individuals are given an explanation for any penalty im-
      posed
(k)   provide a right of appeal and specify the procedure to be followed.[51]

Perusal of a number of procedures shows that it is normal to provide the
person accused with a written statement on the nature of the accusation. The
library manager therefore must be absolutely clear about the alleged offence(s)
and have evidence to support the case. Opportunity for individuals to present
their cases is usually provided by means of a hearing in which witnesses can
be called, and documents produced in evidence. The person accused will
normally have a right to be accompanied by a friend or a trade union official.

A typical hearing opens with the management side presenting its case followed by the accused presenting his or her case. All except the panel withdraw and the panel considers the case and reaches a decision. The decision is
presented orally to the accused, appeal rights are explained, and written con-
firmation of the decision follows.

The disciplinary sanctions available are those allowed in the contract of
employment and the principle usually followed is one of warnings of increasing severity leading finally to dismissal, the starting point being dependent on
the severity of the offence and the past disciplinary record of the individual.
For minor acts of misconduct a written or oral warning can be issued and if
further acts are committed then the result might be a final written warning.
Where gross misconduct is committed, that is misconduct so severe that the
employer cannot tolerate the continued presence of the employee on the
premises, dismissal without notice will be the appropriate sanction with sus-
pension preceding the actual hearing.

Knowledge of internal disciplinary procedures is necessary as librarians are
likely to find themselves on panels or on either side of a case brought before a
panel. Even more important for everyday staff management, librarians must
ensure they are dealing with disciplinary problems correctly and that they are
shown to be good managers when evidence is produced in hearings, but more
especially so that problems can be solved without recourse to the necessarily
bureaucratic, time-consuming and unpleasant procedures that have been described.

When problems do arise it is sensible for library managers to record dates
and descriptions of events in case they are later required. This should be done
immediately after events have taken place to ensure accuracy. It is also a good
idea to call in another member of staff not involved in the problem as a
witness. Choice of the person can be tricky as it may not be desirable for the
problem to be widely known.

Dismissal of staff

Employment legislation in Britain during the seventies tended to favour employees, but with the change of government in 1979 there was a shift towards the employer in the 1980 and 1982 Employment Acts. More protection was given to trade union members who disagree with the union by the 1988 Act, including protection against dismissal of a union member who wishes to leave a union where there is a 'closed shop' agreement. The Trade Union Reform and Employment Act 1993 makes it illegal to dismiss an employee on the grounds of union membership. The legislation serves to emphasize the need for managers to be very careful where dismissals are concerned and this is as it should be because dismissal is a serious matter.

Three different types of termination of employment fall within the definition of dismissal:

1   Where a contract is terminated by the employer with or without notice.
2   Expiry and non-renewal of a fixed-term contract.
3   The contract is terminated with or without notice by the employee in such circumstances that he or she is entitled to terminate it without notice because of the employer's conduct – 'constructive dismissal'. For such dismissals to be judged as unfair a serious breach of contract by the employer must be shown.

Claims for unfair dismissal do not have to be defended by the employer unless certain qualifications are satisfied. Following a House of Lords ruling in March 1994 protection was extended to include anyone with two years' service who works eight hours a week or more. The Equal Opportunities Commission brought the case as part of its campaign for equal treatment for part-timers who are mostly women. The Employment Protection (Consolidation) Act 1978 had restricted protection on unfair dismissal and redundancy to full-time workers after two years, but part-timers working between eight and sixteen hours have had to work for five years before gaining the same protection. Employees must not be over the normal retirement age for their work or in any case aged over 65.

British legislation lists a number of reasons normally accepted as grounds for dismissal:

1   Incapability, which includes lack of skill, attitude, physical or mental qualities. It is normal in many jobs for there to be an initial appraisal so that incapabilities of new staff can be quickly detected. With staffing cuts and lack of staff mobility it has become even more important for libraries to avoid employing staff who are incapable of carrying out their duties in an adequate manner. Dismissal after a few months can be employed where inadequate staff have slipped through the selection net. Though such staff are not able to appeal through the legal system, organizations may still require normal disciplinary procedures to be followed.

Where appeals are made industrial tribunals would have to be satisfied that employees dismissed for incapacity were given adequate training.

2   Absence of appropriate qualifications. Employers may require new qualifications to be attained but must give time for existing employees to qualify before dismissal is possible.

3   Misconduct such as dishonesty. If an employee, for example, makes a secret profit by stealing fines money it is grounds for dismissal. Behaviour is expected to be consistent with the standard expected, e.g. excessive drinking would probably be considered unacceptable in many jobs. Dismissal for a single act of misconduct will usually only be considered fair in very serious cases.

4   Contravention of statutory requirements, e.g. loss of a permit or a licence such as a driving licence which made it impossible for the person to carry out the job.

5   Redundancy. The Employment Protection (Consolidation) Act states that an employee is to be regarded as redundant if dismissal is attributable wholly or mainly to:

(a)   the fact that his employer has ceased or intends to cease, to carry on the business for the purposes of which the employee was so employed; *or*

(b)   the fact that the employer has ceased, or intends to cease, to carry on that business in the place where the employee was so employed; *or*

(c)   the fact that the requirements of that business for employees to carry out work of a particular kind, or for employees to carry out work of a particular kind in the place where they were so employed, have ceased or diminished or are expected to cease or diminish.

Legislation requires ninety days' consultation before dismissal takes effect where one hundred or more are employed at one establishment, and thirty days where ten or more are employed at one establishment. The employer has to disclose in writing the following matters at the beginning of the consultation period:

1   The reason for the proposals.
2   The number and description of employees whom it is proposed to dismiss.
3   The total number of employees of any such description employed by the employer at that establishment.
4   The proposed method of selecting the employees who may be dismissed. (The most popular method has been 'last in first out' but case law has shown that employers are increasingly moving towards retaining those who have the necessary skills for the organization to remain viable.)
5   The proposed method of carrying out the dismissal, with due regard to any agreed procedure, including the period over which the dismissals are to take effect.

In addition the Trade Union Reform and Employment Rights Act extends the information to be given to representatives as a result of an EC directive to include avoiding redundancy, reducing the numbers to be dismissed, the redundancy package and measures to mitigate the consequences of redundancy.

In many organizations which employ librarians encouragement has been given for older staff to take early retirement and in some cases there have been enhanced payments which are a considerable improvement on the minimum redundancy lump sum payments available to those employed for two years or more before dismissal:

1　Half a week's pay for each complete year of service from 18 years to 21 years of age.
2　One week's pay for years between 22 and 40.
3　One and a half weeks' pay for 41 onwards, reduced by one-twelfth for each month in the final year before reaching 64 years of age.

Older staff will wish to discuss their decisions, therefore it is desirable for library managers to be aware of early retirement conditions. It may also be the case that early retirement posts are lost to the establishment and can only be implemented with the agreement of the head of department or senior management equivalent. This is a difficult decision to make but the librarian does have to consider carefully the effect on the library of the loss of posts in such a haphazard fashion. It may be possible to 'trade off' posts to enable the damage to be alleviated. Many organizations now provide support and advice to retirees including courses on such matters as finance, leisure and social security.

Discrimination

A management approach frequently prescribed is one which treats individuals equally according to merit. Burns' and Stalker's theories[52] discussed in Chapter 2, for example, are based on the belief that good ideas should be encouraged irrespective of their origin within the organization. 'If the aim of the organisation is to provide the best service or to produce a profit, then it needs effective staff. Any managers who restrict selection to, for example, men or whites or Protestants are simply not properly fulfilling their duty. The best staff are not obtained by ignoring large sections of the working population.'[53] This practical view of the position of sex, race and religion is enshrined in the legislation. In Britain, the Sex Discrimination Act 1975 and the Equal Pay Act 1970 cover discrimination on grounds of sex and the Race Relations Act 1976 prohibits discrimination on grounds of colour, race, nationality, ethnic or national origins.

The library manager is required to avoid direct discrimination, where a person is treated less favourably on grounds of race or sex than another person would be treated, and indirect discrimination, where a requirement is such that the proportion of one sex or racial group which can comply with it is considerably smaller than the proportion of the other sex or racial groups which can comply. An employer must show that the requirement is justified if it is not to be judged discriminatory.

The effect of these laws is that library managers have to be extremely careful at all stages of personnel management discussed in this book. In particular it is considered necessary for managers to be systematic in that they are clear about what they are trying to do, spell it out to all those involved, and monitor the results. In practice, however, some managers may act in a quite different way saying and writing down as little as possible in order that it will not be misinterpreted and held against them. As might be expected the Equal Opportunities Commission's own 'Code of Practice' advocates 'the establishment and use of consistent criteria for selection, training, promotion, redundancy and dismissal which are made known to all employees. Without this consistency, decisions can be subjective and leave the way open for unlawful discrimination to occur'.[54]

In recruitment it is unlawful to discriminate on arrangements made for the purpose of determining who should be offered employment or the terms on which employment is offered or refusing or deliberately omitting to offer employment. For example, advertising should be clear and unambiguous and avoid anything, such as illustrations and wording, which is, or could be construed as, discriminatory. It is very easy to slip into discriminatory habits without being aware of it, but case law suggests that it is irrelevant what the advertisers subjectively intended the advertisement to mean. The test is whether the advertisement, when read as a whole and interpreted according to what a reasonable person would, without any special knowledge, find to be the natural and ordinary meaning of the words used, is considered discriminatory. Staff giving verbal information about jobs should be careful not to indicate any bias. Application forms should be as simple as possible and cater for minorities. It is usual to ask for race and sex on application forms and the Institute of Personnel Management recommends this in order to furnish statistics on recruitment.[55] Some managers have been reluctant to do this because they feel it highlights differences about which selectors may otherwise have been unaware and which they consider irrelevant. A very difficult problem arises where there are clear cultural differences between selectors and the candidates which make it difficult for them to understand each other. This has to be reconciled with a requirement frequently contained in job specifications, written or not, that a person is required to work well with others in a team. At a time when mistakes are difficult to repair selectors will tend not to take chances especially when the employment situation is such that there is a wealth of good candidates.

The selection interview should be unbiased and this is discussed in Chapter 5. During employment discrimination can arise through the way an employer affords a person access to opportunity for promotion, transfer, training or any other benefit, facility or service, or by refusing or deliberately omitting to afford that person access to them.

The question of sexual harassment at work has received more attention in recent years particularly by trade unions. The Trades Union Congress has defined it as 'repeated and unwanted verbal or sexual advances, sexually explicit derogatory statements or sexually discriminatory remarks'. The European Commission adopted a 'Code of practice on sexual harassment' in July 1991. Although not binding, its intent is to establish practical guidance to employers, unions, and employees to ensure that sexual harassment does not occur, or where it has, to establish proceedings to respond to it.[56] Cases in the UK have confirmed that sexual and racial harassment are unlawful under the Sex Discrimination Act and the Race Relations Act. It has also been shown that the employer is liable for discrimination if the employees who cause the disadvantage to the individual were acting in the course of their employment. An employer may avoid liability where it can be shown that the claim has been investigated though no subsequent action was taken because of lack of evidence. The Equal Opportunities Commission code of practice recommends that particular care is taken to deal effectively with all complaints of discrimination, victimization or harassment and not assume allegations are made by those who are over-sensitive.

Maternity rights

All pregnant employees have a right not to be unreasonably refused paid time off to attend ante-natal care recommended by a doctor, midwife or health visitor.

The Trade Union Reform and Employment Rights Act 1993, which comes into effect in 1994, incorporates the provisions of the European Commission's Maternity Directive. The main provisions, as described by Olga Aikin,[57] are:

Every woman, regardless of hours worked or length of service, will be entitled to 14 weeks' maternity leave, during which she remains entitled to her full contractual terms and conditions other than remuneration, e.g. use of a car, accrual of holiday entitlement and insurances. The leave can start at any time the woman may choose, beginning with the eleventh week before the expected week of childbirth. At least 21 days before her leave begins she must inform her employer of the date of commencement. From the manager's point of view it is essential to be aware of such events as soon as possible in order to fill the temporary vacancy.

She will be entitled to maternity pay during this period.

Dismissal on the grounds of redundancy will be unfair where selection is based on maternity grounds or when available alternative work has not been offered.

Dismissal on maternity-related grounds will be automatically unfair.

Any woman dismissed while pregnant or on maternity leave is automatically entitled to written reasons for dismissal.

Where the health of the woman or her child is likely to suffer as a result of her work, she must be moved to safe work or suspended on full terms, including pay. For example there are the dangers of radiation, certain chemicals, physical agents which could cause foetal lesions and/or are likely to disrupt placental attachment such as shocks, vibration, movement, handling loads, noise, extremes of heat and cold, movements, postures, travelling, mental and other fatigue and other physical burdens. Jobs will therefore need to be reviewed and safe jobs identified.

A woman who has two years' continuity of employment (five years if working between eight and sixteen hours per week) has the legal right to return to work anytime up to 29 weeks after the birth of her child. This can be extended once by four weeks. She must be allowed to return either to her own job or a suitable alternative job on terms and conditions no less favourable than they would have been had she not taken maternity leave. She must give her employer at least 21 days' notice of her intention to return to work. Women do not therefore have the right to return to precisely the same post they previously occupied and this does provide a certain amount of flexibility. A practical problem frequently arises when a temporary vacancy is filled, particularly where the appointment is an external one or when an internal candidate is given temporary promotion. In both cases the temporary person may feel he or she is entitled to the post should the woman on maternity leave not return to work. It is therefore necessary to make it clear that the post will be advertised in the usual way and that the person must compete against other applicants. If this is not done there will be a feeling of resentment by staff who did not believe they had a fair chance. On the other hand it increasingly seems to be the practice for temporary posts to be filled without public advertisement by appointing from within the staff or from a pool of temporary workers, often former employees, known to the librarian. Some employers are more generous with maternity leave and allow up to 52 weeks' absence. Managers therefore need to plan well ahead in order to plug the gaps created by such prolonged absence.

Health and Safety

According to the Health and Safety at Work Act 1974 employers have the duty of ensuring, so far as is reasonably practicable, the health, safety and welfare at work of all their employees. Every employee has a duty to take reasonable care of his or her own health and safety and that of others, including users of the library.

The matters to which the duty extends include the provision and maintenance of equipment; use, handling, storage and transport of articles and substances; provision of information, instruction, training and supervision; maintenance of buildings and the provision and maintenance of the working environment. With increasing concern for the protection of employees from violence and from such hazards as passive smoking there is scope for using the 1974 Act until the legislation is updated.[58] In addition EC directives require a number of health and safety measures to be taken, such as display screen regulations which are designed to regulate the use of VDUs. Organizations are required to have an up-to-date health and safety at work policy and this will probably be carried out by a Health and Safety Committee together with a Health and Safety Officer.

The library should be represented on the organization's committee and many libraries will have their own Health and Safety Committee. This should meet regularly to ensure attention is given to matters appertaining to the Act.

Time off work

The Employment Protection (Consolidation) Act 1978 allows for officials of trade unions recognized by the employer to be allowed a reasonable amount of time off work, with pay, to discharge their duties, though the Employment Act 1989 restricts duties to those concerned with negotiation with the employer. Similarly employees should be allowed time off to take part in union activities other than industrial action. Time off is also allowed for public duties such as those of a Justice of the Peace and for training and educational purposes. With reductions in staffing levels the granting of time off has become more difficult and puts a greater strain on libraries. At the same time it is acknowledged that such activities have an important role to play in combating professional stagnation when opportunities for advancement are so limited.

The library manager needs to be aware of the role of the trade union within his or her organization, liaise with the library's union representatives and know the main union officials. The strength and power of unions varies considerably from organizations in which the union is involved in areas normally reserved for management, to organizations in which the union has little influence.

2

Motivation and job satisfaction

The theories on which the study of job satisfaction is based are motivation theories. These are concerned with the factors that cause an individual to develop and sustain a particular mode of behaviour. They are also concerned with the subjective reactions of the individual during the behaviour. A distinction is usually made between 'content' theories of motivation and 'process' theories. Content theories try to identify needs that should be met or values that should be attained if a worker is to be motivated. Thus it is generally accepted that people at work need security and reasonable working conditions and adequate pay. Beyond those basics however it becomes more complicated. People's higher level needs, for recognition or responsibility, say, may be difficult to meet in routine work. Some staff may want more sociability from their work, others want more sense of achievement than a traditional hierarchical structure gives. 'Process' theories suggest that the variables in a given work situation should all be considered, and that their relationship with each other or their mutual influence is very significant. The assumption is that 'satisfaction is a function of the correspondence between the reinforcer system of the work environment and the individual's needs'.[1] While the individual worker brings his or her own needs to the workplace, the nature of the tasks, the style of the supervisor and the overall management climate are equally significant in determining the degree of motivation that may be developed on the job. Thus the interrelationship between these variables (the 'process') must be considered, not just the 'content' or worker's own needs.

Motivating staff is therefore a complex and delicate business. An individual's sense of job satisfaction, or lack of it, does not depend only on his or her own motivation as, say, a professional librarian with a sense of service and trained expertise to support it. Nor does it depend only on the management styles and structures operating in the library. It is derived from the interaction between the individual's own attitudes, the nature of the task and of the work

23

group, the management styles and the influence of the outer environment – financial constraints, political policies, technological innovation.

Symptoms of poor motivation

The dangers of *not* applying some knowledge of motivation theories in staff development and supervision are that staff may suffer from endemic low morale. There will always be exceptions among the strongly self-motivated or 'self-starters', and the determined careerists, but among the rest of the staff the warning signs to look out for are a high turnover of junior staff (senior people may find it harder to move to other jobs because of low mobility at that level), more than average days off sick, persistent unpunctuality, and increasing complaints by users. There may also be a tendency for staff to identify with user complaints rather than to identify with the library and take responsibility for remedying the user's problem. A defeatist spiral develops in the worst cases, whereby staff and user expectations of the library decline mutually towards a nadir of apathy and inertia. Rules and regulations continue to be applied, but few staff know or care about the reasons that lie behind them, so readers are often fobbed off with bureaucratic excuses rather than explanations. If one tries to elicit from poorly motivated library staff what they are trying to achieve, they are likely to give an account of their routines and procedures, without any reference to purpose or justification. In the same way our experience with staff who are persistently off sick and are not chronically ill is that they will often blame working conditions or bad luck. It is important that such staff are interviewed regularly to indicate that their record is unsatisfactory and that it handicaps the library in meeting its objectives. Staff who are persistently away sick can be referred for medical examination to the organization's medical officer so that an objective view can be obtained and further counselling given. Serious cases may be subject to disciplinary procedures.

These are some of the symptoms that develop when staff are required to operate a service about which they are never asked for their opinions, which they do not monitor for effectiveness to users, and where they cannot see beyond their own tasks to the overall service. The need for consultation, feedback on one's performance, positive as well as negative, and acknowledgement of one's contribution to the library's goals are expressed in all surveys of job satisfaction in library and information work. They match up quite closely with the findings in surveys of other professions and occupations, upon which the theories have been constructed. A résumé is now given of the main schools of thought on motivating people at work, which have influenced managerial styles and affected for better or for worse the job satisfaction of staff. Job satisfaction is itself a complex individual matter – 'a perception or an emotional response on the part of individuals based on their own view of how well these expectations are fulfilled'.[2] The assumption often made that job satisfaction leads to greater productivity is not borne out by recent studies which show some positive correlation but at a low level. Rather they argue that satisfaction comes from the various rewards which follow from improved performance. This seems a more realistic assessment of the complex problems facing the staff manager who is trying to help his or her staff get to 'lift-off', in terms of both performance and job satisfaction.

Scientific management and economic man

The scientific management school had its origin in the behavioural sciences at the turn of the century. Two of its main proponents were F. B. Gilbreth[3] (1868–1924) and F. W. Taylor[4] (1856–1915). They took the view that the average employee is motivated primarily by economic needs, so a pattern of status and financial rewards need to be built into the career path to provide the main incentives. Employees are assumed to be inherently lazy, to lack any self-discipline, so they need to operate within a firm hierarchical structure, with clear lines of control and close supervision. The 'carrot and stick' approach of incentives and punishments is considered to be important, since it is assumed that workers have a natural inclination to 'slacking' and 'soldiering'. By 'soldiering' Taylor meant workers conspiring with each other to carry out an agreed minimum of work, just enough to keep their bosses off their backs, but not enough to stretch them. The concomitant argument about the role of managers was that they were generally incompetent. They only guessed how long it took workers to do tasks, when they allocated work. They knew little about workers' skills and abilities, and operated in a largely arbitrary and ill-informed way which encouraged workers to 'get away with it'.

The Taylorian response to inefficiency, of both employees and managers, was to introduce work study methods leading to job fragmentation. Tasks were broken up into clearly defined subtasks, and the time taken to do them was worked out using a group of the 'best workers for the job'. Workers were not supposed to think about their work, since their supervisors were paid to do that for them. Nor were they supposed to take any initiative, for that was what the bosses were there for. They were to do 'a fair day's work for fair pay', and were to be given the necessary technical training to achieve this.

The implications of the scientific management school, which is by no means extinct in contemporary organizations, are that all decisions are taken by the manager, without any consultation with employees. Authority is concentrated at the top of a tall narrow hierarchical staffing structure, with little delegation. Figure 2.1 provides a checklist of characteristics by which scientific management may be recognized (see the lefthand column headed 'Mechanistic'). There is heavy centralization, closely defined job descriptions, and an emphasis on routines rather than the taking of initiatives. Communication tends to be largely one way, from senior management downwards, and favours written memos and instructions rather than face-to-face discussion. Staff development is confined to technical training, for new processes, say, resulting from automation. The manager's job is seen as planning, controlling, inspecting and punishing. Staff are expected to be loyal to their section, and obey instruc-

Mechanistic/organismic paradigm

		Mechanistic	Organismic
AUTHORITY		Authority concentrated at 'the top'; little delegation. Low and localized; bureaucracy tends to take its place.	Dispersed; much delegation. High and dispersed.
PROFESSIONAL EXPERTISE		Hierarchical. Favours centralization.	Network. Favours decentralization.
STRUCTURE		Closely defined job description; sharp division of duties; fixed function of posts; emphasis on PROCESS (routine).	'Open-ended' job description; duties defined rather by purpose and staff interrelationships; team organization; emphasis on PROJECT.
STAFF DEPLOYMENT			
COMMUNICATION	– lines of;	Little. One way, 'top' to 'bottom'.	Much. Multi-directional.
	– content;	Mainly instructions, 'cut-and-dried' decisions.	Mainly information, advice, opinion-seeking.
	– format;	Emphasis on written communication.	Oral, 'face-to-face' is important.
JOB SATISFACTION		'Hygiene' factors important; reward and punishments.	Herzberg's 'motivators' important. Opportunity for self-development and socially useful work.
COMMITMENT		Obedience and loyalty to an individual leader or/and a part of the organization	To the organization as a whole, or, more likely, to professional goals, or, more likely, to a sense of social 'mission'.
STAFF DEVELOPMENT		Claims a relatively small share of the organization's resources; confined to formal training in new skills and introduction of new knowledge.	Claims a relatively large share of the organization's resources; employs a wide range of means to assist self-development; is concerned with attitude-change, as well as acquisition of knowledge and new skills.
DEVELOPMENT CAPACITY OF THE ORGANIZATION		Works best in relatively static environments, meeting predictable demands; inflexible, and unreliable under stress.	Adapts readily to rapidly changing and unpredictable situations; flexible, and reliable under stress.

(*From* Ross Shimmon (ed.) *A reader in library management*, London, Bingley, 1976, p. 126.)

Figure 2.1   An adaptation of Burns' and Stalker's framework for organizational analysis

tions, without looking to wider goals derived, for example, from their professional education or their social commitment.

The scientific approach to staff management may appear as the pervasive management style in a library, or it may co-exist alongside more people-centred styles. For example it may be identified in some technical services sections of academic libraries, where the reader services are managed in a more participative or consultative style. The findings of the Sheffield Manpower Project indicated that in the mid-1970s it was more common in public libraries than in academic or special libraries. It may be that the problems of lack of consultation and emphasis on downwards communication were a result of the turbulence experienced in the public library sector as a result of local government reorganization in 1974. In the late 1970s it was the turn of academic libraries to experience turbulence as a result of mergers of colleges of education with other institutions (polytechnics or colleges of higher education) and the structural changes which continued into the 1990s with the incorporation of polytechnics and colleges and the changes in status resulting from the Education Reform Act.

In both sectors the inadequacies of scientific management approaches were highlighted. There was resistance to centralization by staff on sites with their own local loyalties and ways of doing things. They felt threatened by the loss of autonomy and the shift in decision-making from the local level to a seemingly remote senior management. Communication tended to be from the top down, and modes of consultation were experienced as unsatisfactory, because they did not appear to feed back into the actual decision-making process. Delegation appeared to be a hollow promise, since increasingly systems and procedures were 'rationalized' at the top of the hierarchical structure.

From the viewpoint of senior management, of course, a different picture emerges. To provide efficient and effective services in multisite library systems it was logical to centralize acquisitions and cataloguing, and to try to achieve consistent procedures and regulations (on lending, reservations etc.) across all service points, even when this meant bringing previously autonomous libraries under centralized control, and leading to complaints that 'headquarters is slow to take decisions, unresponsive to suggestions, and out of touch with local needs'.[5] In a sense autocratic management of the scientific school was forced on some senior management, because staff lower down the hierarchy at middle and junior management levels were reluctant to exercise authority and take decisions or initiate action. They preferred to sit it out, to wait and see what senior management would do. In a word, they engaged in a considerable amount of 'buck-passing', when they were not positively clinging to their traditional ways of doing things as autonomous libraries. The situation was aggravated by what Ashworth calls 'motivation by self-preservation' on the part of some middle managers, who had reached 'the level of their own incompetence', known in management circles as the Peter principle.

Special library staff were not immune to the pressures of change in the 1970s, though it took different forms from the organizational changes in the public and academic library sectors. Technological innovation was the main change agent in special libraries, and their reactions were early documented by Roberts:

> Staff resistance to change involving computers is less likely when systematic attention is paid to the need for consultation and keeping staff informed.[6]

By the mid-1980s much more precise questions were being asked, and recommendations made on how to manage the new technology by, among others, the Industrial Society. These include an attention to staff and union participation which is quite alien to the scientific management approach. Participation considerations are listed:

> What are the systems of participation at present?
> Are people involved in issues that affect them?
> Are they being consulted specifically about the introduction of new technology?
> Is involvement early enough? Regular enough? [7]

These examples may indicate some of the shortcomings of scientific management in an era of rapid structural and technological change. However in the neo-conservative 1980s and 1990s there is evidence of a renewal of interest in some of the old-fashioned virtues associated with the scientific approach, with its emphasis on control and productivity. Partly this is a result of financial pressures, leading to shortage of staff and the necessity for greater efficiency to get the most from diminishing resources. There is also a certain amount of disillusion with early participative staff structures, where it was found that staff were not ready for, or skilled in, participative modes of behaviour. There are many routine and operational activities which library staff are engaged in which do not lend themselves to consultation. They are most efficiently done by providing clear written instructions and regular supervision. When any problems arise they are best sorted out on the job, between staff member and immediate supervisor. There is little opportunity or need for meetings, decision-making working parties or other time-consuming group work.

Another point in favour of the scientific approach is that it provides a great deal of security for the many staff who are not particularly ambitious or seeking responsibility. There is a clear hierarchy of authority, in which the more senior staff take all the decisions, as their status and salary indicates they should. There are fixed function posts with clear job descriptions which, while being perhaps inflexible and unchallenging for more aspiring librarians, provide for many a comfort in 'knowing where I am, and what I have to do'. However a recent research report[8] indicates that younger professional librarians are becoming disillusioned and frustrated because they cannot find interesting and responsible jobs to move to after their first professional post. There is a suggestion in many job satisfaction surveys that new library staff feel overqualified for the work they do. Is this because their managers and supervisors belong to the scientific school of thought, which leads to tight control and lack of delegation? Or is it because they are given the expectation at library schools that they will be working in mainly participative structures, whereas in reality they find jobs in authoritarian structures? In one research report[9] only a third of the library staff responding named team membership as 'of interest to them in an ideal job, resulting in 23rd place [out of 31] for this factor'. Is this because they prefer scientific to participative management structures, or is it because team systems have not evolved satisfactorily into genuinely participative vehicles for decision-making? Barlow, in a more recent study of team librarianship, has considerable doubts about its participative nature in Leicestershire, the pioneering authority, in which he detected a 'move away from organic, participative, or at least cooperative structures, towards more hierarchical forms'.[10]

Human relations school of management

The human relations school of management had its origins in the United States in the 1920s. Since then it has undergone a massive popularization. Particularly since the 1950s it has been widely used in organizations, and a vast body of literature embodies its approaches, from the theoretical academic tome to the staff management textbook studied by every student in business schools both sides of the Atlantic. It has been just as massively attacked, by a wide range of critics across the left–right continuum. Right-wing economists consider human relations approaches to be 'soft' because they reject money as the main incentive to workers. Left-wing critics condemn it because it shows workers to have very complex and not necessarily rational needs at work, and this gets in the way of straight economic and power bargaining between bosses and workers. They may also consider human relations techniques to be manipulative, on the grounds that some staff managers may go too far in exploiting staff's complex needs, for the benefit of the organization. It could be argued that the human relations approach encourages 'workaholics', and can turn people into willing slaves of the organization.

Any exposition of the human relations school must begin with Elton Mayo, who carried out a series of studies in the 1920s in the Hawthorne Works of the Western Electric Company in the United States. One of his most significant discoveries was the importance of the 'informed organization' in any workplace. Alongside the formal staff structure or organization chart there exists an informal social system which acts as an alternative communication channel, and may indeed in some cases subvert the official channel. A common manifestation of this is what people call 'the grapevine', a more or less accurate information network which can be highly influential in forming attitudes (for or against innovation, for example).

Mayo identified employees' need to have a stable social relationship at work, thus questioning the validity of the 'rabble hypothesis' of the scientific school, that each individual pursues his or her own self-interest irrespective of the work group. It follows that people at work need to be provided with a

secure base for 'spontaneous co-operation'. This need can be met by deploying staff in a team or work group with which they can identify, and have a
sense of belonging. Such an approach will, he argued, diminish conflict and
disagreement, and enable individuals to commit themselves through the group
to the aims of the organization. From the manager's point of view leadership
and counselling are indivisible, and it is through skilful communication between manager and workers that teams are built and sustained, because this is
the way that supervisors can develop their staff's 'desire and capacity to work
better with management'. His view that money means less to people than
satisfying their non-logical need for being in a social group at work, has led
unkind critics to say that he substituted the 'tribal hypothesis' for the 'rabble
hypothesis'. It is an important argument against the human relations school
that they elevated the importance of the work group and social collaboration
to a point where other significant factors were ignored, such as the relationship between the nature of the tasks and the work group, or the basic differences between people in their individual or group orientation to work. Everyone was assumed to be primarily social-oriented, obsessed by the need for
'togetherness'.

There has been criticism of Mayo's methodology as well, since it appears
that he was selective in writing up the results. It has been argued that some of
his work groups were inevitably in the end good examples of co-operation
and social belongingness, because:

> (1) members were deliberately selected for their co-operativeness; (2) two unco-
> operative members were soon replaced; (3) one of the replacements urged her
> associates to make high bonuses because she had unusual family responsibili-
> ties; and (4) the second relay assembly team responded to financial incentives.[11]

Bearing these criticisms in mind, one may now consider some of the results of
actual experiments carried out by Mayo at the Hawthorne Works of the Western Electric Company in Chicago. He found that the work group was a major
determinant of behaviour, and also that when supervisors and managers
showed an interest in their workers and were prepared to consult them, there
was improved productivity, whereas there did not appear to be improved
productivity when material conditions only were improved. This was unexpected, since the scientific school of management had always argued for the
'carrot and stick' approach. By tinkering with material working conditions,
like longer tea breaks, for example, it had been assumed you could create
greater productivity. Now it seemed that a more significant incentive was the
interest taken by management, and their willingness to consult.

In another series of experiments, known as the Bank Wiring Room studies,
Mayo observed also that employees have a way of controlling their own work
activities, irrespective of the official management controls. The group of workers in this study was observed to have its own informal social structure and
code of behaviour, which in fact clashed with that of management. They had a
standard of output which no individual would exceed, and they were indiffer-

ent to the company's financial incentive scheme. Too much work was seen as 'rate-busting'; too little would be 'chiselling'. The company had assigned formal roles to the workers, but the really influential roles were the informal ones developed within the group by the employees themselves.

Maslow's hierarchy of needs

After the Second World War the work of the humanist psychologist Abraham Maslow[12] was influential in the development of the human relations school of management. His approach continues to concentrate on the 'content' or 'substantive' theories of motivation, which try to arrive at a set of needs which must be fulfilled if workers are to be satisfied. It emphasizes, that is, the social rather than the technical factors present in the workplace, in contrast to the Tavistock School[13] which in the 1950s in Britain was studying the interrelationship between technology and worker behaviour (a 'process' approach to motivation).

The assumption in Maslow is that it is necessary to understand the different levels of need which people experience, because only then will it be possible to create a work environment which will satisfy staff needs and thus lead to high morale and, it is assumed, high output. Maslow drew up a hierarchy of needs (see Figure 2.2) which is intended to have wider application than the workplace. It has been used by psychologists in helping people draw up 'whole life' programmes of self-development.

Figure 2.2   Maslow's hierarchy

In Maslow's view people are not able to progress to the satisfaction of their higher level needs (such as social needs, esteem needs) until they have first satisfied their more humble needs (those which appear lower down the hierarchy such as safety needs). In western countries most workers earn enough to take care of the basic material comforts of food, clothing and shelter. Once this level is met, people aspire to the next level, which is the need for safety and security. In this area is included not just security of income and tenure, though these are of increasing importance in an era of rising unemployment, even among the graduate population. Also included is the need for information, which can be an important source of security for employees. They need to know where their organization is going, what its future is likely to be, and how this may affect their jobs. This is why house magazines, bulletin boards and other such simple devices are so important. Equally important is the communication climate in an organization, the ease or difficulty with which important developments get passed on, formally and/or informally. Another source of security at work is adequate training for the job one has to do, and the support of backup written guidelines as well as verbal instruction. In periods of rapid technological and structural change in libraries, staff are made to feel insecure if they see their jobs under 'threat' of change, but they feel a great deal more insecure if inadequate provision is made – too little, too late – to retrain them. This applies not only to technical skills, needed in automation, for example, but also to interpersonal skills – learning to work effectively in a team structure, for example, or learning how to be an effective intermediary in on-line searching, between the end-user and the database.

When the needs for material comforts and security are adequately met, Maslow argues that people then aspire to the next highest level, the social or 'belongingness' needs. Once staff have reasonable working conditions, reasonable salaries, and a certain level of security, they will still not be positively motivated, because their needs are more complex than was assumed by classical or scientific management theorists. This is not to say of course that the lower level needs are not important. It is to emphasize that by themselves they will not spur staff on to feelings of positive satisfaction and high achievement. There will always be employees whose expectations of work remain at a fairly basic level of need, and this applies to libraries as to other organizations. However, since library and information work is now a graduate profession, it must be accepted that professional staff are likely to aspire to the higher needs of the Maslowian hierarchy.

The implications of fulfilling staff needs for social contacts and belongingness lead to a consideration of group membership at work. We have already seen how Elton Mayo's experiments showed the value that employees attached to their work group, whether it is formally structured by management or informally arranged by the employees themselves. In libraries team structures have been on the increase since the 1970s. In public libraries in particular, area teams have been formed to combat the isolation of branch librarians and draw them more fully into professional projects for the whole area, in some allocated specialism, so that within the team there is someone with responsibility for developing community information services, children's and schools' work, special services to the housebound, or to institutions etc. In addition to these area teams, public library staff may belong to temporary *ad hoc* working parties where, for example, automation projects are under way. There are also in some authorities groups for 'young professionals', to bring together people with ideas which might not otherwise find expression. In many public library structures a matrix management system operates, cutting across the traditional hierarchy. Thus an individual member of staff may take part in area team meetings, in meetings of specialists, say children's librarians or community information librarians, from across the whole system, and sometimes also in special interest meetings, say new technology applications.

In academic libraries the basic 'team' has remained the group of professionals and assistants who serve subject communities reflecting the primary need for the library to involve itself with the communities. Like public libraries many have regular meetings of management groups and working parties set up to meet particular short-term needs, such as designing a system of charging for services or standing groups concerned with continuing services such as staff training and user education. Nottingham Trent University Library, for example, formed a group to improve its library induction programme and also has a standing user education group. However informal the structure, the number of library staff working as isolated individuals is decreasing, and the majority of academic librarians have some sense of belonging to a work group, if not a team.

The categories that appear to suffer most from isolation are school librarians and information workers in the smallest special libraries. It is often not possible for them even to get away on courses or conferences to meet kindred spirits, because of the practical problems of being a 'one person unit'. Thus they may suffer from a lack of professional self-identity, and in the early stages of their career, a lack of role models. They are dependent for their social and belongingness needs on users acknowledging their value, which may leave them relatively deprived, compared with the collegial support which many public and academic librarians experience.

The message which the Maslowian hierarchy has for managers about social or belongingness needs is important, because if the staffing structure does not allow for work groups and the encouragement of a sense of identity within the work group, staff are likely to form their own informal groups, which may end up pursuing different goals from senior management. There are many notorious examples of the flouting of this principle in the workplace. The open-plan office, for instance, diminishes the sense of identity and makes more difficult the formation of work groups with a common purpose. Some aspects of library automation, such as buying-in centralized cataloguing services, may similarly undermine an existing work group of cataloguers, by deskilling the activities and introducing more clerical workers rather than professionals.

As libraries have become larger and more complex in management structures – through mergers in particular the multi-site problem has grown and continues to grow – careful thought needs to be given to deploying staff in small work groups with which they can identify, and from whom they can draw support. It is the 'primary' group, the people we meet face-to-face in our daily activities, with some common purpose, that matters to people, rather than the 'secondary' group which consists of the more formal official forums within the organization, usually named as management teams. Social psychologists argue that the best size for the primary group is between eight and twelve. The primary group is significant in moulding staff opinions, goals and ideals. If there is conflict between these and the secondary group (the larger organization) goals, the primary group is likely to prove stronger, and no amount of management 'propaganda' will change this. One solution in that case is to start with the primary group, 'where they are at', and see if attitudes and entrenched ideas may be modified by involving them in planning their work in relation to the concerns of senior management, as well as their own concerns as a work group. It is important that all members of a senior management team are able to view matters from a systemwide perspective as well as through their own group interests. If this is not the case then centrifugal tendencies can develop which are harmful when the wish is for the service to make progress as a whole.

The Maslowian hierarchy has at its highest levels people's needs for achievement, challenge, self-expression and 'self-actualization' or fulfilment of one's potential. Surveys of job satisfaction among library and information workers tend to show that people want to be fulfilled on these levels as well as the lower levels, but there may be an element of wishful thinking in the completion of such interviews and questionnaires, if one takes account of views expressed by senior management about the problems they have in establishing participative systems. There is, it seems, a reluctance to take a positive role in teams, a shortage of ideas-generation, a disappointing lack of response to new staff structures intended to stimulate initiative, and get projects off the ground. How can this be, when surveys of newly qualified librarians all seem to show that there is frustration caused by:

1   Lack of opportunity to exercise one's professional expertise.
2   Lack of opportunity to exercise responsibility.
3   Dull and repetitive routine work, rather than being trusted to apply the skills learned during one's professional course.
4   Insufficient contact with users, because of high proportion of technical services work in relation to reader services work so sense of achievement gained by recognition and feedback is seen as inadequate.[14]

As Roberts commented in 1978, 'professional librarians are often not employed to best institutional or user advantage. Or it must be said, to their own',[15] and in 1991 he was expressing grave concern for the de-professionalization being experienced by all types of library who are 'forced to make do with fewer professionals and/or to distribute previously acknowledged professional duties among non-professional staff'.[16]

The question is how to ensure that staff are encouraged to operate at the higher levels of their potential. The answer is not clear cut, because there are so many variables. The nature of the tasks may not require much initiative or creativity, because library and information work contains a fair, or more than a fair, share of routine rather than decision-making. The management structures may not be conducive to delegation or 'trusting' new professionals to carry out genuinely professional work. Some recruits to the profession may have been attracted by the safe nature of the job, and prefer routines to responsibility or innovative projects or they may have had their expectations lowered by the contrast between their professional education and what they are permitted to do in their first posts. Financial constraints are a further factor, and in some libraries they have led to staff reverting to a larger proportion of purely housekeeping routines and day-to-day administration, after the brave new moves towards outreach, community analysis and expanded information services.

McGregor's Theory X and Theory Y

Douglas McGregor took Maslow's ideas and developed them in the staff management context. In doing so, it has been argued, he oversimplified Maslow's sophisticated thinking about the 'role of association, habit and conditioning', and 'the relation between needs and cultural patterns', which may heavily influence individual needs.[17] His three major types of need are physiological, social and self-fulfilment. He considered that the scientific school of management, the 'hard approach', might satisfy staff needs for physiological or material security, but it frustrated their social needs and their need for self-fulfilment. He encapsulated the two extremes that managers could take up, and called them Theory X (representing the scientific approach) and Theory Y (representing the human relations approach).[18]

According to Theory X employees are, in general, indolent. They lack ambition and are resistant to change. They are inherently self-centred and indifferent to the organization's needs. Without the active intervention of management people would be either passive or resistant to the organization's goals. It follows that management must impose firm direction and control on its staff, and attempt to modify their behaviour to fit in with the organization's goals.

There can be a hard or a soft interpretation of the Theory X approach by individual managers. The hard approach favours very tight inspection, checking and control. A certain amount of threat and coercion is usually implicit, though often concealed. There is little communication except downwards from seniors to juniors, and what there is tends to be rather formal, in writing rather than face-to-face communication. The experience of Theory X hard-style managers in industry over the past fifty years suggests that workers respond in quite predictable ways. They restrict their output to the minimum demanded, undermine whenever possible the objectives of senior management, and form their own 'resistance' groups, which can take the form of informal groups of 'mates' playing the system, or of a more overtly political struggle between workers and bosses, in the form of militant trade unionism.

The soft approach to Theory X involves management in speaking softly, but still using the 'carrot and stick' approach of rather crude incentives and punishments, derived from Theory X assumptions about workers' laziness and lack of commitment if not driven. In this case workers' reactions are likely to be equally predictable, since few are deceived by the appearance of the velvet glove on the iron hand. The usual response is to take advantage by lowering output or giving an inferior performance at work. There may be a kind of superficial harmony, because people are not anxious to rock the boat by bringing to the surface fundamental divisions, but there is a lack of real commitment to the organization, because there is little trust and expectations of workers' capabilities remain low.

McGregor argues that in many workplaces observation might appear to confirm the assumptions of Theory X about workers' laziness, lack of commitment and passivity. However he says that this is a consequence of management policies and practices, rather than the inevitable outcome of man's and woman's natures. He is much indebted to Maslow for his views on needs at work, and he emphasizes that in many workplaces only the lower level needs are satisfied. This leads to the frustration and anomie which is what causes people to behave in a lazy, uncommitted, irresponsible manner. Therefore, he says, we need an alternative theory based on more adequate assumptions about human nature. This is provided in the set of propositions called Theory Y.

Theory Y asserts that employees are capable of assuming responsibility and supporting the goals of the organization. It is the responsibility of management to provide the right conditions in which staff are able to fulfil their potential, and satisfy their higher level needs for esteem, recognition and a sense of achievement. By being given more say in their work, people will not only achieve their own goals better, but will contribute more to the overall goal of the organization.

It sounds rather Utopian, and McGregor admits that there are problems putting it into practice. After people have been treated as passive and incapable of responsibility for some time, they are unlikely to be able to make the switch to being mature, self-activating beings, just because there has been a change of management style. People who are used to being closely directed and strictly controlled at work are likely to turn to other spheres of their life for higher level satisfactions, and offer only a minimal commitment to their jobs. Also, it must be faced, many jobs are not worth more than a minimal commitment, and this is a problem highlighted in the job satisfaction surveys in librarianship, which point out the problem of dull, routine procedural work in many areas of the profession. However there are clearly areas for improvement and Theory Y undoubtedly has an appeal in humanist terms, with its emphasis on individual responsibility, self-starters, and the dignity of man and woman *vis-à-vis* their superiors. McGregor is anxious to point out that Theory Y approaches to staff management need not be 'soft', that it can lead to high performance as well as a more satisfied staff. If it works, staff will to work is strengthened and they commit themselves more sincerely to the service aims of their libraries. This may, unfortunately, be offset by a certain anarchy, and less willingness to plod through the duller work with competence and discipline, as they might be obliged to do under a Theory X régime.

It is important to note that real-life organizations rarely fall neatly into the Theory X or Theory Y category. Rather there is a continuum from X to Y, with the majority of libraries, for example, grouped to left or right of the middle. That is, most libraries display a complex mixture of Theory X and Theory Y structures and styles. The head librarian may favour traditional hierarchical management (Theory X) but this may be offset by the deputy, who organizes participative (Theory Y) structures here and there in the organization, and encourages staff to work together and to take initiatives. Or the head may encourage (Theory Y) staff participation by restructuring the hierarchical pyramid so that staff have more meetings and work on projects with colleagues at their own level. But this may be subverted by Theory X long-serving staff lower down the hierarchy, who do not wish to consult their subordinates or to move beyond their own patch, or take an interest in the overall goals of the library.

Rensis Likert[19] and participative management

The human relations approach supposes that participative management structures and styles create conditions at work which enable staff to realize their potential, make greater use of their professional training, and thus improve the effectiveness of the service offered. Likert is one of the leading proponents of participative management, and holds the view that the majority of workers prefer this approach, and that it also results in better performance. Figure 2.3 is a summary of the range of management styles which are found in the workplace, in Likert's analysis.

1	2	3	4
← Authoritative →		← Participative →	
Exploitative authoritative	Benevolent authoritative	Consultative	Participative group

Figure 2.3   Range of management styles

Examples of all four management styles are to be found in libraries, and different styles may operate in different sections of the same library.

Stages 1 and 2 of the diagram show the two variations of authoritarian management styles. The more extreme is the exploitative. This assumes that 'buying a man's time gives the employer control over the employee's behaviour', and that 'the organization must put direct hierarchical pressure upon its employees to produce at specified levels'. This is rare in libraries, perhaps because it is not common for libraries to measure their outputs and to impose clearcut standards or levels of productivity on their staff, so that this approach would scarcely be feasible, even if it were considered desirable in human relations terms. Stage 2 is more common in libraries, and this 'benevolent authoritarian' style is marked by some show of representation of staff views, while retaining all the decision-making at the top of the hierarchy. Thus authority remains concentrated among the few, with little delegation. The organization structure is likely to be tall and narrow, favouring centralized decision-making. The emphasis is on downward communication rather than lateral or upward communication.

The consultative style, stage 3 in the diagram, involves supervisors in asking staff for their opinions and views, but not necessarily incorporating these into their decisions, which they still make on their own as 'the one in charge here'. Or they may take account of staff views in relation to their immediate day-to-day work, but not consult them on any wider issues, though these may affect their work. This kind of consultation often goes with the *laissez-faire* management style which is quite common in libraries. There are few considered management strategies, and so people 'manage' without much conscious awareness of the effects on their subordinates.

The genuinely participative style, stage 4, means that individuals share in decision-making through their activity in the work group, and through meetings which have the power to arrive at decisions, rather than simply making recommendations to the people at the top. This is rare in libraries, where many meetings may be held, but the power to take decisions is quite limited, except at senior management team level.

The applications of participative approaches in libraries have not been entirely successful. In spite of expressed preferences for consultative and participative group approaches, as shown for example in Stewart's 1982 survey of job satisfaction,[20] Ritchie found that the obvious example of participation, working in teams, was not rated high as a source of satisfaction.[21] She suggests, however, that this may be because some teams are authoritarian rather than genuinely participative in the way they are run. So it appears that participative structures are not a guarantee of real participation. This is borne out by Barlow who criticizes team-based structures in which it was thought that participation in the decision- and policy-making processes could not work because staff 'do not want to take responsibility for the decisions they are involved in making'. Unfortunately such an attitude seriously misinterprets the role of senior management in a participative system, as Likert defined it.[22]

Likert's research techniques include asking *subordinates* some questions which may help to analyse just how genuinely participative work groups are:

1 To what extent does your supervisor try to understand your problems at work, and your personal and family difficulties?
2 Is he interested in helping you get the training which will help you in your present and future jobs?
3 How much confidence and trust do you have in your supervisor, and how much does he have in you, do you feel?
4 Does he ask your opinion when a problem comes up which involves your work? Following this, does he attach any value to your ideas, and try to use them?

Other significant findings in Likert's research (which was carried out in American industrial organizations, and may not necessarily be confirmed in public service organizations like libraries) were that the managers able to achieve high output are those who make more use of work groups in decision-making, and who involve their staff in work-related discussion. An important aspect of high performance also appears to be that high performing people act as models for others and provide an incentive, particularly in group working, or team working. The problem is that it can take a long time to develop co-operation rather than competitive individualism in a team, though if it can be achieved it is rewarding both for the individuals and the organization. Some libraries recognize that training is needed in how to make teams more effective, and have devised practical exercises based on simulations of the team situation.[23] Training strategies are discussed in Chapter 8.

Blake and Mouton's managerial grid[24]

The managerial grid is a device for managers, or anyone who supervises staff, to plot, by means of self-scoring questionnaires, the extent to which their management style shows concern for output and concern for people, and in what proportions. The grid is shown in Figure 2.4. Blake and Mouton's view is that the most satisfactory position on the grid, which staff managers should be aiming for, is the 9,9 position. This indicates both a high concern for output and a high concern for people. The practical value of the grid is as a starting point for training for supervisors. Having found their present position on the grid, they can be given in-service training or external courses which enable them to move closer to the 9,9 stance.

The 9,9 position of high participation, commitment to the workplace, and concern for output, is 'not for social purposes or to maintain morale as an end in itself, nor does the team concept provide a cloak of anonymity within which inadequate performance can be buried or hidden. Rather, sound interpersonal relations are seen as the *best* way to achieve or to maintain production at peak levels'.[25] Personal conflict can be worked through, rather than repressed or avoided (as in the 1,9 'country club style', or punished from above (as in the 9,1 style).

Outside observers tend to see libraries as representing the 1,9 style – of low concern for output and high concern for people. There is seen to be a fairly relaxed work tempo and a friendly atmosphere (not competitive or aggressive) among staff work groups. There does not seem to be overt effort to keep improving the quality and quantity of work done by individual members of staff. However generalizations are rash since there may be wide swings within a library from time to time, for example academic libraries might seem to display 9,1 characteristics during their busiest periods in term time, but shift to 1,9 characteristics during vacations. Also within the same library countervailing positions may be displayed by staff at different levels, for example 9,1 by line managers, 1,9 by a personnel officer, 9,9 by the head librarian, 1,1 by stagnating time-servers.

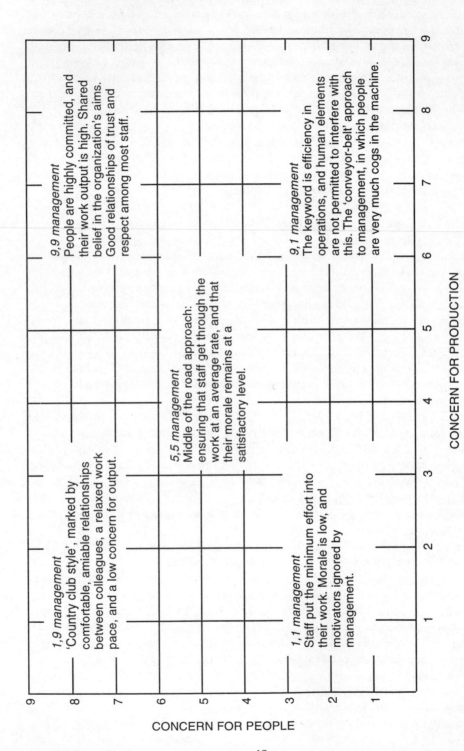

CONCERN FOR PEOPLE

1,9 management
'Country club style', marked by comfortable, amiable relationships between colleagues, a relaxed work pace, and a low concern for output.

1,1 management
Staff put the minimum effort into their work. Morale is low, and motivators ignored by management.

9,9 management
People are highly committed, and their work output is high. Shared belief in the organization's aims. Good relationships of trust and respect among most staff.

5,5 management
Middle of the road approach: ensuring that staff get through the work at an average rate, and that their morale remains at a satisfactory level.

9,1 management
The keyword is efficiency in operations, and human elements are not permitted to interfere with this. The 'conveyor-belt' approach to management, in which people are very much cogs in the machine.

CONCERN FOR PRODUCTION

Figure 2.4   The managerial grid based on the Blake and Mouton research

40

There are also environmental and personality factors to be considered in discussing the feasibility of the 9,9 position. Limitations in resources may mean that staff do more routine operational work and get less satisfaction than if they were in a position to develop services. Personality may limit moves towards 'team socialization' and cause reluctance, if not actual subversion, of management efforts to provide more participative structures. In recent years there has been considerable emphasis on objectives, performance indicators based upon the objectives and formalized staff appraisal systems. These are attempts to move towards a 9,9 position and librarians are having to learn how to make the best use of these techniques.

Herzberg's satisfiers and dissatisfiers

Herzberg is best known for the studies he carried out on groups of engineers and accountants, to elicit their attitudes to work. Later studies applied his 'two-factor theory of job satisfaction' to other occupations, and Plate and Stone[26] applied it to American librarians (1974). Herzberg's theory may be summarized as follows:

> The factors involved in producing job satisfaction (and motivation) are separate and distinct from the factors that lead to job dissatisfaction. Since separate factors need to be considered ... it follows that these two feelings are not opposites of each other. The opposite of job satisfaction is not job dissatisfaction, but rather, *no* job satisfaction; and similarly the opposite of job dissatisfaction is not job satisfaction, but *no* job dissatisfaction.[27]

In other words, it is not enough to remove certain causes of dissatisfaction, by raising pay or improving supervision or providing better working conditions. These will not in themselves increase satisfaction; they may merely remove sources of dissatisfaction. In order to provide positive satisfaction, Herzberg argues, it is necessary to bring into play 'motivators'. These are reminiscent of the higher needs in the Maslowian hierarchy. They include a sense of achievement, recognition, responsibility, advancement, and the nature of the work itself. The motivators must be present to create worker satisfaction; they relate more to the intrinsic nature of the job than to contextual factors. Contextual factors, external to the work itself, include pay, security, status, technical supervision, company policy and administration, and interpersonal relationships. These are Herzberg's 'hygiene factors' which may cause dissatisfaction if they are not acceptably worked out by management and employees. He uses the medical analogy of the hygiene factors to imply that by paying attention to these factors an organization may *prevent* dissatisfaction, without however providing positive motivation. Nonetheless the removal of dissatisfiers is important, just as hygiene factors in the medical context are important, since it clears the way for the benefits that may be obtained from the positive motivators.

It follows from Herzberg's studies that staff managers should be more concerned with job enrichment strategies, and with job content changes, rather than assuming that it is the low motivated employees who are somehow at fault and that the job content is inviolate. He is sceptical of sacred words like 'achievement', 'challenge', 'growth', and 'responsibility', unless they are translated into practical strategies such as job enrichment and actual delegation.

The problem with Herzberg's two-factor theory is that the choice of methodology determines the results. D'Elia warns that the two-factor theory 'is a consequence of its simplistic methodology', and more sophisticated attempts to replicate its results have been unsuccessful or inconclusive. It is therefore a misleading theory on which to base practical strategies of staff motivation:

> This method, by its very form, forces the employee to describe satisfying factors and dissatisfying factors separately, it permits the employee to accept responsibility for his good feelings and to ascribe to others the responsibility for his bad feelings, it is open to subjectivity on the part of the researcher who interprets and codes the employee's responses.[28]

This rather undermines studies like Plate and Stone's, which used the Herzberg methodology and replicated his results accordingly. However it would be a pity if the 'critical incident' approach to exploring job satisfaction were to be thrown out because of its association with the two-factor theory. It is a useful device in a semi-structured questionnaire or interview to include questions like 'Please describe briefly an occasion at work when you felt particularly satisfied', and 'Please describe an occasion at work when you felt particularly dissatisfied'. In the authors' experience the answers are illuminating, and do not divide neatly into Herzberg's motivators and hygiene factors, unless the researcher has set out with that particular methodology in mind. For example, library assistants' responses to automated circulation systems were collected during a student field study, and it was found that the decrease in sociability between staff and users was a source of dissatisfaction for some assistants, but a source of satisfaction for others, who liked to get their work done more quickly and efficiently. Thus the same factor could be a source of satisfaction or dissatisfaction according to individuals' differing needs at work – as in the Maslowian hierarchy, where some staff may seek mainly social and belongingness needs, while others seek esteem or recognition for work well done.

The Minnesota Job Satisfaction Questionnaire[29]

The Minnesota University Industrial Relations Center produced a number of questionnaires in the late 1960s for collecting information on job characteristics and job satisfaction. D'Elia's study[30] in 1979 of beginning librarians in the United States, and Russell's study[31] in 1984 of non-professional library assistants in the United Kingdom both used the Minnesota approach. Bundy[32] also used the Minnesota Satisfaction questionnaire in evaluating the job satisfaction of subject librarians in British and Australian polytechnics. He compared his findings with those of Burgess[33] who had used the technique in surveying reference librarians and cataloguers. This involves getting respondents to rate the degree of satisfaction they derive from a range of job characteristics. The 'job-related dimensions' which are measured include ability utilization, sense of achievement, nature of activity, opportunities for advancement, authority, company policies and practices, one's colleagues, independence, recognition, security, working conditions, and satisfaction at providing a service. It also covers the whole area of supervision, which is seen to have two aspects: the human relations dimension and the technical competence dimension, both of which are important to staff supervised, but in different degrees depending on their particular needs at work.

D'Elia's findings were that the satisfaction needs among beginning librarians were quite similar, and that their job environments provided the characteristics which caused them satisfaction or dissatisfaction. The most important characteristics in providing job satisfaction were 'supervision–human relations' and 'ability utilization'. When these are translated into job dimensions the former means library policy and practices and the supervisory climate. Ability utilization covers factors intrinsic to the job itself, such as use of one's training and expertise, which involves being allowed to exercise some responsibility and professional autonomy, and being given recognition for doing so. It would appear that there is an important relationship between the supervisory climate and opportunities for the beginning librarian to use his or her expertise creatively and autonomously. The climate may be deliberately participative, or it may be merely *laissez-faire*. It is suggested that the performance of library supervisors may be usefully diagnosed and evaluated by reviewing the job satisfaction of their staff.

Bundy found that the job satisfaction of subject librarians was significantly greater than that of reference librarians and cataloguers. He found that activity was the most satisfying dimension for subject librarians but it did not rank in the first two for either reference librarians or cataloguers. Creativity, ability utilization and achievement were ranked 2, 3 and 5 by subject librarians but were not ranked at all by cataloguers and reference librarians. Bundy concludes that it is likely that the additional elements in the role of subject librarians beyond basic information work contributes to the higher level of general job satisfaction. The factors that create the most dissatisfaction are those which are controlled by institutional and library management such as security, recognition and authority. Burgess concludes that 'the dissatisfaction expressed by the respondents with library administration may be due to inept management, but it may also be due to lack of initiative on the part of librarians in not creating opportunities for participation and implementing decisions'.

The Russell survey of non-professional library staff, part-time and full-time, in six British academic and public libraries received replies from 341 or 60 per cent of the library staff contacted. The Minnesota Job Satisfaction Questionnaire was modified in two ways. The dimensions of social status and moral values as constituents of job satisfaction were omitted as 'not relevant to the context of this study', and eight other dimensions were added: career prospects, communication, comparison of self with professional librarians, education utilization, physical demands of job, supervision–participation, task completion and training. These, when added to the original Minnesota dimensions of job satisfaction – ability utilization, achievement, activity, authority, company policies and practices, co-workers, creativity, independence, pay, promotion, recognition, responsibility, security, social service, supervision, variety and working conditions – provided a total of twenty-six dimensions. They were tested by asking the library assistants to tick on a Likert scale of one to five their degree of satisfaction with various aspects of their job representing the Minnesota dimensions.

Russell's findings were interesting both in relation to the methodological problems of investigating job satisfaction, and in terms of the results. A direct question about job satisfaction revealed that 85 per cent of non-professionals were satisfied or very satisfied, but when these results were tested by asking direct questions, it found that 'the percentage dissatisfied may be somewhere between 30% and 40%'. The causes of their dissatisfaction were the nature of the supervision received and lack of freedom of action in the performance of their duties. The most unsatisfactory aspects of their jobs were 'library policies', particularly their promotion and career prospects, their treatment by library management and their relationship with professional staff. Sources of satisfaction centred on their actual duties and their co-workers. Thapisa's survey[34] of full-time library assistants with at least two years' continuous experience in university libraries in England also found lack of promotional opportunities high on the list of causes of dissatisfaction. Sixty-eight per cent felt they were in dead-end jobs with no promotion prospects and 'nothing to work towards'. Very little was done to encourage library assistants to take up higher qualifications leading to feelings of low esteem and unimportance. The greatest source of dissatisfaction, however, was pay – 'the most prevalent feeling was that library assistants should be paid more since they were the ones that kept the library running' and it certainly was not considered adequate for young single people or people who were just married or setting up a new home. Banks,[35] who carried out experiments with student assistants in academic libraries, supports the view that pay is the most important motivator for casual workers who generally do not work full-time, have only a partial psychological commitment to the organization and have no career notions. She found that a pay increase across the board rather than pay tied to goals was the most effective motivator.

The alleviation of the problems experienced by non-professional staff in libraries, particularly those in academic libraries and those who work in technical services, for these are the most dissatisfied categories, would involve a multidimensional strategy. Recruitment policies are the starting point and should begin with job analysis and job design, and the appointment of staff who can carry out those duties effectively. A particular problem has been the employment of over-qualified people in library assistant posts. This is more likely at times when jobs are scarce and where applicants believe that contact with users will provide compensatory rewards. Our own experience has been that this can be successful if the routine nature of the job and lack of promotion prospects are forcefully stated and the particular circumstances and personality of the applicant are taken into consideration. Once library assistants are in their jobs it is of paramount importance that their contributions are appreciated – 'What I am trying to say is, although my job may be routine it is how I make my living and I need to be appreciated. All it needs is for someone to notice something I have done and the whole attitude to my work changes'.[36] This view is supported by Miletich,[37] who speaks out on behalf of the non-professional – 'your front line of defense against time-robbers and energy-wasters' – compared with professionals whom he considers as often transients on the look-out for better pay, more responsibility, always scanning the ads in various professional journals.

Many libraries have been restructuring over the last decade and this has usually meant giving more of the clerical and administrative routines to non-professionals, and increasing the job satisfaction for professionals as well, by ensuring that a higher proportion of their work content is actually professional and therefore appropriate to the graduate profession that we have become. By 'actually professional' we mean a role in which:

> library needs are identified, problems are analysed, goals are set, and original and creative solutions are formulated for them, integrating theory into practice, and planning, organizing, communicating and administering successful programs of service to users of the library's materials and services.[38]

Often the incentive to restructuring seems to come from outside financial pressures (one professional salary equals three non-professional salaries) or for technological reasons, mainly automation, which not only alters non-professional jobs, but deskills, for example, cataloguing posts which were once the preserve of graduate librarians, but now only require trained non-professionals. It is an opportunity to reassess the tasks that make up jobs and analyse the responsibilities carried by jobs. Many job descriptions list professional duties but do not make it clear that most of the job is not professional duties, but routine administration. This is not an exercise that can be carried out quickly or simply. There are many vested interests and entrenched attitudes involved. Participation and consultation with unions are essential, and even then the implementation is likely to be slow and disruptive, since it is a human characteristic to prefer the devil you know to some great beast slouching towards your library to be born. The trend is establishing itself, however, towards a better more economical balance between professional and non-professional staff, leading not only to increased job satisfaction at both levels, but to more effective services to the public, as staff are encouraged to develop projects, and consider that change and the generation of better ways of doing things is as much part of their work as keeping the daily routines ticking over. The trend is encouraged by the wider introduction of career grades, if limited, for non-professionals, who are thereby given an incentive to take BTEC or City and Guilds certificates in library and information work. The introduction of National Vocational Qualifications in library and information work will encourage this trend.

More complex models of motivation

Some theorists in motivation have evolved more complex models to explain people's behaviour and aspirations at work, than the scientific or human relations schools provide. Vroom,[39] for example, stresses the effect of individual differences among staff on their motivation. Fiedler[40] stresses both differences in the work situation and in the kind of supervisors or leaders which an organization has recruited. It is accepted that staff motivation depends on a complicated interplay between the supervisor's management style, the organizational climate and the immediate work situation, where there may be significant differences in the management or technical services, say, compared with readers' services, in addition to the individual's needs of security, esteem etc.

The 'complex systems' approach is usefully summarized by Schein.[41] He emphasizes in his research findings that any organization consists of a series of subsystems – in a library these would include, for example, technical, social and environmental systems – and argues that the interplay of these subsystems is as important, if not more important, than the individual's propensity to certain kinds of work behaviour. Staff can be motivated or demotivated as much by the work group to which they belong, and the roles and norms of their colleagues, as by their individual needs for self-identity, self-fulfilment etc. Someone who is alienated in one library or section of a library may be motivated by moving to another post, or may find self-expression through union activities, while remaining inert and repressed on the job:

> Ultimate satisfaction and the ultimate effectiveness of the organization depends only in part on the nature of the motivation. The nature of the task to be performed, and the abilities and experience of the person on the job, and the nature of the other people in the organization all interact to produce a certain pattern of work and feelings. For example a highly skilled but poorly motivated worker may be as effective *and satisfied* as a very unskilled but highly motivated worker.[42]

Pirandello says that truth in a particular situation is a collection of what each person in the situation sees. If, in addition, everyone is wearing a *commedia del organizatione* mask (scapegoat, joker, token woman manager, Big Boss), whatever is the poor personnel manager to do? Plate and Stone, as a result of their survey of job satisfaction among American librarians, say:

> Libraries, despite their homogeneity, differ considerably with regard to their organizational history, leadership climate, and even goals and objectives. Library procedures vary from library to library, and so must personnel practices and supervisory styles ... library managers must therefore be skilled in the adaptation of existing principles of motivation to local requirements.[43]

A final approach to the 'process' school of motivation theories, as compared with the 'content' approach of analysing categories of needs experienced by people at work, may be loosely summarized as the 'action approach'. This involves analysing the workplace as an arena in which workers take part in 'social processes', and their interactions – between bosses and subordinates, between peer groups, between professionals and clients – are explained in terms of the meanings they have for the 'actors', which are dependent on different value systems and cultural backgrounds of the people involved. They are also, of course, subjective rather than objective meanings, and criticisms of this approach to analysing the workplace are that it ignores the realities of objective power. Some people have more power to impose their meanings on a situation than others, and ability to have one's definitions accepted, whether from a formal or informal power base, is part of the situation. For an organization to work at all, there has to be at least a working minimum of shared meanings among the people in it, and an acknowledgement if not an acceptance of objective structures and pressures within and without the organization. However, the contribution of the 'action school' of theorists is significant in that it draws our attention to the ways in which people at work attach their own meanings and values to their situation. There is no such thing as a purely objective view of the workplace, its technology, its staffing structure, its hierarchy of power. All these features are mediated by the subjectivity of those who experience them, and each person's subjectivity is a varied mix of individual aims and perceptions which are the result of that person's socially structured experiences and expectations. A useful derivative of the action approach is expectancy theory. This theory states that people act in ways that they think are likely to benefit them. Following the work of Vroom, Howard[44] has developed an expectancy theory in which motivation is seen in terms of four primary process variables:

E – P expectancy: an individual's perception of the likelihood that his or her effort will result in the successful performance of specific behaviour(s).

P – R expectancy: the perception of the likelihood of being rewarded for successful performance.

R – N expectancy: the perception of the likelihood that these rewards will meet important personal needs.

Valence: the value the individual places on the object, e.g. performance, reward or need satisfaction, of any of the above expectancies.

These concepts have been applied to *The motivation to train* by Crowder and Pupynin[45] and can readily be seen as important contributions to our understanding of motivation in other areas of librarianship.

The action approach is a useful antidote to the scientific systems analysis of organizations, which assumes that logic and reason are all that is needed to understand and manage staff, that central planning and more high technology will solve all problems. It is European rather than American – the seminal theorist was Touraine[46] who carried out studies among industrial workers at Renault in France – and is an attempt to reinvest 'organization' man and woman with individual dignity and meaning, rather than being dependent on their status and function in the work machine (as seen by management) for their (assigned) meanings.

Practical applications of motivation theories in libraries

The work of motivation theorists such as Maslow provides a range of useful background information on the factors underlying staff behaviour and attitudes at work. This is a valuable starting point for supervisors, to help them analyse people's needs at work, and take account of these needs in their strategies of staff deployment, allocation of duties, and job design generally – shaping the set of tasks and responsibilities which go to make up the job of any one individual. Understanding the importance of leadership styles in motivating staff is another area where motivation studies help, for they have a great many findings on how staff respond to the range of styles from paternalist authoritarian through consultative to genuinely participative. Many large academic and public libraries are impelled from time to time to redraw their organization charts and restructure their staff, to take account of changes introduced as a result of new technology or newly emerging user needs or financial cuts leading to reduced staff numbers. Here again an understanding of motivation theories is desirable, to provide for staff needs for security, recognition and identification with their own work group.

Motivation theory can also prove helpful in alleviating specific staff problems. The initial step the supervisor has to take is analysing the problem accurately, and often motivation and morale lie at the heart of the matter. In trying to find a solution, techniques which are derived from the human relations school of theorists may be relevant. Can a job be enriched or enlarged to fulfil the post-holder's frustrated need for recognition of professional expertise? Can a larger element of professional work be assigned to a member of staff whose job has been 'impoverished', by automation for example, or 'deskilled'? Can staff be restructured into small work groups or teams, to enhance their sense of identity at work and diminish isolation? Can initiative be encouraged rather than stifled by supervisors delegating more responsibility, and giving them more opportunities to develop their particular talents, expertise, specialisms and enthusiasms?

Motivation theories of the human relations school argue that concern for output and concern for people go hand in hand, and that a satisfied staff will be a high-performing staff. This has never been conclusively established (the research findings are contradictory or inconclusive), and would be especially difficult to establish in libraries, which do not in general have adequate measures of staff output. There may well be a conflict between the aims of employers and the aims of employees, centring on the following:

Aims of employer	*Aims of employee*
Work specificity (clearcut tasks)	Work flexibility(variety)
Output (high-performing)	Input (able to use expertise/interests)

| Uniformity (emphasis on rules, procedures) | Individuality (emphasis on initiative, judgment) |
| Performance (what one does) | Personal qualities (what one is) |

Supervisors responsible for allocation of tasks and job structuring can at least try to take account of the likely areas of conflict between their aims and their subordinates' aims at work, to effect a compromise.

Participative management and the human relations school of motivation

The human relations school places great emphasis on participative management as a method of satisfying a greater proportion of people's needs at work. It is considered conducive to high staff morale to provide more delegation, to push decision-making lower down the staff hierarchy, and to involve staff in setting their own objectives (projects, tasks to be completed by the end of a term/year) and in evaluating their achievements. The emphasis in organizational communication shifts from formal written memos and directives from the top down, to more informal face-to-face communication, through group and team and working party meetings. There is an increase in down/up and lateral communication. Emphasis is laid on 'self-starting' qualities, the capacity of staff to develop themselves in their own jobs, to grow professionally and reflect this in how they interpret their work.

It can be seen that these characteristics of participative management are derived from the thinking of Maslow, McGregor and others of their school. They follow from a conviction that people at work need to satisfy their higher level needs, for success, self-respect and self-actualization, as well as their basic needs for material support and security. As soon as people have achieved a secure job, with reasonable pay and working conditions they will escalate to higher level needs for social and self-expression rewards at work. Some at least will express their higher level needs, and expect work to provide them with opportunities for self-actualization.

An example of how participative management approaches were applied in an ICI information unit is described by Dutton.[47] The main features were that individual staff adopted their own individual targets; having defined these objectives, they were encouraged to attend relevant meetings and courses to get training, and feed back their increased expertise to the unit. All jobs, including counter jobs, were subject to 'self-examination'. Everybody was expected to question the way they did things, and assess whether it could be improved. For example, a small study was done on the success rate for borrowing interlibrary loans from various sources, and standard practice was reversed as a result of the findings. The general approach was to involve the staff at every level in dealing with problems and introducing and planning new systems. The more participative structure led to the elimination of excessive control and checking of minor matters. This meant economies in the use of time, besides encouraging staff at all times to differentiate between the essential and the trivial in their tasks.

Dutton sums up the value of motivation studies for the library managers as follows:

> These studies (Maslow and Herzberg) suggest that in developing staff we need to recognise two fundamentally different types of effect on motivation relating to hygiene factors and to motivation factors. Further, whilst the hygiene factors must be considered first, it is only necessary to ensure that these do not get out of line. The only practicable method for doing this is through comparison with similar units. It is not profitable to become continually preoccupied with improving these aspects ... Rather we must concentrate on trying to improve the motivation factors through the better organization of work, and experience points to staff participation as a highly effective means for doing this.[48]

In the academic library sector Ashworth notes that with the development of multisite polytechnic libraries from the late 1960s the old hierarchical staffing structures with strong central control and little delegation proved inadequate:

> For example a local academic librarian can be faced with demands from a Board of Studies which conflict with the total library policy, and an embarrassing division of loyalties ensues. If the secondary centres take independent action, the whole model fails.[49]

But if the site libraries are not able to take independent action, there are the universal complaints from staff and users that the centre is out of touch with local needs, that it is slow to act, unreceptive to communications from periphery to centre. If these problems are to be resolved, Ashworth argues, library management must move away from the 'mechanistic' hierarchical model towards the 'organic' model (see Figure 2.1). The organic, or 'organismic' as the Americans call it, model derives from the human relations school of motivation. Behind its assumptions about human nature in the workplace lies the Maslowian hierarchy of needs, with its emphasis on social needs, needs for esteem and recognition, and the need to fulfil one's potential. The organic model represents McGregor's Theory Y, the optimistic image of employees, which sees them as capable of assuming responsibility, and of supporting the aims of the organization, provided they are given the supportive context of participative rather than mechanistic management. Ashworth selects certain features of the organic structure which he sees as specially relevant to the problems of academic library management.

First the head librarian's role needs to change from omniscient being to pilot of a team, all of whom may be more professionally expert in their own specialisms than he can be. Second, staff are expected to take part in setting their own work goals, and evaluating their achievements as a matter of course. The emphasis should be on open-ended job descriptions, rather than very rigidly structured and detailed job descriptions, so that staff are encouraged 'to stretch themselves and set their own reach for the stars standards'. Third, a good communications network is an essential characteristic of the organic model. This can begin, Ashworth suggests, with interbranch working parties to make recommendations about standardizing as many routines as possible, to remove low-level causes of friction. These working parties should be drawn from all strata, and will form the basis for building up networks which can be used later for more important matters such as designing new services. To reduce the amount of time spent on round table discussions, the 'network' idea is to use wherever possible 'nodal' individuals who have emerged from group discussions as the people who will most efficiently facilitate specific developments and activities. This kind of communications network is more informal, *ad hoc,* and decentralized, than the traditional hierarchical communications system, which emphasizes one-way, top-to-bottom written communication, of mainly cut and dried decisions.

In the public library sector of the UK, the impetus towards more staff participation in management has come mainly through the spread of team structures, since local government reorganization in 1974. Typically, an area team consists of six to twelve professional librarians responsible for all the service points in their geographical area. Each has additionally a specialism to contribute to the development of the services in the area, information services, say, or publicity and promotion. He or she may also belong to a systemwide working party, for example to develop staff training or automation, in the library as a whole. Responsibility is delegated from headquarters to the area teams. Individual professional librarians enjoy greater autonomy in shaping their work, and developing their jobs, within the guidelines of overall aims and objectives, and with the collegial support of team members. There is more face-to-face communication, through area team meetings, and the attendance of the area team leader at senior management meetings, to provide a bridge between centre and periphery. There are also meetings of specialists throughout the system, of children's librarians, say, so that as well as being a member of an area team, a professional librarian may develop particular interests with other enthusiasts. The role of non-professionals is enhanced, since they are in charge of the day-to-day operations in service points.

A further development of the team approach has been in large central libraries, where some public libraries have adopted a subject approach rather than the traditional division by function – lending, reference. McClellan pioneered this deployment of staff in subject groups at Tottenham in the 1950s, to get away from the rigidity of 'reference' and 'lending' concepts and to provide the readers with 'service-in-depth'. The team of subject librarians at the central library would be engaged in selection of stock, stock editing, readers advisory work, promotion (booklists etc.) and evaluation of their services.

A number of public libraries have tried setting up 'project groups' which in effect leads to a matrix management structure, where staff are drawn from different levels and sections of the library to take part in a project group working on particular problems or development areas. They thus retain affiliations with their line manager (their area team leader, for example), but at the same time have other loyalties to their project team leader, who may be appointed for his or her expertise rather than seniority. Bryant notes that 'staff used to conventional organisations find it difficult to adjust to such a structure with its dual loyalties and temporary inversions of certain superior–subordinate relationships'.[50] This matrix approach is comparable to the 'networking' in academic libraries mentioned above. Both are intended to take participation to the point where the staff with the greatest expertise, rather than the most senior status, in a particular problem are drawn in to a project group.

The team approach to public library staff management has had mixed reactions. At its best 'the team provides a valuable training ground for newcomers. It meets their affiliative and support needs, helps them to discover their role, socializes them to the kind of professionalism which the team is endeavouring to practise, and offers safe space for individual venture'.[51] In service terms, teams can be high-performing mission-oriented groups for moving a library onward towards its goals. But Jones notes two important reservations – 'They are inappropriate to the routine type of operations so important in librarianship', and they 'can flourish only where the human resources ideal is to some extent made flesh':

> They require numbers of mature and enthusiastic people who are able to acquire social skills and the necessary nose for management, and, above all, are keen to learn ... when used appropriately, in the soft systems/human resources context, they are probably the most potent organizational phenomenon that there is. However, a third rate team system may be worse than useless.[52]

Where teams are imposed on a traditional hierarchy, without careful attention to developing group skills, and without real delegation of decision-making power, staff may be unnerved rather than motivated. They may be made insecure by being removed from their fixed function post in a branch library, and given a wider roving commission. They may have been rendered incapable of initiative by many years of routine work in a Theory X mechanistic environment. They may see librarianship as routine clerical work, basically, and therefore not requiring meetings to discuss it. They may even envy the non-professionals who are left to run the branches, and on their visits there, may try to take over their work, rather than engage in professional project planning or implementation. Theory X people conditioned by their past experiences cannot be turned into Theory Y people with the wave of a wand and the production of a new staffing structure plan.

Practical applications of the scientific school of motivation

The problem with motivation as revealed by studies in job satisfaction, is that there appears to be a credibility gap between what people say they want from their jobs, and how they actually behave if given, say, more responsibility or opportunities to participate and take initiatives. Would-be Theory Y people revert to showing Theory X tendencies, unless moves towards participation are made very slowly, with training and developmental support at every step. This perhaps indicates that the scientific school of management should not be too hastily condemned in fashionable moves towards human relations management. It seems to have quite a bit to offer library workers, whether one agrees with its basic stance on human nature or not.

The advantages of centralized decision-making and fixed-function posts are that they provide staff with security. People have clearly defined duties, and the day-to-day routines give an operational framework which many people seem to need from their jobs. Straightforward line management means that everybody has one boss to report to, and to approach with problems that arise. There are none of the complications of a matrix approach, where in addition to one's line manager one has responsibilities to project groups or working parties which report to somebody else again. Library managers who take a mechanistic approach argue that the majority of library tasks do not demand much creativity. What is wanted is efficiency rather than originality, skill rather than imagination, endurance and application rather than flair and insight. Most library staff for most of the time, it is argued, are engaged in predetermined procedures, whether in running acquisitions, streamlining interlibrary loans, or cataloguing a special collection of eighteenth-century French literature. These are more typical of library jobs than designing and planning new services, which only happens from time to time – setting up a community information service, introducing on-line searching in a special library, or automating some of the housekeeping routines. Against this stance are the library managers who try to encourage creativity in their staff, or at least expect their graduate professionals to analyse their work critically and have some ideas from time to time on improving services, or increasing efficiency or effectiveness. They argue that the pace of innovation is now unprecedentedly high in library and information work, calling for a more creative response from staff.

In fact it is negativist attitudes derived from mechanistic approaches that can frustrate creativity and change. Rooks[53] gives helpful advice to managers faced with negative attitudes which can infect others and make progress difficult especially when such attitudes are held by persons with influence. Practical responses include:

1   Demonstrating that positive rather than negative thinking will be rewarded.
2   Examining closely the worth of some of the negative points made, as they may have substance.
3   Arguing the consequences of not acting in a positive manner.

Resistance to change is often based on fear of the unknown and of failure. Therefore adequate training should be given where necessary and changes made gradually where difficult to implement. Sometimes it is desirable to have an experimental period with monitoring and a review at the end of it. On a practical point it is always very difficult to withdraw services to users once they have been implemented.

Sources of job satisfaction in the mechanistic model are confined to the lower levels of need in the Maslowian hierarchy. In other words people's needs at work are met mainly in the areas of material reward and security – using security to include not just security of tenure, but the security of working in a clearcut hierarchy, and knowing exactly what is expected of one, and having adequate technical aids to do one's job. Is this enough, or do library and information workers expect more from their jobs? Let us now consider the findings of job satisfaction surveys in the profession.

Librarians' views on job satisfaction

There are serious methodological problems in investigating job satisfaction, which cast a certain dubiety on the many research reports into librarians' degree of satisfaction with their work, and the reasons for it. As has been indicated earlier in discussing Herzberg's two-factor theory, the use of the methodology powerfully predetermines the results likely to be found. Furthermore the components of job satisfaction are extremely complex, especially in their interrelationships, therefore it is not very helpful to try to get staff to say what their overall degree of satisfaction is. It may be positively contradictory to other things they say when given an opportunity to answer more detailed questions about their work. Again there are problems arising from the stances of the researchers. No research is ever impartial. The individual's ideological stance, for example a strong attachment to the scientific school or the human relations school of management, has a powerful influence on what he or she is looking for and how they go about trying to find it. It has been questioned whether, as is assumed by the 'participative' enthusiasts, the majority of people really want challenge and responsibility at work:

> Largely based on academic surroundings which afford them opportunity for creativity and self-actualization, have organizational humanists inadvertently infused their own values into the theories, and over-generalized their perspectives to all workers?[54]

A related argument put forward by Jones[55] is that Marxist theorists attack the whole approach of 'human relations management', on the grounds that it ignores the real sources of power and control in organizations, and tries to overlook the inevitability of conflict between management and workers. From this viewpoint the human relations approach can be seen as manipulative in a more fundamental way than the scientific school, since it tries to use people's higher level needs in the service of an organization over which they ultimately have little control. Such 'meaning of life at work' questions are rarely discussed in job satisfaction reports, although they are clearly relevant, if the surveys are to consider the whole person, rather than some curiously fragmented being who exists or subsists between the hours of nine and five.

Having stated the shortcomings of job satisfaction surveys, let us consider now what are the most commonly stated sources of satisfaction and dissatisfaction, where librarians are asked questions about their work and their motivation. Table 2.1 summarizes the findings. Note that the survey findings all identify 'intrinsic factors' (related to the content of the job) and 'extrinsic factors' (related to the context of the job) as important to people at work. The purpose of listing staff needs in this oversimplified way is to provide those involved in managing staff with a basic toolkit for taking action along the

	Job Content *(intrinsic factors)*	Job Context *(extrinsic factors)*

S A T I S F Y I N G	Variety
	Involvement with users
	Satisfaction with books/
	   library materials
	Service orientation
	Personal/professional
	   growth
	Intellectual satisfaction/use
	   of professional expertise
		Colleagues
		Atmosphere/work climate

D I S S A T I S F Y I N G	Routine
	Physical demands
		Management and
		   organization (staffing
		   structures, supervision)
		Working conditions (physical
		   aspects, unsocial hours
		   of work)
		Status
		Undermanning
		Pressure of work
		Salary
		Career prospects

Interaction Needs of Librarians at Work

To give and receive recognition for work done
To feel a sense of achievement
To have opportunities for feedback about their work
To experience positive supervision ('affective' as well as task-oriented)
To identify with the system through a work group or team
To participate in decision-making about their own work and related areas

Table 2.1 What motivates librarians? Summary of satisfaction and dissatisfaction in library work

lines suggested in Table 2.2. Characteristics related to the job itself which are satisfying are variety, involvement with users, and the service ethic (thus readers' services work is on the whole preferred to technical services work). 'Ability utilization' is very important, particularly at the beginning professional level, when many newly qualified librarians are deployed, it seems, below their capabilities. The job content may also determine the sense of achievement, though that is a complex area where acknowledgement of one's supervisor may also be a factor, as may the overall management climate. Autonomy, a sense of responsibility, and creativity or a chance to take initiatives, are higher level sources of job satisfaction, which are partly intrinsic to the job, but partly determined by the supervisory structures and styles.

	Staff Needs	*Action*
Job Content	Variety	Job rotation, job exchange, job enlargement
	Reducing routine	Systems analysis, organization and methods (O & M), automation
	Involvement with users	Job rotation (e.g. between technical and readers' services)
		Modify staffing structure, to give more staff contact with users
	Use of professional expertise/intellectual satisfaction	Increase delegation, job enrichment, assign projects to individuals/working parties
	Personal/professional growth	Involve staff in developing their own area of work (projects to be achieved in a term or year), and reporting on their progress
		Appraisal (formal or informal) and follow-up (e.g. training)
		Supportive staff structures, e.g. attention paid to teams, work groups, working parties, to improve their effectiveness, and quality of the group process
		Quality circles (informal groups of interested staff reading and running seminars on relevant issues/current problems)
		Networking (encouraging staff to develop contacts inside and outside the library with key people in their specialisms)
Job Context	Quality of supervision	Coaching skills, positive and negative feedback, task-centres and people centred approaches (See Chapter 8)
	Communication styles and structures	Up/down only, or two way? Lateral communications, matrix approaches. Written or face-to-face. Diagnose failures of communication to pin-point bottlenecks/ authoritarian supervisors
	Career prospects diminished for older staff	In periods of low mobility, match jobs to individuals in restructuring caused by fewer posts or automation. Include staff in task groups, and include senior staff in training.

Table 2.2 Staff needs and management action

Sources of satisfaction related to the work environment or job context are colleagues (more important in one's first professional post) and the supervisory climate, or general atmosphere or overall work climate. This may be analysed into a number of significant factors, which cannot be entirely separated from intrinsic factors of a job, especially for staff who are engaged in any supervisory work and are therefore themselves contributing to, as well as being on the receiving end of the supervisory climate. It has been observed that librarians filling in questionnaires on job satisfaction have a tendency to attribute unsatisfactory aspects of their work to other people and to give themselves credit for the satisfactory aspects. It is important therefore to see oneself as a contributory factor, at least, to the supervisory climate, and to ask whether one is a democratic manager who regularly seeks the views of one's staff, or only insists that one's own supervisor be democratic. This seems to be widely wanted, according to the CLAIM survey of 1982, which found 80 per cent of the respondents expressing a preference for democratic managers.[56] It is noteworthy that staff could have confidence in, and trust their managers, while at the same time be dissatisfied by the quality and quantity of consultation and communication.

Intrinsic sources of dissatisfaction are the amount of dull routine work in librarianship and, for beginning librarians especially, lack of information to be able to carry out a job. This is related to extrinsic factors, since it connects with complaints that training and induction are poor, and that brings in management and the supervisory climate as a main area of dissatisfaction, highlighted in all the surveys. The connections between intrinsic and extrinsic factors are graphically shown by the CLAIM survey, which points out that staff ability to get intrinsic satisfaction from their job depends upon the resources and training available to them from management. It is significant, in a time of recession, that the 1988 cohort, surveyed in 1991,[57] placed 'resources available' high on their list of least satisfactory aspects of their jobs. Furthermore ability to get satisfaction from achievement is restricted by 'predetermined work flows' in many lower level jobs. Only as staff get promoted to higher levels do they begin to have any real flexibility in how they interpret their work, and use their expertise, and set their own performance standards.

Communications between staff at different levels – senior, middle and junior, central or site – and between professionals and non-professionals leaves much to be desired, according to the job satisfaction surveys. Stewart makes some recommendations in this area:

> Professionally experienced staff should make others aware of the overall objectives of the library and should draw their attention to proposed changes and development, and better still involve them in discussing changes; they should praise and compliment employees as well as suggesting improvements in performance.[58]

Strategies for increasing job satisfaction

Since there is a large proportion of routine work in libraries, both at professional and non-professional staff levels, it is important to build in variety, which all the surveys indicate is much appreciated by library workers. Job rotation may be used particularly to alleviate boredom in the humblest jobs – technical services routines or counter work. There are various patterns of rotation used in libraries, from daily to weekly, monthly or annually. In the US it is becoming fairly common for headships of libraries or library schools to rotate on an annual or three-year basis. This has not yet happened in the UK, in spite of models in the academic world. Indeed there has been reluctance among professional librarians to become involved in job rotation when it is their own job that is under consideration. There are both sound and unsound reasons for this. Some argue that they have developed specialisms and knowledge of user communities, which would be wasted if they moved around at two-year or three-year intervals and that stability is important when other changes are being made. Others, it seems, are reluctant to have revealed how they actually spend their time. In threatening circumstances of recession and change staff may develop protective ploys to conceal rather than reveal what they do:

> We don't admit we have spare time on our hands in case something happens. You'd be a fool to admit you had spare time on your hands, but, on the other hand, you want something to do.[59]

As the writer of that research report indicates, such attitudes militate against the introduction of job rotation or exchange schemes within a library. Konn therefore goes on to recommend that when internal job exchange schemes are introduced they 'need to include all members of staff without exception in order to avoid being regarded as a personal threat to particular individuals'. If this proves too difficult in practice, there is a more limited strategy which has been tried in Sheffield Public Libraries:

> In Sheffield we have developed the concept of training posts for professional staff. These are generally senior assistants' posts in specialist departments and are filled for a maximum of two years. This controlled turnover together with natural wastage is usually sufficient to allow anyone wishing to broaden their experience to transfer to a different kind of work within a reasonable period of time.[60]

The objective of job rotation is not only to increase job satisfaction for the staff, but also to give them a wider knowledge of the library system, or at least of what goes on elsewhere in their own section, which can improve the quality of the operation. At senior levels it has been our experience that good quality staff who have changed posts at the same level are better able to effect desirable changes than staff new to the system, because they are already aware of the library's aims and practices. However, job rotation which merely involves an increase in the variety of tasks undertaken is job 'enlargement' rather than 'enrichment' and at lower levels can be seen as having a number of boring tasks instead of only one.

A more satisfying strategy which can be introduced is to add to people's jobs tasks which are of a more interesting or demanding kind, so that they have a mix of humdrum routines and a certain amount of responsibility, or at least the satisfaction of seeing a task through and getting recognition from colleagues or users for the end result. This is known as job enrichment. It has been introduced in libraries mainly through staff restructuring schemes, though it can also be introduced by concerned supervisors for their own sections, by sharing out the work to take account of job enrichment strategies. The most common examples of job enrichment are subject specialization structures in academic libraries, where staff are given responsibility for a particular area, and within that have the satisfaction of carrying out a variety of work, using their own initiative and specialist knowledge, and getting feedback from a known user group of academic staff and students. The problem is that as staff cuts take place the job of the subject specialist may be impoverished rather than enriched, because it becomes necessary to spread the load of more procedural and administrative work, and they have to take their share, thus reducing the time they have for the more 'enriched' and rewarding side of subject specialization – user education, readers' advisory work, collection development.

In public libraries team staffing structures are an indication of job enrichment strategies at work, though their degree of success has varied considerably. The intention is to give professional staff a higher proportion of challenging work, by taking them out of their solely branch library concerns, and putting them with other professionals for the purposes of developing projects to make the services more effective over the whole area covered by the team. When it works well, staff jobs are certainly enriched. They spend some time out in the community making contacts with other information providers and with community groups and opinion leaders. They use this 'community profile' insight to develop relevant community information services, or children's activities like story hours, or support services for identifiable disadvantaged groups. They get feedback on their efforts by monitoring the take-up of their services, and gauging the value of their projects to the community. This approach only seems to work well when staff are 'self-starting', and support the other members of the team. It requires a certain capacity for self-development, so that ideas are forthcoming and action taken as a result of team deliberations. As with subject specialization the team approach can lead to job impoverishment rather than enrichment if it goes badly. Staff may miss the secure daily routines of branch librarianship including the supervision of staff, and the contacts with a known clientele of local users. Failure to work with others as a project-oriented team may be another source of dissatisfaction, giving the impression that team meetings are a waste of time, and that nothing significant ever comes out of them. These symptoms make a clear case for staff development in the form of team skills and self-appraisal techniques based on agreed targets.

The responsibility of individual supervisors to provide job enrichment for their own staff is also fraught with problems. Supervisors may be exclusively task-oriented rather than people-oriented, and they may have an underdeveloped understanding of staff management strategies. Proctor observes that the success of job enrichment depends on:

> supervisors being willing and able to delegate authority as well as responsibility. Many are over possessive or over prescriptive. Some lack the imagination to see how a job can be enriched and lose sight of the priorities in a surfeit of clerical routines.[61]

Techniques which may lead to job enrichment include more genuine delegation by supervisors, a project or 'mission-oriented' approach to work (agreed projects and timetables for their achievement), and staff development strategies of an organic kind. Dutton provides a good example of the latter in his report on a staff development scheme at ICI which included the library staff in a companywide application of Herzberg's motivators:

> To encourage the widest sharing of experience, in addition to homogeneous work groups, representative groups comprising staff of different grade levels and in different disciplines explored common problems. As anticipated, hygiene factors predominated initially, but a constructive approach to these moved attention to motivational factors. Thus individual staff from the most junior began to analyse and discuss their individual jobs, in the light of library operations; to single out and express the most important elements and existing shortcomings, and to suggest methods for improvement. A number of such operations, previously spread out over several individuals, were reconstituted and total responsibility allotted to one person.[62]

Problems in the application of motivation theories and strategies

Cultural bias

Much of the research into motivation originated in the US, and the results may not be transferable to other countries. It may be that the 'achievement ethic' is not as highly developed in Britain, for example, particularly as Britain declines in power, prestige and prosperity relative to other advanced industrial countries. A lack of employment prospects even among graduates has led to lowering of expectations. It may not even be practicable to subscribe to the achievement ethic any longer, since there are limited opportunities for practising it.

The 1960s and 1970s witnessed the growth of an alternative stance in the professions. This may be defined as a socially committed viewpoint, which asks the question, 'What can I do in my profession to help the disadvantaged and deprived?' rather than 'Where am I going in my professional career?' In public librarianship especially this has been an important impetus behind the growth of the 'welfare librarianship' concept, which starts with a 'commitment to reducing inequalities in knowledge and information deriving from a realisation of the structural rather than the residual nature of these inequalities' in our society. 'Relevant services...would include community information, basic education and services for the unemployed and ethnic minorities. In general terms the library would take an active stance on issues such as racism and sexism, with stock selection policies being adjusted accordingly.'[63]

A further problem which the human relations approach to motivation seems to provoke among British librarians is that it invites self-analysis, and this may be anathema, agony or sheer bad form. It is all very well for Americans to be articulate and open about their motivation, by charting their needs at work using, say, the Maslowian hierarchy. The British shy away from such self-exposure, or condemn it as airy-fairy theory (the concept of self-actualization, for instance), which runs counter to their stolid pragmatism. This means that researchers must be most careful to speak the language of their respondents rather than assume any acceptance or even familiarity with motivation theory. When concepts like 'self-actualization' and 'identity needs' are translated into everyday terms like 'a sense of achievement at work', 'using one's intellectual or professional capacities to the full', or 'acknowledgement of what you do by your supervisor', it becomes possible for the gap between theory and practice to be bridged.

The situation may improve as more interest is taken in library education and training for interpersonal skills (see Chapter 8), which inevitably gets librarians into the habit of analysing group process and gives them toolkits for doing so. There is also growing interest in the UK in transatlantic approaches to self-growth through group work. The American encounter movement, and the work of the therapist Carl Rogers[64] have had an impact in approaches to education and training, as well as in the original area of counselling and psychiatry. However there are clearly problems in transferring self-development and group development strategies from one culture to another. Motivation theories which have been based on studies in one country may not be transferable to other cultures.

Some interesting research has been carried out by Hofstede[65] on the impact of different national cultures on people's attitudes to work. His thesis is that organizations and management are culture-bound, and he based his findings on an investigation into the problems that multinational companies experience in transferring management styles and structures from one country to another. He identified four measures for determining significant cultural differences between countries, which need to be taken into account when assessing people's behaviour at work, and in understanding their motivation. First there is the Power Distance Index. When this is high employees are used to close supervision and display deference to superiors. They prefer (perhaps only because they are subject to it) paternalistic structures and styles of management, and staff managers need to provide clearcut guidelines and close supervision to satisfy the needs of their workers. Allied to the Power Distance Index is the Uncertainty Avoidance Index, which measures the degree to which staff are at home with definite rules and regulations, and prefer to avoid taking any decisions of their own. They prefer security provided again by paternalistic managers, who make it absolutely clear what has to be done and leave little to the initiative of their staff. Hofstede's third index is a 'Masculinity' rating, which places countries on a scale depending on a masculinity–femininity axis. He construed 'masculine' cultures as those where women were less likely to be employed in technical and professional work, where there was less concern for the physical environment, higher traffic speeds, and more road deaths etc. The more strongly masculine countries display tendencies at work towards individual achievement rather than group or team achievements, and there is correspondingly more work-related stress and emphasis on career aspirations. Women in this kind of culture have to be more assertive to break into the male-dominated higher echelons at work. By contrast in the more 'feminine' countries, typically Scandinavia, professional women can afford to be less assertive, a sense of achievement is more likely to stem from working co-operatively with a team or group than from individual success, and there is less career pressure and job-related stress. Hofstede's fourth index measures the degree of 'Individualism' to be found in different cultures. Where this is low, for example in Japan and Latin America, satisfaction at work is derived from loyalty, or indeed favouritism, within family firms or paternalistic organizations. Where it is high, for example in Britain and the US, the emphasis is on satisfaction gained by individual achievement and recognition rather than submersion of individual effort to the greater glory of the organization.

Ouchi's Theory Z[66] is based upon these cultural differences following his analysis of Japanese productivity. He believes that the Japanese approach to management offers valuable lessons. For the Japanese everything important in life happens as a result of teamwork or collective effort which conflicts with the American concept of individualism. The Japanese organizations also hold a holistic view of people involving a concern for employees at work and outside work which stems from a rapid move from a feudal to an industrial system and the provision by companies of accommodation and welfare for workers. Type Z organizations, on the Japanese model, tend to have long-term employment, non-specialized career paths and decision-making is a participative process. Broad concern is also shown for the welfare of employees and informal rather than hierarchical relationships are emphasized.

In Hofstede's analysis Britain and the US score high on individualism and masculinity, low on power distance and uncertainty avoidance. The implications for staff motivation are that these cultures produce people capable of Maslowian achievement up to the highest level of self-actualization, even if many of them do not realize this potential, or at least not at work. However the Maslowian hierarchy cannot be meaningfully used in trying to understand motivation in countries where the rating is low on individualism and high on power distance and uncertainty avoidance, such as Islamic countries and Latin America.

Hofstede provides a helpful starting point for understanding the problems of cultural bias in motivation theories. However he seems to beg some questions. Do staff 'prefer' a paternalistic style, for example, because it is the only one they know, and would they in fact 'prefer' a more open participative style if they were offered it and trained to benefit from it? Third World librarians attending courses in the UK have expressed the need for such a shift in their own library management back home, but that may be only because they are influenced by the Anglo-American motivation models presented to them in seminars. When they tackle case studies they tend to produce solutions which are relatively more authoritarian or paternalistic than those produced by English students, perhaps supporting Hofstede's views about cultural bias in management.

A further problem with intercultural comparisons is that they perforce have to make generalizations about each country, which conceal a vast range of different stances which comprise a national trend. Job satisfaction surveys in librarianship, for instance, reveal differences between young less experienced managers, who are more human relations-oriented, and older managers, who are more disposed to the scientific school of management.[67] They also suggest job satisfaction is influenced by the kind of work done – technical services or readers' services – because that generates sources of satisfaction, or fails to in technical services, derived from user contact and recognition of services successfully delivered. Again it is suggested that satisfaction of employees is to a greater or lesser degree dependent on their supervisors' management strategies and styles.[68] The variables are seemingly endless and the truth of the matter highly complex, since it apparently lies not in any one set of criteria for job satisfaction – based on a hierarchy of needs, or one's cultural background, or the management climate in one's library, or the nature of the task assigned. Rather it lies in the interrelationships between all these variables, which takes us back to the point made at the beginning of this chapter. Theories of motivation which emphasize 'process' rather than 'content' are more helpful and realistic, because they give due weight to the interrelationship between variables, rather than leaving it at identifying variables, such as Maslow's hierarchy of individual's needs, or Likert's continuum of management styles, or Blake and Mouton's grid. In making use of 'content' theories to understand a particular situation, it is essential to consider their interaction with such variables as cultural background, state of development of technology, staffing structure, supervisory styles, and the level of sophistication of education and training.

Closed system approach in motivation theories

Work is only one facet of a person's life and his or her responses to it are affected to a greater or lesser degree by other aspects, such as personal relationships, domestic circumstances, individual interests and leisure pursuits. Yet when reading some of the human relations school of motivation theories, one forms the impression sometimes that the work situation is a world in itself, a closed system not affected by the varying situations and stances of all the people who operate within it. It must be recognized that for a large number of people the various levels of need – for self-identity and social recognition, for esteem or sense of achievement – are met by situations and activities outside work, correspondingly reducing their needs at work. In some cases, for example, people deliberately take jobs which include less responsibilities because they have responsibilities outside work. It could be argued that the human relations school of management has a tendency to idealize the satisfactions to be had from work and that for the majority of people the expectations they have about work remain low, often justifiably in terms of their past experiences of work. In times of economic recession, when choice of jobs, promotion prospects and job mobility are diminished, many people, whether beginning librarians or the middle-aged in posts where they are likely to remain till they retire, find their expectations lowered even further.

Consensus or conflict in the workplace

Both the scientific school and the human relations school of management seem to imply a greater degree of consensus in the workplace than experience suggests is justified. Theorists of the Marxian school make the important point that conflict must be recognized. Motivation looks very different from the point of view of senior management, lower levels of staff, or the trade unions. Trade unionists naturally are sceptical about job enrichment schemes, because from their standpoint it may mean that management is getting more higher level work done 'on the cheap'. Participative schemes often look very different to different levels of staff. Senior staff may think they are good communicators and are consulting staff regularly, and engaging in delegation. Seen from the level below it may not look like that at all. Stewart's findings were that in British libraries in the early 1980s 'consultation and communication at all levels and in all types of library organization appeared to be unsatisfactory'.[69] And Konn, in her survey of continuing education needs in academic libraries, found that:

> there were glaring contradictions between the image which top librarians wished to project, indeed thought they were projecting, and that perceived by their staffs. Individuals from this top group expressed concern for the welfare of their staff ... Yet ... members of staff could complain at the lack of practical manifestations of such concern, or point to the neglect of human matters in favour of procedures and machines.[70]

Another example of different perspectives occurs when supervisors are put under pressure to delegate more, and to give their subordinates more participation in decision-making. The pressure most often comes from above, when there is a new head librarian with a less authoritarian attitude than his or her predecessor. The supervisors may resent these efforts to change their approaches, and find ways of keeping up a superficial appearance of participative management (meetings are held and bits of paper are circulated), while in the eyes of their juniors they are actually undermining participation. Typically such supervisors retain for themselves all the decisions that really matter, they only attend to their staff's views when they happen to coincide with their own, and they tend to ignore suggestions or initiatives from their staff which have not been sought by the supervisor. There are more extreme ploys, when the supervisor 'accidentally' leaves some important matters off an agenda, or makes the excuse that there was not enough time for consultation, so that he or she can make the decision on their own.

The associated problem stems from the supervisor who is willing to delegate and be participative, but does not know how, because of long-term working experiences in very hierarchical mechanistic libraries. Chapter 8 suggests ways in which supervisors may learn, and encourage their staff, to be more responsive and to share in the organization of the work, through delegation, coaching, self-appraisal, and positive as well as negative feedback on their performance. McGregor's categorization of staff as Theory X – lazy, indifferent workers, at best passive, at worst resistant to the organization's needs, only moved by material rewards or punishments, with no intrinsic motivation – or Theory Y – people ready to assume responsibility, take initiatives, identify with the organization, satisfy higher level needs for recognition and achievement in the workplace – has been criticized for its naive assumptions. Is it really feasible to transform Theory X workers into Theory Y workers? How can delegation and participation be introduced in a library where staff have been rendered fairly passive and inert during a long régime of more authoritarian management? The management literature offers only limited prescriptions, because the solution will be long term and organic, rather than instant and mechanistic. A strategy adopted in industry (Sears Roebuck) forces authoritarian managers to delegate more by giving them more staff to supervise, until the wider span of control compels the managers to delegate. Thus they are 'got off people's backs', leaving staff more space to plan and organize their own work within the company's objectives. The authoritarian manager may also be circumvented by adopting matrix management approaches, so that staff are engaged in projects which require them to report to others besides their immediate line manager.

The organic long-term approaches are summarized in Figure 2.1 in the righthand column of Burns' and Stalker's checklist. It should be noted however that an all-out participative approach is by no means a universal panacea to increase staff satisfaction and performance. In recent years a note of cynicism has crept into the literature, and the problems of participative management have been revealed by library managers' own experience. First, it is very time-consuming because of the increased number of meetings, so time-management courses are now becoming necessary to get people through their meetings effectively. Second, it has been found that team structures and similar participative frameworks can turn out to be as authoritarian as those they replaced, because of how they are practised by staff who either do not agree with participative stances, or do not know how to practise them. Third, staff attitudes are influential, not just their rational responses. Attitudes are a complex set of responses, the product of cultural influences from home, education and society at large, as well as the more immediate outcome of organizational experiences. They are much more difficult to change than knowledge or skills, and so training very often confines itself to the latter. This may not get to the root of the matter. It has been found, too, that in libraries many managers are over optimistic about their communication skills. Communication only exists when the message has been understood by the recipients, not when it has been transmitted by the sender. Until more effective communication is established, participative structures will invariably work at lower than their potential.

The problem of socialization also needs to be taken into account. When staff join a library they are under heavy pressure to adopt its norms and values, or at least the norms and values of one section where they will mainly be working. The problem is that although human relations management is:

> ... inherently or culturally appealing ... people are forced to depart from it in their working lives ... It is possible that the classical and pluralist models are so pervasive and strongly held in the workplace that people who enter the work force with different perspectives find themselves being socialised into adopting these approaches.[71]

Bowey, however, goes on to point out that the type of organizational structure affects the organization's capacity for adapting to change. In periods of rapid change, foreseen for library and information services till the end of the century, as a result primarily of information technology, it is particularly important for libraries to move towards a more participative structure. In her study of attitudes to change in organizations Bowey's findings were that change is more difficult and stressful where staff see the organization as 'essentially hierarchical, with rules and regulations to be conformed with, and with authority vested in senior positions', compared with staff who see the organization as an 'interdependent system of parts, all making their contribution to the development and survival of the organization in its environment (characterized by threats and opportunities)'.

Women and motivation

The growth of a feminist perspective since the 1960s is reflected in the literature of management, though to a limited degree. In library management both in the US and in Great Britain it is reflected also by the formation of groups such as 'Women in Libraries' (in the UK) and The American Library Association Committee on Status of Women (in the US). In management generally the need has been recognized to develop women as managers through all-women training groups on interpersonal skills, and on assertiveness in particular. There has been a growth in the UK of workshops or courses specially for women librarians, in order to meet the need to develop women as managers. The Library Association's survey of 1991[72] found that 4.5 per cent of women members earned £20,000+ per annum compared with 19 per cent of men, although the situation for women had improved over the last three years. There have been some notable female appointments in libraries and library schools in the UK over the last few years but 'equality' is a long way off as 75 per cent of Library Association members are female.

The main problems faced by women managers are derived partly from attitudes, partly from the work environment, and partly from social pressures from the wider environment. In the first category lies the problem of how women see themselves, which is influenced by their education and training, but also by the presence or absence of role models. Clearly in UK libraries there are few women in senior enough positions to provide these important models. This may help to explain the often repeated generalization that women are not as ambitious as men. As Ritchie points out:

> ambition is not an attribute which is stable over time ... It is likely to fluctuate markedly according to a person's motivation, self-image, perceived likelihood of advancement, present status, and numerous other variables...[73]

Ritchie's findings were that women aspire to better things as much as men do, but 'relative to their present inferior status', which may indeed lead to the appearance of 'less ambition'. Among non-professional staff in public and academic libraries surveyed by Russell,[74] of whom approximately 93 per cent were women, lack of promotion and career prospects was a serious source of dissatisfaction, which is another sign of women's 'relative ambition'.

Russell also found that part-timers, who are always more likely to be women because of the way in which domestic responsibilities are allocated in our society, expect less from the job than the full-time non-professional library worker, because 'work is very much an adjunct to family life'. Their 'ambition' lies in a different direction from work, and so they are less concerned with promotion prospects of the competitive 'achievement ethic' kind. This links up with earlier criticisms of human relations motivation theories as making rather sweeping assumptions that work is the main source of recognition, self-expression and self-actualization. This ignores the possibilities in the post-industrial society of men as well as women leading more balanced lives by channelling their energies more equitably between organizational employ-ment, domestic and personal commitments, and self-actualization through intellectual, aesthetic or social commitment activities. These possibilities may indeed be forced upon the attention of society by the permanent decrease in employment that has resulted from new technologies. There are some signs that the necessary structures are beginning to emerge. These include accept-ance of job sharing by leading employers, more open access to higher and further education for people at all stages in their lives, and increasing oppor-tunities, pioneered by the Open University, to take courses in one's own time by distance learning packages. The nature of these courses has also broadened considerably to include family and home-oriented programmes, as well as vocationally-oriented and traditional programmes in humanities, social sci-ences and science and technology.

Women have to face the criticism – or the prejudice, since it is generally unsupported by reasoned argument – in our society that somehow they are not 'management material'. This assumes that managers are born not trained, or that men but not women develop qualities essential to leadership. No one is entirely agreed as to what these essential qualities are, and in any case they keep changing as fashions for authoritarian or participative approaches change. It could be argued that as participative styles and structures have become more widespread, women are more likely to succeed than men, if we attribute to them alleged gender-specific tendencies of co-operation and consultation, or 'caring and sharing' as the popular mind sees it.

It is assumed in the world of business management and industry that women managers need special training workshops, which encourage them to develop skills of self-marketing, assertion, and communication skills needed to be an 'organization person'. There are two schools of thought on this. Those in favour argue that since women are lower profile and contribute less in mixed groups than in all-women groups, they need to engage in self-development with other women, and then use the interpersonal skills acquired in the workplace. The other side argue that such workshops are in danger of turning women into 'organization men', with characteristics of aggressiveness, competitiveness and generally dominating behaviour, which will in the end make the workplace even worse than it is now. In the library and information professions there have been some moves towards helping women develop in their own workshops, and also build up women's networks to begin to offset the 'old boy network' which in every profession gives men an advantage in such areas as promotion, invitations to publish, to speak at conferences etc. For example the British group Women in Libraries runs workshops with creche facilities, and has held annual conferences on such themes as 'Images of Women' (1986), including the image of the librarian, and how women are depicted in the library stock. A number of continuing professional development events have recently been held by The Library Association looking at ways forward for women.

In the US there is more fully developed monitoring of sex discrimination in the profession, through the work of the permanent Standing Committee of the American Library Association. Its remit is to represent women's interests in the ALA and to ensure that the 'Association considers the rights of the majority (women) in the library field'. Specifically they try to take action by identifying gaps in education and training resources for women, by developing guidelines and programmes 'to enhance women's opportunities and image' in the profession, and by monitoring all the other ALA units to ensure proper consideration of the rights of women, and to prevent sex discrimination.

In the United Kingdom The Library Association established an Equal Opportunities Working Group in 1986 which has been very active. An Equal Opportunities Pack has been compiled containing leaflets, among others, on job sharing, sexual harassment, and recruitment and equal opportunities. Two surveys which examined equal opportunities were funded and are referred to in Chapter 3. As in many other areas of management the responsibility of individuals themselves to act in ways which ensure opportunities are equal is stressed in The Library Association's leaflet:

As professionals we cannot expect The Library Association to take all the responsibility for ensuring that equal opportunities permeate our relationships with our users, or our employment practices. We need to take responsibility ourselves for ensuring that everyone's opportunities are equal.[75]

3

Workforce planning

Workforce planning, a non-sexist term for manpower planning, covers a range of activities designed to ensure a satisfactory balance between the supply and demand for library and information workers, in both qualitative and quantitative terms. It is concerned with what kind of people, and how many, are needed now and in the future, to run library and information services at all levels from junior assistants through para-professional to professionals. It is equally concerned with government policies at national and local levels, since it is central Government and local authorities who ultimately determine what funding is made available for staff, irrespective of the 'ideal' establishment in public and academic libraries. Central Government also has an important say in the numbers of students recruited to library and information studies schools (LIS) and to a large extent controls the funding for these students – with the exception of part-timers, overseas students and those few recruits who can afford to pay their own fees – through mandatory grants for undergraduate courses, and bursaries or postgraduate studentships for postgraduate courses.

At the national level the 1980s have witnessed a spate of reports on workforce planning for library and information work. These emanated from the professional associations, the Library and Information Services Council (LISC) and from the Transbinary Group on Librarianship and Information Studies which was set up by the Department of Education and Science in 1985 to carry out an overall 'review of likely demand (both in terms of numbers and expertise) for library and information professionals'. Although these reports address themselves to similar problems of workforce planning, their motives for doing so are very different. The Transbinary Group (University Grants Committee and National Advisory Body) study was one of a series – including architecture, pharmacy and agriculture – of investigations intended to achieve economies in higher education by 'achieving a closer balance between supply and demand' as welcomed by the Government green paper 'The development of higher education into the 1990s' (Cmnd. 9524). The LISC documents were intended to provide advice, in the Whitehall manner, on workforce planning. Their Working Party on Manpower Education and Training (MET) produced a number of consultative papers on basic and continuing education in the library and information fields.[1-3] These were circulated in the profession for comment, as was the 'keynote' paper from which they stemmed, 'Library and Information work in a changing environment'. The ultimate intention was to provide a 'unified policy framework' for workforce planning, though it was admitted that any definitive statements would be difficult 'because of continuing environmental changes and because of the ways in which the library/ information community, and especially educational institutions, react to these changes'.[4]

There were other investigations in the early 1980s which took a more structured approach, and collected quantitative evidence on the numbers and qualifications of the library and information workforce, as well as providing a qualitative review. Nick Moore's report published by Acumen in 1984[5] looked at wastage rates, age structures, mobility and the position of women, as well as considering the nature of the work.

The other strand in the literature on workforce planning may be called the 'apocalyptic', which is represented by the 'visionary' approach of Blaise Cronin, who believes, with Ralf Dahrendorf, that 'research has a seismographic function: that is, it indicates rumblings of what is going to happen in the future'.[6] In *The transition years* and numerous other writings, he advocates educational pluralism for a profession that must diversify to cope with 'l'informatisation de la société' and with the rapid development of 'infobusiness' which may lead to librarians cutting their links with traditional libraries, and making contracts with businesses, community groups and others who need their information organized and automated. Information management is the name of the game for the 1990s.

Amid this surge of interest in workforce planning from bodies and individuals concerned with the long-term future, employers and library schools continue to engage in the day-to-day, year-to-year evolutionary approach in education and training. The library schools are also concerned with long-term developments and in responding to the changing skills demanded of entrants to the profession and the shift of emphasis towards the private information sector without jeopardizing provision to the traditional public and academic sectors. Janet Shuter, in a highly critical article, seeks to demonstrate that surveys carried out in the early 1980s greatly underestimated the number of information workers in the private sector. Using figures from the report of the Technical Change Centre she concludes that 'the norm is now not a person working in a large public library system but a person working in a small industrial unit'.[7]

It can be seen that there are numerous conflicting interests in workforce planning, ranging from the professional associations and the Library and Information Services Council, to national planning bodies such as the Higher Education Funding Council (HEFC) for public sector higher education, the individual library schools in the context of their own institutions, the employers, and entrants to the profession whether at professional or non-professional or para-professional level. Let us turn to a consideration of some of these conflicting views about the quantity and quality of people needed by our library and information services between now and the end of the century.

Library Association and its Futures Working Party

In 1981 The Library Association Council set up a Working Party on Manpower Forecasting to consider the qualitative and quantitative aspects of manpower. Education policies were to develop in this context, and would be under radical review, in the light of 'developments in information technology, government policies in promoting commercial and industrial information matters and the resultant changes to the career patterns of many people'. An Education Policy discussion document was debated in 1984 by the Council, which held that the Association should become more hospitable to other workers in information-related activities, and should find ways of expanding membership. The Futures Working Party was set up and, after much consultation throughout the country, produced its Final Report in late 1985.[8]

There is informative basic data on membership – fairly static at around 24,000 from 1980 onwards, with 43 per cent working in public libraries, 19 per cent in academic libraries and 14 per cent in special libraries. The total membership in 1992 was 25,171 which is the second highest in Library Association history. There are background factors which are interesting in their contribution to the debate on workforce planning, and there are recommendations on changes in the future role and membership, and even name, of The Library Association. Recommendations however on 'the scope and future manpower requirements of the library and information community' are acknowledged to be almost impossible to make, since:

(a) public sector provision of library and information services is heavily dependent on government policies and perceptions about public spending,

(b) traditional private sector provision is highly sensitive to the prevailing financial climate and ... libraries and information units are (like research departments) often among the first to be axed in unfavourable economic circumstances,

(c) it is difficult quickly and accurately to 'fine tune' numbers of students to actual or perceived requirements.[9]

The report nonetheless emphasizes certain points relevant to any attempts at workforce planning, and the Association submitted these in its evidence to the Transbinary Group on Librarianship and Information Studies, which was at that time engaged in a workforce planning exercise. First it was noted that any reduction in numbers could restrict the qualified people needed for the newly emerging 'non-traditional' market for 'information professionals'. Second, the point was made that there is a need for qualified librarians in a number of traditional areas, schools for example, but the posts are not being filled for economic reasons. Third, emerging markets in 'such fields as commercial, professional and voluntary organizations and in the media and service industries' were noted. The general conclusion was that library and information skills 'are potentially transferable to a wide range of other occupations, especially in the communications field', and that indeed there are already jobs in these areas which are unfortunately occupied by people without professional training. Thus any attempts to cut down numbers of entrants to the profession could be misguided, and dangerously ignore such significant social factors as the new centrality of information technology and information management in the context of education, leisure, community service, business, commerce and the professions.

Library and Information Services Council (LISC) views on workforce

The views of the Library and Information Services Council were expressed in the series of papers circulated for discussion in the profession, from 1982 to 1984. The 'keynote paper' suggested that the quantity and scope of information sources will continue to expand, and that this will inevitably demand an increase in the numbers of people engaged in 'the generation, management and marketing of databases'. With the accelerating advances in information technology, there would be a need for more 'systems designers and managers who understand the content of what they are handling, and library/information workers who can interact with systems specialists and together with them tackle the management problems of computerised services'.

Another impact of technological change is the blurring of distinctions between producers and end-users of information, with the advances in electronic publishing. This means that people will be needed who can cross this traditional barrier. Another factor is changing demands and skills in information users, as the younger generation takes for granted computer access to information. Users may 'put a premium on information analysis and repackaging in local community information as well as in scientific, technical and economic information'. It follows that:

> a wide range of specialities will be required in the future provision of library/information services – authorship, editing, printing, primary publishing, document delivery, collection management, conservation, data-base and catalogue production, thesaurus construction, systems design and management, on-line computing and searching, the management of resources, records and archives, information analysis and repackaging, question-and-answer services, marketing, research, advice, brokerage, signposting and referral, exhibitions, consultancy etc.[10]

The Transbinary Group (UGC/NAB) Report 1986

The University Grants Committee and the National Advisory Body's working group to review education for librarianship and information studies in the UK finally reported in July 1986. Their recommendations were concerned with both quantity and quality, in the context of newly emerging markets and resource constraints in higher education.

They did not recommend any reduction in numbers, since they felt that schools should have an opportunity to gear their courses to the emerging marketplace, and prepare students for wider opportunities in information technology, before any cuts were made.

The Group was in favour of both undergraduate and postgraduate courses continuing, since they could find no significant differences, over a seven-year period, in prospects or attainments, except that those with master's degrees entered a wider range of jobs and did better in emerging markets. Recommendations were that undergraduate courses should have more imaginative curriculum design, and that applicants for postgraduate courses should all do a year's training to gain practical experience before joining the course.

Attention was directed to the skills which were relevant to all LIS courses. These included communication skills, effectiveness in selecting, organizing and promoting services, ability to influence decision-makers, and user-centred skills for understanding and analysing information needs. Applications of information technology were considered particularly vital, with the general recommendation that IT should permeate the whole course, rather than be treated as a bolt-on unit. Management skills were poorly taught.

Following the Transbinary Group's report the British Library Research and Development Department identified research into the size, structure and nature of the workforce as a key priority area and two projects were funded. One looked at longitudinal career developments of a nationwide cohort of students graduating from Schools of Library and Information studies in 1988 and the other – 'Monitoring the library and information workforce' reported in 1991.[11] The aims of this project were to establish a forecasting model, based on Unesco guidelines and to measure the development of the library and information workforce in Britain, and identify any emerging trends by collecting quantitative data on the flows into and out of the workforce. The data was collected in 1988 by questionnaire and the main findings were that the workforce (see Table 3.1) had remained fairly static overall but the special library/information sector was growing faster than any other sector (5 per cent in 1988 compared with 1 per cent elsewhere). Women occupied 82 per cent of the workforce including 65 per cent of professional posts compared with 59 per cent in 1981. The bulge identified in 1981 in the 30–39 age group has moved into the 40–49 category producing a glut of individuals competing for promotion. The numbers in the 20–29 age group had dropped causing concern for the future especially with the expected skills shortage resulting from demographic trends.

It was considered likely that the workforce will continue to grow steadily and the report recommends that 'strategies should be developed to try to attract more trained personnel back from the latent supply', i.e. the trained or experienced individuals who are not participating in the workforce.

Over the last decade there has been more interest in discrimination in employment, particularly racial and gender discrimination, which has therefore resulted in more activity in monitoring the workforce. 'Manpower planning' has become 'workforce planning' to rid it of sexist undertones. Bray and Turner showed that there has been an increase in the proportion of qualified women in the profession since 1981 and The Library Association's survey of 1991[12] found that the proportion of women earning in excess of £20,000 per annum increased nine times between 1988 and 1991 whilst the proportion of men in this salary band increased by less than three times. There were, however, still proportionally far more men in this top salary band (19 per cent) than women (4.5 per cent) although approximately 75 per cent of Library Association members are female.

In addition the overall proportion of unwaged Library Association members fell from 14 to 11.5 per cent between 1988 and 1991 but the proportion of unwaged men remained unchanged at 4 per cent. This means that considerably fewer women were unwaged in 1991 compared with 1988. The report surmises that contributory factors are likely to include economic necessity to work in a recession, greater availability of flexible working arrangements, such as job sharing and part-time posts and the demographic 'time-bomb' with fewer school-leavers, meaning that women are being encouraged back into the workforce.

Library Association membership is heavily dominated by those of European origin (97 per cent) as is also the Library and Information Studies student population (94 per cent). Gil Burrington concludes that, because the ethnic groups are better represented in the student population this should be reflected later in the membership as a whole.[13]

Employers' views on workforce needs

Workforce planning is concerned not only with the quantity of the workforce but also with the quality and the supply of good quality entrants into the profession and is heavily dependent upon the quality of the Library schools and their ability to attract good quality students on to their courses.

Concern for the attractiveness of undergraduate courses in library and information work was the impetus for a British Library study published in 1989.[14] It found that the number of applications had not dropped significantly overall although the majority of the schools were experiencing difficulties in filling their quotas by the beginning of the academic year. The response was seen as a willingness to relax entry standards and 'accept people who are not fully committed to LIS work'. The researchers' conclusion was that this certainly dilutes quality – 'while there are still many good students, there are perhaps larger numbers than there used to be who are lacking the qualities necessary to make a high calibre LIS professional'.[15]

Prior to the investigation problems had been reported by public libraries, particularly in London and the South East of England, in recruiting junior professional staff. The investigation therefore included discussions with librarians about the supply of good quality recruits. The public librarians in the main supported the view that quality had declined.

Although this study was largely concerned with undergraduates, its findings and conclusions resemble closely those of recent studies which have concentrated on the period following the library school course.[16,17] In a changing world the schools are having to adapt their courses to the market in a number of ways. The most obvious is the shift towards information technology. This ought to attract good quality candidates, especially men, who are discouraged by 'librarianship' which is perceived as 'an unexciting environment populated by quiet perhaps rather dull people on low salaries'.[18] The Brenda White Associates' study took place when schools were moving quickly towards information technology in their curricula and the researchers felt that it had had very little impact on recruitment and yet had diminished the librarianship element in courses thus affecting their traditional markets. Information technology is much less obvious in public libraries. Students attracted to this element in courses are therefore more likely to seek posts in academic libraries or in the emerging markets of information work. Additionally the schools have to find room for the growing information technology element and this has led to an absence of teaching on matters which specifically relate to the public library such as the climate in which they operate and current issues such as income generation, contracting out, community involvement, ethnic minorities etc.

The Class of '88 cohort project[19] followed the early career patterns of those leaving library and information studies schools in 1988. Most respondents, whether in library and information work or not, felt their courses had introduced or broadened their skills and in particular information technology, self-discipline, communication and organizational skills, time management, information handling and management were noted. The conclusion reached by the investigators was that 'the courses do develop skills and knowledge which enhance employability of newly qualified workers, and a key factor is the extent to which curricula equip students to be more resourceful in applying specialist skills and knowledge in a variety of contexts'.[20] As Freeman points out, the schools are under constant pressure to add specialist areas into a finite curriculum and have largely taken the view that a generalist course which produces practitioners 'who can add in later life the specialism appropriate to the professional post they then occupy'[21] is the best solution.

The debate about theory and practice is frequently raised. It is easy to say that education and training, theory and practice can be neatly split up with the responsibility for the conceptual allocated to the schools, while the libraries look after the practical applications, but that is a recipe for professional schizophrenia which leads to the sort of criticism voiced by employers surveyed for 'Curriculum change for the nineties', a report published by the British Library in 1983,[22] that schools concentrated too much on the theoretical rather than practical content. Theory on vocational courses has to be taught in the context of its applications and on-the-job training must be connected to theory if it is to have much lasting significance for the trainee. After all good theory will have been derived from empirical evidence of practice and seeks to explain what is happening. There is nothing as practical as a good theory.

Freeman's remarks also point to another dilemma facing schools: what should be acquired on the initial professional course and what should be left to continuing education? Librarians' preferred continuing education activities are discussed in Chapter 7. Those of the 1988 cohort employed in library and information work were asked about training received.[23] Information/computing skills and management headed the list which suggests that, like theory and practice, subjects should not be designated as appropriate to initial professional education OR continuing education but that basic skills should be taught at library schools and built upon and updated by continuing education.

All the recent reports stress the need for library educators and employers to work together to ensure that curricula on courses match the needs of employers and employees alike. The traditional scenario, described in 'Education and recruitment of junior professionals',[24] in which employers – notably public library chiefs – say that the library schools do not produce the sort of junior professional librarian they need, whilst library school heads say that 'librarians are unable to say what they need, and anyway, sniping at the library schools has always been a popular sport', is not the way forward.

To what extent are supply and demand mismatched?

This is a complex question, to which there are no easy answers. To take the quantitative approach, are we producing too many library and information workers? Well, that depends on whether you take the view that our library school graduates must find jobs in the traditional academic, public and special library fields, where opportunities are fairly static (and probably falling in the public and academic libraries, thanks to public expenditure cuts and staff restructuring exercises). If you take the contrary view, that library schools are producing people with information skills applicable in the emergent 'information profession/industry' triggered by IT, then the question changes into

> ...how to quantify the submerged part of the iceberg and, more importantly, what proportion... is susceptible to colonisation by the information professionals of the future.[25]

Within the traditional sectors library schools have observed in the 1980s a significant growth of jobs in the commercial and professional sector of special libraries (in law, accountancy and architects' firms). But there has not yet been any discernible breakthrough into the 'emergent information society' for a number of reasons which are pinpointed in a series of reports conducted for the British Library from 1984 to 1985 by Davinson and Roberts.[26-28] They investigated information-based courses outside the Schools of Library and Information Studies (SLIS), to see whether they were serious competitors to SLIS and to consider what knowledge and skills they were developing in their students. It emerges that most were entirely technology-based, with little or no interest in the user orientation to information provision, which is emphasized in SLIS courses. They were not likely to produce job hunters, therefore, in the fields traditionally grazed by SLIS products. On the debit side, however, it emerged that there were considerable obstacles in the way, should SLIS wish to break into the wider information market. Much centred around the question of resources. Any such moves would have to be centred on a heavy investment in IT resources, and substantial additional funding would not be readily available, due to the poor public image of library and information work and its credibility as IT-based. Current SLIS courses were seen to be 'IT-related' rather than 'IT-based', in that they were centred not on the technology, but on a 'commitment to information and knowledge that comprehends a range of issues – social, cultural, educational, political – that demonstrably falls outside the likely preoccupations of IT-based information specialists with organisational concerns'. The perspective is that of 'knowledgeable user of the technology and its products' rather than the perspective of systems designers or systems analysts. The conclusion is that:

> Those SLIS wishing to make claims upon emerging IT-based information markets must, however, attempt more than the provision of modified programmes based largely on issues previously thought suitable for librarians.[29]

The other aspect of this question is more of concern to library educators than to library practitioners. It would seem, from the Davinson and Roberts' investigations, that the SLIS have a kind of information education to offer that aims to 'integrate, in a balanced fashion, user, information and systems elements'. This is rare in UK information courses outside the SLIS. The suggestion is that SLIS have a significant role, if they are flexible enough to take it, in setting up innovative information programmes, with other departments, which would 'complement the currently dominant model of technology-driven programmes'. How this would mesh with their existing role of producing library and information workers for the traditional library markets remains to be seen. One can with some certainty predict a backlash centred on the criticism that librarian-

	Public	National	HE	FE	Special	Total
Professional	7,839	913	2,618	841	4,426	16,637
Total	30,701	2,385	7,056	2,128	7,912	50,182

(From Felicity Bray and Christopher Turner, *Monitoring the library and information workforce.* British Library Research and Development Department, 1991.)

Table 3.1   Estimated size of the library and information workforce in the UK

ship has become 'technology-driven', at the expense of clients, materials and the service ethic. Indeed there have already been whispers… and so far the profession is only 'IT-related', not even 'IT-based'.

Workforce planning in the individual library

Figure 3.1 summarizes the stages necessary in drawing up a workforce plan for an individual library. It will be seen that the basic aim is the same as in national workforce planning attempts: to create a balance between supply and demand, in both quantitative and qualitative terms. The supply side of the formula involves collecting accurate information on existing jobs and expertise of the people doing them; then calculating likely wastage rates over the period under review, say over the next five years. The demand side of the formula concerns making a realistic assessment of staffing needs, taking account of existing services, new projects, and necessary cuts. The final plan brings together supply and demand factors, and often is incorporated into proposals for restructuring staff and/or services, which take account of ways of improving performance and providing staff with greater job satisfaction. The main stages of workforce planning are shown below.

Analysis of existing staff and their jobs

All libraries keep personnel records, though the nature and extent of their contents differ markedly from one organization to another. Sometimes application forms, references and other material from the selection interview make up the entire record. Increasingly, however, schemes of staff appraisal or 'performance review' are being introduced (see Chapter 6 for details). Appraisal may be carried out on a regular basis, usually once a year, and a record kept of the appraisal interview, sometimes with input from both supervisor and member of staff being appraised. Staff appraisal systems, when linked with job analysis and description (see Chapter 4) enable a manager to make more regular and systematic links between allocation of staff and effectiveness of services. This is a necessity whether a complete staff restructuring is in the offing, or simply to achieve a closer match between staff expertise and the jobs that have to be done. It is particularly important in periods of rapid change when a library is introducing new services – on-line searching, or community information services, for example – or undergoing new ways of carrying out existing services – such as automated circulation, serials control or acquisitions. In these circumstances existing job descriptions may become redundant, but staff may go on pretending their job is not changing, because of security needs or fear that any admission of spare time will only attract a new heap of work which they may not feel like taking on. Such situations must be handled sympathetically by managers, and support provided in the form of retraining.

Analysis of staff in existing posts may also be used to spot 'high fliers', such as those with management potential. The use of 'potential reviews' in making

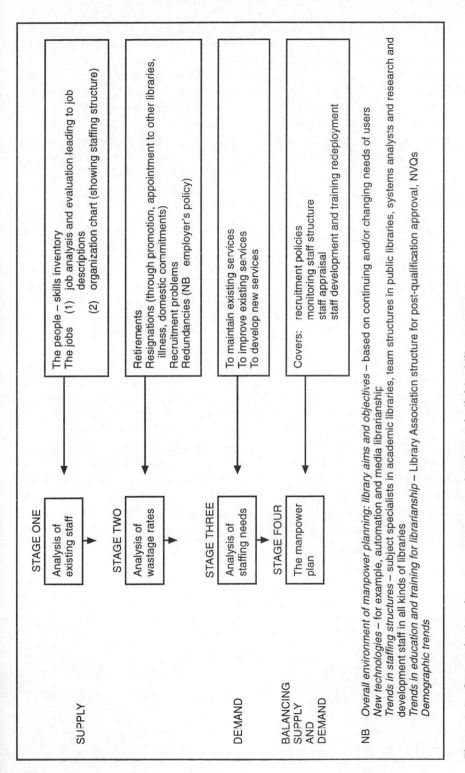

SUPPLY

STAGE ONE

Analysis of existing staff

The people – skills inventory
The jobs (1) job analysis and evaluation leading to job descriptions
(2) organization chart (showing staffing structure)

STAGE TWO

Analysis of wastage rates

Retirements
Resignations (through promotion, appointment to other libraries, illness, domestic commitments)
Recruitment problems
Redundancies (NB employer's policy)

DEMAND

STAGE THREE

Analysis of staffing needs

To maintain existing services
To improve existing services
To develop new services

BALANCING SUPPLY AND DEMAND

STAGE FOUR

The manpower plan

Covers: recruitment policies
monitoring staff structure
staff appraisal
staff development and training redeployment

NB *Overall environment of manpower planning: library aims and objectives* – based on continuing and/or changing needs of users
New technologies – for example, automation and media librarianship
Trends in staffing structures – subject specialists in academic libraries, team structures in public libraries, systems analysts and research and development staff in all kinds of libraries
Trends in education and training for librarianship – Library Association structure for post-qualification approval, NVQs
Demographic trends

Figure 3.1   Stages in drawing up a manpower plan for an individual library system

this analysis is described in Chapter 6 but some organizations also plan at a systemwide level, particularly in the private sector. Here there is frequently a policy of recruiting internally for posts at the top. Andrew Mayo of ICL describes a model which visualizes the organization as broadly pyramidal and divides it into a number of hierarchical levels. At each level it is calculated that 40 per cent or so will need to be people with some potential. The exercise started at ICL with an 'organizational audit' assessing the ratio of people with upwards, to people with lateral, potential. As a result of the analysis ICL increased their numbers of young entrants substantially. They discovered also that they were not accelerating high potential people fast enough. 'Frustrated ones left for greener pastures. So we have brought the average age of entry to "senior" management grades steadily downwards.'[30]

Analysis of staff wastage rates

It has been noted in the introductory section on national workforce planning for library and information work, that social and economic and technological trends have a significant impact on the reality of library staffing levels, irrespective of what might be considered an ideal establishment by senior library managers. Local variations in unemployment figures, in local authority expenditure on libraries, and in policies on early retirement and redundancy agreements between employers and unions, all affect the wastage rates which can be predicted over a five-year period, or more or less. National social trends, such as women staying on in their professional jobs and postponing having children until they are in their thirties, so as to get a better foothold in their chosen careers, may also vary regionally (the north being more conservative in this particular instance than the south east). It is therefore rash to generalize, but it is probably safe to assert that in staff wastage in the last decade or so the push–pull ratio is changing significantly. Figure 3.2 identifies

Push factors	Pull factors
Induction crisis, or adjustment problems in a new situation	Higher earnings
	Promotion to further one's career
Interpersonal conflicts	Alternative job opportunities
Redundancy or early retirement schemes offered by employers	Alternative roles, e.g. motherhood, self-employment, voluntary work, or a combination of alternative roles, including:
Pressures from changed working requirements, e.g. impact of automation, staff restructuring, or loss of contact with users	Emerging work structures, e.g. job sharing

Figure 3.2   Influential factors in job change

the most common 'push' and 'pull' factors which are influential when staff leave jobs.

Because of the changing age structure of the profession there was a greater number of young professionals seeking promotion, or at least a change of job opportunity after their first post, but a blockage was caused because not enough people were of the age to retire. This led to low mobility and job stagnation, which was not particularly alleviated by early retirement schemes, since often staff taking advantage of these were not replaced by the parent organization. Thus pressure of work increased for those left, without any corresponding reward in the way of increased salary or a rise in status. A changing 'push' factor was that people were more inclined to put up with not very satisfactory or motivating situations at work, because the possibilities of moving to another job were diminished by the economic recession and cuts in public expenditure. Security became more significant, and so staff might be more tolerant of traditional push factors such as interpersonal conflicts or unwillingness to be socialized into an apathetic time-serving work group, when previously they would have been driven to look for other jobs as soon as possible.

Over the last decade the fall in property values particularly in the south-east of England and the sluggishness of the housing market has seriously affected mobility. Our experience has been that strong shortlists for senior staff have been difficult to compile.

There are a number of quantitative formulae for calculating wastage rates, in order to establish yearly trends and work out likely needs in the years ahead. The simplest of these is:

$$\frac{\text{Number of staff leaving in a year}}{\text{Average number of employees}} \times 100 = \text{percentage wastage}$$

This may conceal, however, a high turnover in one area of the library, or at one level of staff, such as junior non-professionals on the counter. So it is more representative of the true wastage rate to calculate:

$$\frac{\text{Number of staff with over one year's service}}{\text{Number of staff employed one year ago}} \times 100$$

The result is a 'labour stability index', which can be used to keep a check on staff trends in a specific library. This kind of information may be politically useful in drawing up arguments to safeguard a library from staffing cuts, but should be allied to other common formulae, such as number of library users per staff member (full-time equivalents – student numbers in education – FTEs; population served in public libraries; number of researchers who need SDI in a special library).

Forecasting the demand for staff in an individual library

An accurate forecast is almost impossible as so much depends on changing social, economic and political factors affecting funding. Clearly there are dangers in making comparisons between apparently comparable libraries. The outcome may be that the better staffed may be cut rather than the worse off improved. It is noteworthy that there are wide variations, for example, in staffing ratios in polytechnic libraries. The Council of Polytechnic Libraries (COPOL) figures for the period 1984/85 to 1990/91 show that the number of staff has been falling in relation to the number of FTE students served (1:117 in 1984/85, but 1:141 in 1990/91). But there is a very wide range, as shown by the 1990/91 figures, where the worst off poly is serving 234 FTE per one staff member. A further fact emerging from the COPOL statistics is that the percentage of the whole library funding spent on staff salaries in 1990/91 ranged from 40 per cent to 63 per cent, although the services offered in polytechnic libraries were at least superficially the same. Significant factors which affect such statistics are the number of site libraries, and degrees of centralization of, for instance, technical services. But beyond this professional judgements are involved, on the priorities attached to certain services, or to the book fund, or to automation projects. For the latter it may be easier to get capital funding than for other projects, though the subsequent costs of upkeep may prove crippling to the materials fund.

Cutting staff is often forced upon library managers by higher policies, but certainly in public libraries in the 1980s restructuring often took place with the deliberate intention of making more effective use of staff by reducing the number of professionals to non-professionals. Traditionally the workforce in libraries has been underused in terms of skills and professional expertise. Professional posts have often had a high proportion of routine administration, which could as well be carried out by trained clerical assistants. This change is naturally very threatening to professional staff, particularly to those who have done long service entirely engaged in routine operational tasks and do not see that there is anything more to library and information work. Therefore the argument often put forward that restructuring will free professional staff for more demanding professional tasks, does not always prove true. Staff may not be flexible enough, or may not be given sufficient retraining, to cope with their new role:

> It is the professional's ability and willingness to question current practices which distinguishes him from the non-professional (who is not able to question), and from the minor bureaucrat (who is not willing, even if able, to question).[31]

'The manpower shortages of the 1960s was one of the main factors which led to consideration of strategic approaches to labour market problems and a much greater interest in manpower planning'.[32] With the recessions of the 1980s and 1990s there have been fewer manpower shortages and therefore less interest in manpower planning but, as David Bell explains, 'this is about to change. Skill shortages loom once again. The demographic issues, of which personnel managers and their organisations have at last become aware, are beginning to prompt a return to longer-term planning of the human resource'.

The fall in the birth-rate in the mid to late 1970s has meant that there will be two million fewer young people in the labour market by 1995. Live births in the UK fell from 901,600 in 1971 to 657,000 in 1976 and they are unlikely ever to reach their former level. Mary Auckland[33] provides evidence that libraries, especially in the south-east, are already having difficulty recruiting and many organizations are now devising strategies designed to attract and retain staff especially those with much needed skills. It has been predicted that by the year 2000 over 70 per cent of jobs will be cerebral, requiring brain skills rather than manual ability. She recommends a number of solutions:

- Encourage job sharing.
- Encourage part-time working.
- Introduce a 'flexible working year' in which some employees contract to work a specified number of hours in the year which will vary at different times, e.g. term-time and vacations.
- Encourage para-professionals to become professionals. Patricia Kreitz[34] considers they are 'a ready-made pool of potential recruits' and recommends the provision of opportunities for them to learn about the work of professionals – 'active role-modeling could be something as simple as a bag lunch or a series of meetings in which librarians share their professional activities with library staff'.

Beryl Morris is strongly of the opinion that 'the employer who thrives in future will be the one who takes steps now'.[35] In some organizations, however, there is considerable reluctance to change from working patterns which have so far been successful. In addition those strategies that increase the size of the workforce and are perceived as giving benefits to some and not to others are considered potentially damaging. Although job-sharing has been around for some time it has not been universally popular with managers. The increase in staff numbers can create communication and span of control problems, though our experience has been that two job sharers who are known to be valuable members of staff contribute more than many full-time equivalents. They bring enthusiasm and commitment to the job and are not worn out at the end of the week. They are also reasonably flexible, filling in for each other where needs dictate. Most job-sharing in libraries is undertaken by women. In the past organizations had assumed 'that career-oriented employees will devote (sell) the majority of their time during their working years to the organization, while women's biological cycles demand major allocations of time during that same life-stage to child-bearing and child-rearing'.[36] The skills shortage as much as anything else is changing this view.

Problems of control and communication are likely also to be the main disadvantages of teleworking which many see as the next major change in work patterns. Technological developments have made it possible for a lot of work to be carried out at home and a number of organizations have already recruited workforces.

Retaining and attracting quality staff has always been a management objective and the skills shortage has given it greater priority. Beryl Morris[37] has reviewed the options available to libraries and information units drawing upon strategies being employed by large organizations such as banks, building societies and large retailers. The list below is derived from her article.

Recruitment
- Improve recruitment literature.
- Target specific groups of potential employees who have previously been neglected, e.g. older workers, ethnic minorities, disabled.
- Improve the image of library and information work.
- Stress the personnel and training activities of the organization.
- Attend recruitment fairs and develop initiatives to project a positive image.
- Provide more attractive conditions for women who are likely to provide the majority of new entrants.
- Increase the use of temporary staff.

Retention
- Improve salaries.
- Offer benefits such as extra leave, promotion and training opportunities, job enrichment, to those who stay.
- Examine working hours and introduce flexi-time.
- Introduce career break schemes which permit women (and men) to take a break away from work for family and other reasons.

Until recently few libraries had evolved regular monitoring mechanisms for measuring the effectiveness of their services or their staff. Chapter 1 highlights the increased emphasis on performance indicators and Chapter 6 provides plenty of evidence that staff appraisal schemes have become quite commonplace in recent years. As far as forecasting staffing needs is concerned it is necessary to bring together the information gained by these activities in order to calculate the number and nature of staff needed over the next two, three or five years. The steps required are:

1   Examine the numbers, skills and attributes of existing staff, who currently keep the services going at varying levels of effectiveness.
2   Note any apparent undermanning or overmanning, often resulting from automation projects, altered staffing structures, cuts in services, or shifts in priorities of services.
3   Note any apparent mismatching of people to jobs, usually resulting from poor recruitment practices or from job changes backed up by inadequate training.
4   Consider to what extent the present levels of effectiveness meet the aims and objectives of the service, based on a well-informed analysis of user

needs. Pinpoint specific areas of service which do not seem satisfactory in terms of objectives – requests, interlibrary lending, short-loan service, promotion and publicity, or staff-user relations… Is the problem a staffing one, in whole or in part?

5 Consider the development of new services which are needed, or planned, or in the process of implementation – on-line information services, housebound services etc. Calculate the number of staff hours, and the necessary and desirable attributes and qualifications needed to develop these services.

Balancing supply and demand: writing the workforce plan

In times of public expenditure cuts, it may be useful to produce two workforce plans: a short-term economy plan and a long-term development plan. Each will incorporate the steps summarized in Figure 3.1, starting with a detailed analysis of existing staff quantity and quality and leading on to decisions about high priority services and objectives, if it proves necessary in the short term to cut or reduce some services. Staffing levels are a thorny question – libraries of the same type run similar services on widely differing staffing levels. LAMSAC standards exist for the public library sector, but academic and special libraries have evolved their own staffing levels, often with pressure from their parent bodies to take their share of staffing cuts when necessary. The research undertaken by the Local Authorities' Management Services and Computer Committee in the mid-1970s (the LAMSAC Standards) into public library staffing provided detailed guidance on the staffing levels necessary to maintain the range of services normally operated by public libraries. Time allowances were built in for staff training and for holiday allowances. The project could not in the end be completed, because it was not always possible to arrive at standards, due to wide variations between the libraries investigated. Bibliographical Services, for example, were examined in six local authorities' libraries, but no staffing formulae could be hammered out, since 'differences in policies and practices produced differences in staffing, and the variations were too great and the sample too small to enable the production of standards that could be offered with any degree of confidence'. In some public libraries requests were handled by professional staff, and in others by nonprofessionals. Some bibliographical services departments were highly active in the production of booklists and other guides and so needed more staff. There were conflicting approaches to stock editing, stock revision and 'balance of stock' among service points:

> In one authority there were four stock editors undertaking stock revision, allocation of new stock etc, together with a Catalogue Editor to co-ordinate and balance the collections between service points. In another authority where the figures for total stock and additions were greater the number of staff used was considerably less.[38]

In the absence of definitive standards about the numbers and kinds of staff needed to carry out services effectively, library managers should be capable of reasoning out their own, within the constraints of their institutional environment, and the rather broad guidelines laid down by the professional associations and/or trade unions. An example of the latter is The Library Association's 1991 *Guidelines for college and polytechnic libraries:*

> On this evidence the Library Association believes that higher education institutions should view a point between the median and the 75 percentile as a minimum target (1 F.T.E. library staff member : 115–125 students F.T.E.); in further education the minimum target should be the 75 percentile (1 F.T.E. library staff member : 329 students F.T.E. in large colleges and 205 students F.T.E. in small colleges) and in larger institutions should exceed this level.[39]

The recommendation is that professional librarians and para-professional staff are required, in most institutions in a ratio between 1 : 2 and 3 : 2.

The Library Association has a manpower section which can provide useful information on salary grades at different levels in different kinds of library.

In the small special library or information unit workforce planning is an altogether more informal matter, but of vital importance as there is less scope for absorbing people with the wrong skills and attitudes. Webb analyses the qualities necessary for information services in business and professional firms:

> Whether operating as a one person library or with several members of staff, the role of the librarian is one that is based on relationships and continuous communication with individuals at all levels throughout the organisation... communication involves breaking down barriers, one of which may be that caused by 'the image' of a librarian in the user's mind. This may be an unapproachable, unhelpful character, surrounded by so many inflexible rules and regulations...[40]

When planning workforce in special libraries the essential qualities to look for are flexibility and a wide range of skills, because a tiny workforce has to cover the whole gamut of information tasks. As well as professional qualifications in library and information studies or in information science the staff who will be most useful will have secretarial skills and some experience of, or at least favourable attitudes to, the 'business ethos'. Unfortunately there is still in some special libraries a staffing legacy from the days when companies staffed 'the technical information agencies with workers made available by chance and who are difficult to employ in other divisions'.[41]

Desirable staff–user ratios in special libraries are difficult to specify, since there is such a wide variation in the levels of service provided and in the complexity of enquiries received. Another significant factor is the level of technology in use, for example buying-in information services, using on-line rather than manual searching. In 1979 Slater carried out a survey of 655 special library/information units, and compiled information on staff–user ratios 'for use in forecasting and planning at both the national and organisational level'.[42] One of her summary tables is reproduced (see Table 3.2), to show the average number of staff related to the numbers of actual and potential users. She

	Average number per unit				
	All kinds library information staff	Qualified library information staff	Actual users	Potential users	Total onsite payroll
Whole sample	5.2	1.5	291	703	1,390
Area:					
North	5.3	1.4	263	528	1,031
Midlands	3.3	1.1	252	528	1,926
South	5.5	1.7	307	800	1,392
Type:					
Industry, Commerce	3.8	1.1	217	471	1,181
Government	7.0	2.0	497	1,265	2,191
Society-staff	4.7	1.6	88	180	322
Service title:					
Library	4.7	1.5	365	973	1,896
Information	9.7	2.1	115	297	502
Combined	4.3	1.4	258	509	1,058
Different	8.2	1.9	138	291	684
Medical v rest:					
Medical	3.1	1.1	595	1,218	2,346
Non-medical	5.7	1.6	226	592	1,184

From Margaret Slater, *Ratio of staff to users*, Aslib, 1981.

Table 3.2 Staff user ratios in UK special libraries

points out, however, that information services cannot be planned solely on the basis of the 'inhouse onsite population', as shown in the table. 'This represents only the tip of the iceberg ... Even industrial and commercial organisations have substantial offsite user groups (though distance may mercifully diminish the frequency of demand).' It is clear from the tables that most special libraries employ few staff. Bray and Turner (1991)[43] confirm the average to be five whilst Nakivell's survey of 1991[44] found 16.7 per cent of the cohort with jobs in library and information services were working in isolation compared with 8.3 per cent in 1989.

Slater's questionnaire included a section on the existing level of automation, and future plans, since this was relevant to future staffing levels in such a labour-intensive occupation. The findings were that 46 per cent of the special libraries in her sample were already using computers, 68 per cent had access to them, and 30 per cent had no access and no plans to get access. Of this 30 per cent the majority were very small units, and included a high proportion of Society libraries. The most common uses of computers were, in order of frequency of mention from top down, for on-line and batch searching, use of external commercial databases, creation of in-house databases, current awareness services, cataloguing and indexing, housekeeping routines such as membership and loan records, or periodicals control. It is not yet clear to what extent staff will be reduced as a result of automation, but Slater sounds a warning note that it is possible to detect:

> Rather a deplorable tendency to regard human beings and the latest products of the new technology as interchangeable parts of the system. Eventually this attitude cannot fail to be detrimental to the interests of people, whether broadly or narrowly defined. So one hears managerial statements like this: 'Before I agree to the purchase of this new equipment – how many staff will you be able to get rid of if I do'.[45]

A final aspect of the impact of technology on manpower planning is that new staffing structures are emerging which break down the traditional barriers between different sections of libraries, such as readers' services and technical services. Increasingly libraries are appointing 'systems librarians' to co-ordinate all applications of automation. Their job is to liaise with systems suppliers to iron out problems of maintenance and quality control, to train staff, to promote the systems with users, and to take part in user group activities intended to influence the future development of systems such as OCLC or BLCMP. In libraries where staffing structures are very hierarchical, with each member of staff reporting to one boss, this can cause outbreaks of 'staff and line' problem. In libraries which have already moved towards a 'matrix' approach, where staff have a line manager but also take part in working parties or have a special responsibility (for AV or user education) across sites or branch libraries, there are fewer problems because of greater flexibility.

4

Job description and personnel specification

Staff are the life-blood of any library or information service, and effective re-cruiting and training can make all the difference between a poor or run-of-the-mill service and a high quality service, particularly in periods of limited finance and low job mobility. It has been argued that recruitment is the most vital single aspect of staff management in both financial and human terms. When mistakes are made, and there is a mismatch between person and job, the costs are not just poor performance and output, but often physical ill health or stress symptoms expressed through absences, unsatisfactory behaviour and conflicts with col-leagues. So recruitment is a two-way process, in which it is essential to ensure that the tasks and responsibilities of a post are compatible with the person appointed – their qualifications, skills and aspirations.

The aim then is not just to fill vacancies, but to place people in jobs where they are likely to be well adjusted to their responsibilities and the organization as a whole. However that is not to say that people have to fit into an inevitable status quo. Certainly at the higher levels of recruitment it is important for individuals to have a say in how they would like their job to develop, and how they would interpret it if appointed, rather than assuming that they are required to carry on just as their predecessor did. A further relevant point is that since Britain joined the European Economic Community employment protection legislation (see Chapter 1) has increased security from dismissal, so getting rid of recruitment 'mistakes' can be expensive and time-consuming, involving appearance before industrial tribunals and the possibility of fines, compensation and reinstatement of an employee if the decision is 'unfair dismissal'. Another result of the growth in legislation affecting recruitment is that discrimination on the grounds of race or sex must be scrupulously avoided, and shown to be avoided, by those involved at all stages of recruitment from wording the advertisement through short-listing to the questions asked in the interview, and the reasons why a specific person is appointed.

Later chapters in this book deal with staff appraisal and training. One of the factors influencing the workload involved in these later stages of staff management is the quality of recruitment policies and procedures. If recruitment is poor this may not show up until appraisal systems, formal or informal, reveal that a member of staff needs considerable development to live up to the expectations of those who appointed him or her to a particular post. Figure 4.1 summarizes the connections.

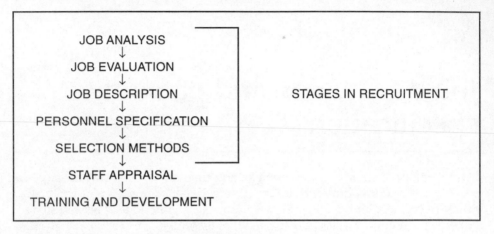

JOB ANALYSIS
↓
JOB EVALUATION
↓
JOB DESCRIPTION   STAGES IN RECRUITMENT
↓
PERSONNEL SPECIFICATION
↓
SELECTION METHODS
↓
STAFF APPRAISAL
↓
TRAINING AND DEVELOPMENT

Figure 4.1   Main stages in staff management

Job analysis and job description

As Plumbley points out, 'There appears to be a built-in reflex which even "head-count" restrictions fail to inhibit; someone leaving must be replaced as soon as possible'.[1] A vacancy is an occasion for analysing what the post holder did, and how it fits in with the organization's purposes, which may be taking new directions, or adapting to new technologies. Furthermore job analysis may suggest that internal promotion or transfer of existing staff may be more appropriate than advertising the particular job that has fallen vacant. There may be staff in other jobs who would be ideal in terms of their qualifications and interests, and who may not be getting full outlet where they are at present. Whatever decision is made about a new appointment or a 'reshuffle' of existing staff, it should be done from a well-informed basis, through careful analysis of the job vacancy. A job may be defined as a collection of tasks and responsibilities making up the work of one member of staff, but in reality some jobs would be better described as only existing because there is a person holding them. Job analysis may reveal this situation, often the result of technology and other changes in the working environment, which causes jobs to become diminished, or in some cases to disappear entirely, although still on the establishment of posts.

The two classic examples invariably quoted in the literature are the extra man in the artillery team, whose job originally was to hold the horses and whose post continued even after horses had been replaced by mechanization; and the civil service post (in its later stages an office job) still on the establishment in the 1950s, the purpose of which was to patrol the cliffs of Dover to give early warning of Napoleon's invasion of our shores. In the library and information context vigilance is just as necessary to ensure that posts are modified or created to make sense in terms of the organization's current and future, rather than past commitments and priorities. This is especially difficult, but even more necessary, when posts are frozen and individuals and trade unions are naturally suspicious that employers are trying to squeeze more work out of a diminishing number of employees.

As resources became more scarce from the end of the 1970s onwards, many academic and public libraries changed their staffing structures to reduce costs. One solution was to allocate more operational activities to non-professional (better called para-professional) rather than professional staff, changing the ratio of professionals to non-professionals, in favour of the latter. Another solution was automation of housekeeping routines which should, but does not always, appear to result in staff savings or redeployment of staff to, say, readers' advisory work. A further idea was to have more centralization, either by reducing the number of site or branch libraries to an economically manageable number, or by centralizing technical services to save on the large number of graduate staff traditionally employed in acquisition and cataloguing routines. Restructuring may also lead to extra duties being added to existing jobs. An example was the tendency in the 1980s for academic libraries to give subject librarians functional duties as well as subject duties. Comparably in public libraries non-professional staff were given more responsibility for the day-to-day running of service points, and the professional staff were assigned to a wider range of tasks and projects. These normally included responsibility for a specialist function – children's work or community information – in the area group of service points, and stock editing in a specific Dewey class, also across the area group.

It should be noted that transferring routines and procedures to para-professionals inevitably leads to a reduction in the numbers of professionals required, unless times are prosperous and the extra staff time released can be channelled to developing, extending and improving the quality of services.

In special libraries and information units it has been important for information officers to develop in-depth information services to prove their worth. Using job analysis to enrich their jobs, and rewriting job descriptions to include more dynamic duties and responsibilities has helped this process.

Practical advantages of job analysis and job description

Job analysis can be seen as a helpful aid to staff structuring and allocation of work. However it may also appear as a predatory activity carried out by parent bodies such as local authority, company, or educational institution,

Designation	Team Librarian: Maidenhead
Grade	Sc 4/6 (Career Grade: See Annex A)
Reports to	Senior Librarian: Maidenhead
	(Professional Services Co-ordinator)
Job purpose	1 To be a member of the Professional Services Team and assist with the provision and promotion of the total pubic library service and its related activities.
	2 To specialise in a particular aspect of service provision across the Area as may be required by the Area Librarian or Professional Services Co-ordinator.
Organisation structure	See attached

DIMENSIONS:

Area budget 1991/92	£514,656 net expenditure including £414,550 for staffing, and an income target of £79, 735.
	The above total includes an element for material which will be under the direct control of the postholder.
Staff supervised	Whilst the postholder does not supervise any staff directly he/she must demonstrate the skills of good staff management through his/her liaison with the Area Supervisor, 6 Branch Supervisors and approx 18 FTE support staff.

NATURE AND SCOPE OF THE POSITION:

Maidenhead Area includes the major towns of Maidenhead (the area base) and Windsor. There are part-time libraries in the villages of Cookham, Dedworth and Old Windsor. A container library serves the Wraysbury, Cox Green and Holyport areas. The East Berkshire Mobile Library serves the rural areas in the east of the county not served by static provision. The Area bookstock is 156,000 and annual book issues are 889,000.

The postholder is a member of the Professional Services Team of the Maidenhead Area and as such should aim to reach the highest possible standards of professional service and customer care. Approximately 50% of working time is spent on lending or reference desks on face-to-face or telephone enquiries. Under the general direction of the Area Librarian and co-ordination of the Senior Librarian, the postholder provides specialist advice, stock knowledge and service delivery to the customers served by the branch libraries in the Maidenhead Area.

PRINCIPAL ACCOUNTABILITIES:

1 *Direct Reader Services*
Provides a general enquiry service at all full-time service points utilising specialist bibliographic expertise and knowledge of County and National resources. This includes face-to-face, postal and telephone enquiries and

Figure 4.2   Royal County of Berkshire Library and Information Service job description

the associated bibliographic work for appropriate specialist requests across the Area.

2   *Stock Management*
Manages the Area wide stock in the appropriate specialism in order to maintain optimum use and ensure its quality and suitability to the community served. This is achieved by stock profiling, planning and monitoring stock circulation programmes, taking decisions on selection and deselection whilst monitoring the expenditure of the budget allocated.

3   *Services within the Specialism*
Manages the assigned specialism in the Area by assessing present and potential demand for the service, liaising with appropriate staff in the Area and County to determine this and to satisfy demand.

4   In the assigned specialism, identifies the training needs of the rest of the Professional Services Team and other members of Area staff. Helps to provide effective training to meet these needs, in conjunction with fellow specialists within the County as necessary.

5   Maintains current awareness in the postholder's specialism.

6   Represents the Area at county-wide meetings of fellow specialists.

7   Helps the rest of the Professional Services Team and other members of Area staff to keep up-to-date with techniques and information associated with the postholder's specialism.

8   Identifies possible income generating services and ensures that maximum income is derived from existing resources.

ANNEX A

TEAM LIBRARIAN CAREER GRADE

Scale 4 – Qualified librarians obtaining first professional appointment.

Scale 4 plus 2 increments – completion of one year's satisfactory service, based on performance assessment.

Scale 5 – Chartered Members of the Library Association subject to performance assessment.

Scale 6 – Subject to the following criteria:

1   Be a Chartered member of the Library Association or other relevant professional body.
2   Minimum of one year's experience since becoming chartered.

Figure 4.2   Continued

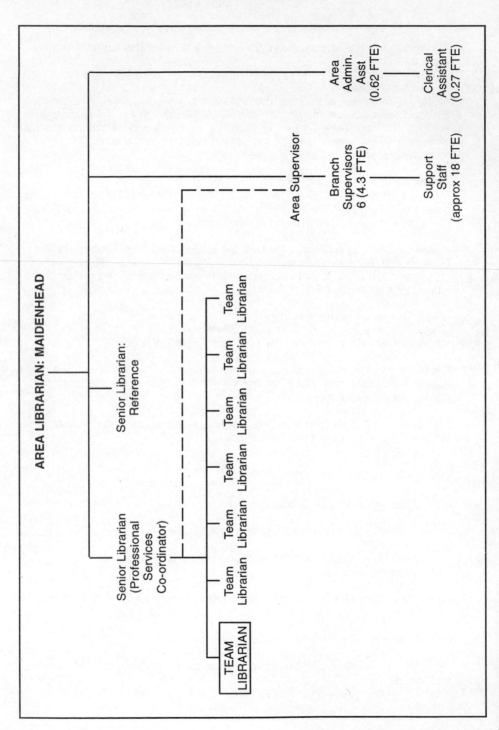

Figure 4.2   Continued

3 Demonstrate initiative in identifying needs and opportunities within specialist area of responsibility, ability to achieve agreed objectives and, in a cost-effective manner, to measure the benefits to the service as a result of these initiatives and achievements.
4 Demonstrate ability to lead by example, to motivate and train staff and to show measurable achievements in service performance as a result.
5 Demonstrate sustained commitment to the service and a consistent standard of excellence in customer care.
6 Demonstrate good inter-personal skills so that colleagues are sufficiently aware of information, techniques and developments in the postholder's assigned specialism and the postholder plays full part in efficient and effective working of the team.
7 Demonstrate in-depth knowledge of assigned specialism so that the postholder is normally self-sufficient in serving customers through own resources with minimal need to refer to co-specialists.

ALL 7 OF THE ABOVE CRITERIA NEED TO BE MET IN FULL

Figure 4.2 Concluded

with a view to cutting staff. Trade unions go on the alert when job analysis or job evaluation is in the offing. It is a signal for them to consider how to protect members' jobs. The employer has to make certain therefore that relevant trade unions are consulted at an early stage, to reach agreement on restructuring.

A job description is a statement of the objectives, main tasks, supervisory duties and place in the staff structure which the job holder is expected to accept. It should be the outcome of careful job analysis, rather than an automatic retention of the previous post holder's duties. During the recruitment process the job description is sent to potential applicants and used as the basis of the advertisement. Examples of good job descriptions are shown in Figures 4.2, 4.3, 4.4 and 4.6. A further use for job descriptions is in diagnosing training needs, when the post holder has been in the job for some time. A job description provides a basis for the training officer to draw up relevant programmes of staff development, since most staff display varying capabilities and competencies, depending on which aspects of their jobs are under consideration. A job description provides a useful checklist for the trainer, in diagnosing training needs.

In special libraries particularly, job analysis is often used as a preliminary to job evaluation, which may be defined as 'the process of analysis and assessment of the relative content of jobs, to place them in an acceptable rank order, which can be used as the basis for a pay structure'.[2] Mason[3] points out that such evaluation is a means of ensuring that salary grades and working status are fair both to the occupant of the job and to the employer. A dynamic information officer may have extended the job far beyond the clerical tasks which it originally covered, so that the job carries higher levels of decision-making, communication outside the unit, and advanced levels of technology in the SDI services. Job evaluation should in these circumstances be welcomed, in order to have the job regraded from clerical upwards.

JOB DESCRIPTION

JOB TITLE: Information Analyst   **REPORTS TO:** Senior Information Analyst

JOB HOLDER: ^C   **DATE:** September 1992

1. JOB PURPOSE

To analyse standards and associated documents to generate subject and bibliographic data in order to develop and maintain the BSI databases of British, foreign and international documentary information and to interrogate BSI and other external data sources on behalf of internal and external clients and to contribute to terminological (ROOT) thesaurus maintenance.

2. ORGANIZATION CHART

Senior Information Analyst

| **Information Analyst x 7** | Assistant Information Analyst |

3. DIMENSIONS

Financial: Current awareness bulletin revenue £12k
           Search service revenue £3k

Staff: None

Other: Foreign and international database   600,000 documents, 1 million records, 2,100 documents analysed per month.
       British Standards database   22,500 documents, 28,400 records, update 2,500 records at bureau, 1,000 per month at online host (Standardline).

   UDC project on behalf of UDC Consortium   100 records analysed and entered per month.
   Searches   External clients 35 per month, international clients 50 per month.
   ROOT project.   Term database of 13,000 hierarchical records.

4. JOB CONTEXT

The library comprises three sections – Collections Management, Data Services and Product Management.

The Collections section maintains and sources collections of documents and provides the working material for the Data Services team.

The Data Services section carries out subject and bibliographic analysis and data entry on this material, in order to generate highly formatted data which may then be used in the production of electronic and hard copy products. The databases and all associated authority files including the ROOT thesaurus are maintained by Data Services.

A commercial search service is operated by Data Services as is the WSI current awareness bulletin. Data is used directly in the production of the BSI Catalogue and Supplement, Standardline, Perinorm, Library retrieval systems etc.

The Product section further develops these products by working on aspects of editorial control, typesetting, print liaison and other commercial matters.

The Collections section is Data Services' main supplier. The main customers are external clients, Products section, Technical Services, Customer Services, Membership Services etc.

5. PRINCIPAL ACCOUNTABILITIES

KEY RESULT AREAS	PRINCIPAL ACCOUNTABILITIES
Indexation and validation for database maintenance	Analyse standards and associated documents according to subject and bibliographic attributes and to validate data resulting from database systems according to timeliness, accuracy, completeness and volume constraints, as determined by Senior Information Analyst.
Database authority files including ROOT thesaurus	Develop and maintain control (authority) files, including the ROOT subject thesaurus, in order to help ensure integrity of the databases and to meet ROOT commercial commitments.

Figure 4.3   British Standards Institution job description

Search and enquiry service	Operate the on-demand search service of BSI and external data sources in order to provide accurate and complete information to internal and external clients and comply with the financial and technical guidelines as determined by the Senior Information Analyst.
Worldwide Standards Information (WSI) current awareness bulletin	Provide a client contact point for discussion/determination/agreement of clients' subject profile which will determine subscription rate for the service. Monitor renewals and subscriptions on behalf of the Manager, Library Data.
UDC Data	Operate and monitor a subject indexing and validating service on behalf of the BSI Universal Decimal Classification (UDC) Consortium, allowing UDC classification numbers to be created and entered into the corporate standards publication system (PIMS), in order for data to appear on published BSI documents according to timeliness, volume, accuracy and completeness targets as determined by the Manager, Library Data.
Presentation and Training	Make presentations to and train internal and external clients on data production/retrieval systems as required by Senior Information Analyst.

6. KNOWLEDGE, SKILLS AND EXPERIENCE

Degree in a technical, scientific or information discipline to enable job holder to have a comprehensive knowledge of technical terms and subjects, in order to undertake detailed analysis of standards in complex subject areas. Intellectual ability and technical/scientific training to enable job holder to readily gain an understanding in subject matters in other disciplines.

Proven experience/qualifications in information work.
High level of accuracy and attention to detail.
Foreign language skills sufficient to enable foreign documents to be analysed.
Computer literacy to a level which enables understanding of how the database works and the methods of inputting data.
Knowledge of Standards information.
Communication and estimating skills.

7. DEGREE OF SUPERVISION OR DIRECTION

i) Received from your superior:

Constraints of weekly, monthly and annual targets, but otherwise freedom of action. Indexing and validating procedures. Estimation and charging guidelines are given. Ad hoc priorities and trouble shooting tasks may be set by superior/s.

ii) Given to your subordinates:

Work guidelines/instructions given to clerical staff who are not direct reportees.

8. KEY CHALLENGES

To maintain a high level of accuracy whilst under considerable time/deadline pressure, where staff resources are static, but volumes are increasing steadily. A very wide understanding of technology has to be maintained. Interpretation of customers' requirements in order to provide them with maximum benefit. Material is diverse and involves a high proportion of foreign language material.

9. ADDITIONAL INFORMATION

Customer search requirements need high order communication/estimating skills, in order to deliver correct results on time and to cost. Computer systems used require use of highly complex coding conventions in a consistent and reliable manner.

Approved by: Job Holder   Date:

     Manager   Date:

     Analyst

101

Figure 4.3 Concluded

Post title:	Assistant Librarian, Periodicals & Information
Department:	Library
Grade:	Assistant Librarian: SALC 1
Responsible to:	University Librarian
Reports to:	Sub-Librarian, Technical Services Sub-Librarian, Readers' Services

Main Purpose

To manage, organise and exploit the University Library's Serials Collection in support of academic teaching, learning and research and to assist in the development and delivery of high quality information services in the University Library.
The main duties and responsibilities associated with the post include:

1. *Serials Management*
   - reporting to Sub-Librarian, Technical Services;
   - to manage the serials collection within the assigned budget by means of the Periodicals Formula and to liaise effectively with academic departments in its application, including acquisitions and cancellations;
   - to manage the abstracting and indexing serials held in the Library, to assess the usage and develop retention criteria;
   - to supervise and perform the routine processes of receipt, recording, binding and storage of serials;
   - to advise the Sub-Librarian and the University Librarian of appropriate forms of serials records and optimal systems for serials management;
   - to arrange effective and economical supply of serials by knowledge of and liaison with subscription agents, publishers and other suppliers, including the timely and careful checking of invoices;
   - to supervise the work of Senior Library Assistants and Library Assistants assigned, within Technical Services, to Serials/Periodicals.

2. *Information Services*
   - reporting to Sub-Librarian, Readers' Services;
   - to participate in the provision of mediated and end-user database search and information services from CHEST and commercial hosts;
   - to use, to demonstrate and to train others to use and exploit databases and information services on CD-ROM and on the network;
   - to advise on selection criteria for information services (on-line and CD-ROM) by single, multiple or networked access;
   - to administer the on-line search service, including the checking and processing of external invoices and the raising of internal recharges for usage;
   - to assist in all aspects of the setting up, installation and maintenance of information services workstations in the Library;

Figure 4.4 City University job description

102

- to acquire and make available in timely fashion documentation for on-line search services, for CD-ROM and for networked information services;
- to write user-guides for information services as required;
- to supervise that part of the Library devoted to Serials/Periodicals;
- to administer the use of the microform reader-printers in the Library, to include ordering of supplies, maintenance, training in the use of and provision of documentation as required.

3.   *Other (general) duties*
- to participate in the Library's enquiry desk rota and assist library users in finding information;
- to participate in the Library's user education programme;
- to take charge of the Library on evening duty and on other occasions as required;
- to supervise Senior Library Assistants and Library Assistants as required.

The above list is not exclusive or exhaustive and the post-holder may be required to undertake any such duties as may reasonably be required of her/him.

Physical fitness and the ability to sustain a degree of manual activity in the handling of printed materials are inherent in this post.

All senior members of staff are expected to be flexible, co-operative and professional within the needs of the post, the department and the University.

Other Working Relationships
(a)   Member of Technical Services Division, required to liaise and work closely with the staff of the division on a day-to-day basis.
(b)   Reporting to the Sub-Librarian, Readers' Services, in respect of operation and staffing, of library services for library users (in addition to Information Services above).
(c)   Liaison with the Systems & Information Librarian.

This post is third tier in the present Library staff structure. Effective and close working relationships with staff of both Library divisions are required.

Figure 4.4   Concluded

The final use of job analysis is in designing new jobs. New jobs become necessary even in a recession, when library and information units find it necessary to appoint, for example, 'systems librarians' with a co-ordinating role in automation, or when priorities indicate the need for services to hitherto neglected user groups, such as ethnic minorities in public libraries, or part-time students in academic libraries. In designing a new job the manager must have knowledge and understanding of what makes a satisfying job, in addition to listing tasks which have to be carried out. Motivation theories are highly relevant here, because it is important to build into jobs some positive motivators such as responsibility, sense of achievement, opportunity to use professional expertise, as well as providing for the 'hygiene factors' of pay, working conditions and status. Redesigning existing jobs is closely allied to designing new jobs, and often happens when staff restructuring is taking place. It is an opportunity for job enlargement and job enrichment. Some examples will illustrate how this may be achieved.

When public libraries introduce team structures, branch librarians, who had hitherto spent a high proportion of their time on routine non-professional tasks, are usually redeployed as members of an area team, each with functional and sometimes also subject responsibilities, as well as geographical responsibility for a number of service points. This is an example of job enrichment – tasks of a higher level are added to a job. Job enlargement on the other hand means adding further jobs of the same level to provide variety and alleviate boredom in lower level jobs. This is a strategy often used in designing non-professional posts. The usual procedure is to give the assistants limited shifts, say two hours at a time, on issues, overdues or shelf tidying. The problem is how to reconcile this with the need to give staff an area of their own to look after, so that they have a sense of achievement. Some academic libraries assign a specialism to each job holder, such as inter-library loans or short loans, or having a specific section of shelving which is their responsibility to keep in correct classified order. Motivation theories suggest that periods of backroom work should be alternated with periods of sociable work, in contact with users or with other members of staff. Most people at work want to have a sense of belonging, and this is satisfied by designing jobs so that everyone is a member of an identifiable work group, whether or not it is a formal team. In very small or one-person libraries this is not possible, and the sociability factor must be built up in the larger environment of the parent company or firm. This can have useful spin-offs in getting to know the user community better, as well as keeping isolation at bay.

Methods of job analysis and evaluation

Job evaluation is the technique used to compare the relative worth of jobs in an organization enabling equitable grading and reward systems to be created.

Many, particularly large companies, employ schemes which were often initiated by legislation, such as the Equal Pay Act of 1970, by labour problems associated with pay differentials and comparabilities, and by the introduction of new skills, particularly those associated with information technology. A recent factor has been the incorporation of educational institutions giving them greater autonomy and the amalgamation of institutions revealing anomalies in gradings. All these factors have produced pressure for change and one response has been to introduce an objective, as far as possible, system of job evaluation.

The methods used are usually divided into non-analytical and analytical, though all systems are analytical in a sense. The non-analytical systems compare whole jobs, the most common being grading. Most libraries in the public sector employ this system usually making use of nationally agreed scales. Jobs are analysed, descriptions written and grades assigned after comparison with other jobs.

Non-analytical methods make no attempt to assign values and often the evaluation is made in a fairly crude manner although it can usually be said to work reasonably well. If recruitment and performance are satisfactory there may be no strong reason to change the system. If rewards are perceived to be unfair there will often be opportunities for review, usually by an objective panel.

Analytical methods have developed because the non-analytical methods appeared to be insufficiently scientific and objective. The analytical methods all involve the analysis of jobs by factors and the assignment of values to those factors. In some systems the factors are weighted according to importance.

Recent schemes which have operated in Manchester Metropolitan University and Aston University involving the library staff are very similar. An evaluation panel was set up representing most areas of the university including trade union representatives. They first decided upon the factors to be used to measure the demands made on the job holder by the job tasks. The factors in each university were similar and have been combined to produce the summary below:

Expertise and experience
Responsibility – for people and resources
Advisory responsibility
Communication and contacts
Judgement and decision-making
Work complexity, adaptability, pressure
Working environment.

For each factor a description is compiled to enable it to be applied consistently. In some cases they were divided into sub-factors. For example, the Communication factor at Manchester is divided into two sub-factors:

A   Contacts: This sub-factor assesses the need for each job holder to contact a range of other people in the course of carrying out duties. These contacts may be at some or all levels internally and may also include external professional counterparts, professional bodies, legislators, members of the public or the media. Both the level of contacts made and their frequency will be assessed.

B   Communication skills: This sub-factor covers the extent to which the job holder requires varying levels of communication skills to carry out duties effectively. These will range from the basic ability to communicate simple written or verbal information to colleagues, through to the ability to write complex reports or give presentations. It also includes the ability to conduct sensitive discussions with others (external/internal) who may hold opposing views to the job holder.

A representative sample of posts (94 at Manchester) was selected to be used as *benchmark* jobs for comparison purposes.

A questionnaire was designed to enable job descriptions of the benchmark jobs to be written.

Questionnaires were completed by job holders and agreed with line managers.

Paired comparison techniques were used to produce a rank order of benchmark jobs and the weightings to be attached to each factor were decided upon. For example, the Aston scheme has a weighting of 25 per cent for Judgement and decision-making and 10 per cent for Contacts.

A factor profile for each benchmark job was then calculated and refined by the judging panel.

The benchmark profiles and the factor descriptions were then used to score all the jobs in the system.

An American example of job evaluation involving a scoring system is shown in Figure 4.5. Rothenberg[4] compiled this for evaluating jobs held by school librarians in the US. She assigned tasks to four groups – high professional, low professional, high non-professional and low non-professional – on the basis of the skills and knowledge necessary to perform the various tasks making up a school librarian's job. The scores for each were added up to provide a 'job task index score', arrived at by dividing the total score by the number of tasks included in one job. In the questionnaire mailed to the sample of school

---

Group 1   High professional job tasks
Score – primary involvement 4, secondary involvement 3

Bibliography	Formal library instruction
Budget preparation	Personnel co-ordination
Choosing publications	Policy determination
Choosing subjects	Program planning

Group 2   Low professional job tasks
Score – primary involvement 2, secondary involvement 1
Assisting readers
Descriptive cataloguing
Informal library instruction
Responding to information requests
Verifying requests

Group 3   High non-professional job tasks
Score – primary involvement minus 2, secondary involvement minus 1

Bindery preparation	Inter-library loan
Bookkeeping	Periodical checking
Data processing	Searching catalogs

Group 4   Low non-professional job tasks
Score – primary involvement minus 4, secondary involvement minus 3

Bookmarking	Repairing and mending
Filing cards	Shelving
Filing and maintaining	Typing cards
circulation records	Typing correspondence
Photocopying	

Figure 4.5   Rothenberg's scoring sheet

librarians the tasks were not of course grouped into professional and non-professional as in Figure 4.5, but were arranged in a single alphabetical sequence. The librarians were asked to tick off all their duties on this list, and indicate whether each was a task of 'primary involvement' or 'secondary involvement'. The results of such an evaluation were intended to help staff managers evaluate job content for the purposes of recruiting the right people for the jobs.

Comparable schemes, if less elaborate, are found in the special library sector. Mason identifies the following significant factors used in evaluating jobs in information work:

1   Amount of specialized knowledge which the job demands.
2   Level and extent of staff management involved.
3   Range of relationships within and without the company which the job-holder needs to maintain or build.
4   Value of the decisions which have to be made.[5]

Methods of drawing up job descriptions

Job evaluation leading to job grading and salary structures is mainly the concern of employing bodies, and the job analysis that takes place in specific libraries includes producing job descriptions for use in the selection, appraisal and training of staff. The usual methods used are chosen from the following:

1   Job holders are asked to write their own description of their job, either freely or within a framework of given headings similar to those used in job evaluation (decision-making, supervisory duties etc.).
2   The immediate supervisor writes the description, with or without the participation of the job holder.
3   The supervisor or an outside job analyst carries out a detailed 'observation' of the work being done.
4   Job holders are asked to keep work diaries over a period.

Often a combination of these methods is used as a check on the reliability of any one method.

Keeping job descriptions up to date is very important. They can become quite misleading after two or three years as jobs evolve or regress due to technological or other environmental changes. In many libraries job descriptions seem only to be used when jobs become vacant and have to be filled, and they remain in the files becoming more and more obsolete. Job descriptions however have considerable potential in other areas of staff management besides recruitment. In particular they serve a useful basis for staff appraisal schemes, providing a yardstick by which to assess the strengths and weaknesses of staff in carrying out the various aspects of their jobs. As a result of such appraisal on a yearly, or more frequent, basis it is possible to plan training and staff development activities with greater attention to established need.

Content of job descriptions

1   *Statement of purpose, objectives of the job*

The examples of job descriptions from Berkshire, British Standards Institution and City University (Figures 4.2–4.4) show clearly how a particular post is related to the overall objectives of the library, and also give specific objectives for the particular job.

It might be argued that such statements of purpose merely state the obvious, but they very often set the scene for a more detailed description of what the job is about, by placing it in the whole context of the library and its community of users. The best ones make strong links between the job and the library's overall aims so that the job holder, if prepared to take the job objectives seriously, could develop a strong sense of playing a purposeful part in the library's complex network of activities and services to its public.

2   *Main tasks and duties*

This section of the job description is often a straightforward list of the activities which the job holder will be expected to perform, but it will be noted from the examples that libraries are tending to take an objectives approach and in some cases giving a weighting to the various tasks or 'accountabilities'. In the Berkshire example (Figure 4.2) weighting is given in terms of the proportion of time to be spent on tasks whilst the British Standards Institution (Figure 4.3) groups tasks into key areas followed by the range of duties or activities related to those key areas. There is an argument for not being too specific, since this may straitjacket the post holder, and prevent or discourage creative or new approaches. Guidelines rather than complete specification may be more supportive of staff development, besides leaving room for flexibility of staff, a factor which may increase in importance as job mobility decreases and staff rotation and exchanges may be desired.

3   *Place of the post in the library's staffing structure*

This part of the job description should indicate clearly to whom the member of staff is responsible, and whom they are required to supervise in turn. It is sometimes conveniently set out in the form of an organization chart as in both the Berkshire and British Standards Institution examples (Figures 4.2 and 4.3). Alternatively it can be simply written as in the City University example (Figure 4.4) which shows to whom the person reports and describes other working relationships. It is important to make clear the range and level of decision-making involved in the job, in addition to a bald statement about position in the staff hierarchy. This involves some indication of the amount of guidance which will be given by the post holder's superiors, the existence or lack of clearly outlined policies and procedures and precedents, the gravity of the problems likely to arise, degree of innovation likely to be required in the work, and the effect on other staff (how widespread and significant) of decisions taken by the holder of this job. The examples indicate clearly the dimensions of the posts and the support which is available.

4   Contacts outside the library

It is useful to indicate the range and level of people in the community with whom the post holder will be required to develop and maintain contacts. In the Berkshire example (Figure 4.2) relationships with the area team and the senior librarian are described and the City University assistant librarian (Figure 4.4) is expected to liaise 'with subscription agents, publishers and other suppliers'.

5   Salary scales and working conditions

These are part of the contextual, as opposed to content of job, information which is essential in job descriptions, particularly when used in the recruitment process. Working conditions include details of hours, holidays, opportunities for staff development such as time and expenses for attending professional workshops and conferences, and prospects for promotion.

6   Organizational factors

In some job descriptions libraries take a lot of trouble to convey the philosophy and structure of the service as they operate it, in order to attract the right kind of staff for them. In all the examples the philosophy of the service comes through in the descriptions, although they do not contain a separate section. The British Standards Institution's emphasis on the provision of 'accurate and complete information to internal and external client', and Berkshire's 'aim to reach the highest possible standards of professional service and customer care' convey their philosophies.

In many cases additional material will be supplied with job descriptions which provide the context of the post and help potential candidates to decide whether to apply.

It is important to recognize that 'both the design and the content of the job description convey an impression of the professionalism, or otherwise, of the employer'.[6]

Problems associated with job descriptions

1   They must be continuously updated, otherwise they become irrelevant and ignored.
2   They must leave some scope for initiative and innovation on the part of the job holder. If they are too specific and detailed, they can encourage the job holder to continue merely to do what the predecessor did, without bothering to create and improve.
3   They are generally careful to state that the post holder may be required to undertake 'such other duties as from time to time the chief librarian may decide'. Otherwise they could become a force for reaction. There may be difficulties in this area when unions consider that duties from frozen posts are being reallocated to increase the workload of other staff. They may instruct their members to refuse to take on extra duties of this nature.

4   If the post holder has not been consulted or personally involved in compiling a job description, it is likely that he or she will not be anxious to carry out its injunctions, and will ignore it as far as possible.
5   The value of job descriptions depends very much on how they are used in a library and extends beyond the recruiting phase, but often this is the only area in which they appear to be used. They should be referred to when staff appraisal and staff development are taking place, and when policy decisions are being taken on workforce planning.

Personnel specification

The job description describes the *job*: the personnel specification describes the *person* capable of doing the job. The job description should be sufficiently informative to enable a realistic picture to be outlined of the attributes required in a successful applicant. What are the qualifications, experience and personal qualities, the skills, abilities and specialist interests required to carry out a particular job?

The job description and the personnel specification are often combined in one document for recruitment purposes. Job applicants who send off for further details receive information on the duties and responsibilities of the job, and also on the qualifications, experience and qualities required in the person who will be appointed. An example from the City of Newcastle-upon-Tyne of a personnel specification combined with the means of assessment derived from the job description is shown in Figures 4.6 and 4.7.

It is sometimes useful to have an intermediate stage after the compilation of the job description and before the personnel specification is written. This is the job specification in which the characteristics of the job are listed, in terms of complexity, responsibility and supervising load. These are then used to determine the characteristics of the person needed to do the job. In library practice the job specification is usually merged with the job description.

The employing organization may not have complete control over the requirements they ask for in job applicants. Professional bodies and trade unions may lay down certain guidelines as to hours of work, jobs which may or may not be carried out by the post holder, appropriate qualifications and salary grades applicable to a particular post. In public libraries Unison (the Public Service Union) is the relevant union for professional librarians; in college and ex-polytechnic libraries it is Natfhe (National Association of Teachers in Further and Higher Education) or Unison; and in university libraries it is AUT (Association of University Teachers). Special libraries cover a wider range of unions because of the diversity of the parent institutions, but some of the commonly found unions are ASTMS (Association of Scientific Technical and Managerial Staff) and Unison.

The Library Association from time to time draws attention to jobs which it has decided to black, because of unsatisfactory salary or conditions of service. It is not necessarily successful, however, in dissuading librarians from applying

LIBRARIES & ARTS

1 **JOB TITLE:** Assistant Librarian (Team Librarian)

2 **POST REFERENCE NO:** CS/3

3 **GRADE:** Scale 3–5 [progression beyond Scale 3 subject to Chartered Librarian status]

4 **RESPONSIBLE TO:** Senior/Group Librarian (Community Services Group)

5 **RESPONSIBLE FOR:** Staff as may be allocated from time to time

6 **KEY ACCOUNTABILITIES:**
6.1 To assist in the provision of an effective, and efficient library service for the Group's area, and to share in providing a comprehensive outreaching service through the service points and staff in the Group.

7 **SUMMARY OF MAIN DUTIES AND RESPONSIBILITIES**
7.1 To share in the Team's work of providing a professional service to the Group's area.
7.2 To develop and promote the library service as directed by the Group Librarian.
7.3 To be responsible to the Group Librarian for stock provision as directed.
7.4 To provide general and specialist services as directed by the Group Librarian.
7.5 To undertake such project work as directed by the Group Librarian in order to meet the library service needs of the area.
7.6 To assist in the training of other members of the Team and of support staff.
7.7 To liaise with senior support staff and other library staff, and with outside organisations as appropriate, e.g. speaking to local societies etc.
7.8 To maintain personal training and development activities and current awareness of relevant fields in librarianship.

This list is typical of the level of duties expected of the postholder. It is not necessarily exhaustive and other duties of a similar type and level and may be required from time to time. All posts are linked to the operating requirements of the service and all appointments are *'to the library system as a whole' and not to an individual workplace.*

Note: THIS IS OUTLINE JOB DESCRIPTION ONLY, FURTHER DETAILS AND JOB APPLICATION FORMS SHOULD BE OBTAINED FROM CENTRAL LIBRARY, PRINCESS SQUARE, NE99 1DX (TEL 261 0691 'ADMINISTRATION', office hours *only* Mon/Fri 8.45 a.m.–4.30 p.m.), to where application forms should be returned.

Figure 4.6 City of Newcastle-upon-Tyne Leisure Services Department job description

POST ASSISTANT LIBRARIAN (TEAM LIBRARIAN COMMUNITY LIBRARY SERVICES) DEPT. LEISURE SERVICES: LIBRARIES & ARTS REF. NO. CS/3

	ESSENTIAL	DESIRABLE	MEANS OF ASSESSMENT
1 SKILLS, KNOWLEDGE AND APTITUDES	Able to work effectively as a member of a team. Good interpersonal and communication skills at all levels. Good organizational skills.	Innovative. Ability to adapt to change.	Interview. References.
2 QUALIFICATIONS AND TRAINING	Qualified librarian.	Chartered librarian.	Application form.
3 EXPERIENCE		Experience of stock selection library work with client/community groups.	Application form. References. Interview.
4 DISPOSITION	Confident, enthusiastic, outgoing, reliable.	Equable temperament. Well motivated.	Interview and discussion. References.
5 SPECIAL REQUIREMENTS	Public service timetable including evenings and alternate Saturdays.	Ability and willingness to be flexible about timetables.	Application form. Interview and discussion.

Figure 4.7 Personnel specification

for, or accepting such jobs, because the sanctions it can impose seem to depend on members' solidarity which is not always evident, probably because of the wide range of levels and types of library. In periods of economic recession, moreover, librarians may have to be less choosey about getting a toehold in the profession, or a step up the ladder.

The Library Association, it should be emphasized, is not a trade union for professionals, and concern over salaries and gradings and conditions of service is very much more in the hands of the white-collar unions, to which an increasing proportion of librarians belong. However The Library Association does have an Assistant Director (Employment and Resources) part of whose job is to advise members and to develop contacts with the main unions, so as to have an indirect say in safeguarding the rights of members. A newsletter, 'Employment News', is produced for all library staff who have an interest in pay and service conditions issues.

How to compile a personnel specification

Provided that the job description gives a clear and accurate account of the content and context of a post, and the levels of performance required in terms of decision-making, policy and planning and such matters, it is comparatively straightforward to decide on the kind of person required for the job. But there are pitfalls. Rodger, the formulator of the widely used Seven-Point Plan for selectors, says:

> If matching is to be done satisfactorily, the requirements of an occupation (or job) must be described in the same terms as the attributes of the people who are being considered for it.[7]

Plumbley adds a further point, that 'it is not helpful to ask for attributes that cannot be assessed by the selector or the selection process'. It might be added that the most common selection process in libraries is the interview, and this is often very inadequate for the purposes for which it is used. It cannot, for example, test people's executive capacity or problem-solving skills, though these are very often needed in library services.

To help managers draw up a personnel specification, there are two widely-used classifications of attributes:

Rodger's Seven-Point Plan[8]	*Fraser's Five-Point Plan*[9]
Physical make-up	Impact on other people
Attainments	Qualifications
General intelligence	Innate abilities
Specialized aptitudes	Motivation
Interest	Adjustment
Disposition	
Circumstances	

Each of these categories (the two classifications overlap almost completely, so are not to be seen as alternative guidelines in drawing up a personnel specification, but rather as suggesting common categories to be considered) is likely to be considered when staff are appointed to library jobs. Although Rodger and Fraser were concerned with recruitment in general and not with any particular occupation, there is much coincidence between their categories and those derived from librarians' own accounts of their jobs and the skills they require (Sheffield Project findings):

1   Special knowledge: bibliographic; subject knowledge; particular type of work or procedure; foreign languages; users' needs; locality.
2   Special abilities and skills: mental or intellectual; organizing or administrative; staff management; social skills; clerical skills.
3   Other qualities: those relating to temperament, disposition, personality, interest, motivation.
4   Formal qualifications and experience: education, previous work experience.[10]

These findings are largely echoed in more recent studies[11] such as the 'Class of '88' project with understandably more emphasis on information technology skills. Communication skills and the development of personal confidence were also highlighted as areas which had increased employability.

The Sheffield Manpower Project also elicited from librarians the factors in their work that put pressure on staff. The replies mentioned pressures arising from the pace of work, from the variety of tasks in many jobs, physical demands (sheer stamina), contact with people, and changing environment and techniques.

It should be noted that in drawing up a specification a distinction can be drawn between 'essential attributes', 'desirable attributes' and 'contra-indicators'. The example from Newcastle-upon-Tyne makes use of the first two categories. This may help the selectors in refining the process of sifting candidates. Another helpful source of information may be provided by the exit interview. The departing job holders may give some useful clues about the kind of person who could best succeed them. Was the departing member of staff able to use his qualifications to a satisfying extent? Did the individual's disposition prove mainly suitable or unsuitable for the range of personal contacts involved in the job? Were there specialist abilities needed which they felt they did not have, or had been inadequately trained to develop? Exit interviews are discussed further in Chapter 7.

The points focused by Fraser and Rodger may be used either as headings in drawing up a personnel specification – the selectors can jot down notes under each heading relevant to the job in question – or as general guidelines to be taken into account when sifting applications for the shortlist, and in interviewing applicants. Some librarians prefer to avoid too much specificity in a personnel specification, on the grounds that it may lead to good applicants being ruled out if their education and/or experience has been unconventional.

Another criticism of using the points to check off an applicant's characteristics is that the whole individual is often greater (sometimes less) than the sum of their parts. The selection process must remain open to overall impressions and avoid fragmentation into stylized categories.

Physical make-up and impact on others
In Fraser's and Rodger's plans, these attributes include appearance, bearing and speech, and the reaction they elicit in other people, both colleagues and users. Aspects of health and physique necessary for library work are also covered. Very closely related is Rodger's 'disposition', the set of attitudes and personality traits which to a large extent determine the impact made on the public and on other staff in the work group.

When recruiting library staff it has often been the subjective impressions of the interviewing panel that count in determining applicants' general disposition and impact, but there is now an increasing tendency to emphasize the informal parts of selection. Other members of staff, particularly the colleagues who will be working with the new recruit, are given an opportunity to show the applicants around, and lunch with them, and sometimes even take part in the interview. They can give their views on how well they think candidates may fit in or, as necessary, not fit in, and act as a lively stimulus.

Ability to express oneself reasonably fluently may be more effectively assessed informally rather than in the awesome atmosphere of the interviewing room. Desirable qualities include articulacy on matters where knowledge might be expected (previous work experience, professional issues, higher education courses, studies); an ability to be clear in communicating; and a degree of amiability in responding to other people.

In terms of physical stamina, some library jobs (counter work, for example) make quite high demands, perhaps surprisingly so in the light of the public image of librarians. There are plenty of jobs however which are mainly sedentary and selectors should take account of the policies of their employing organizations on providing jobs for the physically handicapped. The Disabled Persons (Employment) Acts 1944 and 1958 state that employers with more than 20 regular workers must employ a quota of registered disabled workers. This is generally 3 per cent. 'Failure to do so can result in a fine, but prosecutions are very rare'.[12]

Qualifications and attainments
Fraser distinguishes between general education, specialist training and work experience. Rodger likewise includes under 'Attainments' all those educational and professional experiences which the applicant has had from school through higher education to the previous job.

The requirements differ from one type of library to another. Academic and special libraries, for example, may be more concerned with the subject and level of the first degree, than with the applicant's professional education in librarianship or information science. In traditional university libraries more weight is likely to be given to research degrees in, say, history or theology or literature, than to professional research in librarianship. The argument seems to be that assistant librarians should be able to communicate with academics in their own terms, and display some personal experience of the research process which is the *raison d'etre* of the academic way of life. It is also felt that status might be lowered if it is based on professional rather than academic attainments. This seems a curious argument when most professions have now built up an educational framework reflecting the academic framework at every level, from first degrees, to taught master's degrees, to research degrees at M.Phil. and Ph.D. level. It is unusual in these circumstances for a professional group to argue, as some academic librarians continue to do, that to improve one's prospects in the profession it is important to work for a qualification in a different discipline, such as English literature or history, although newly qualified graduates in librarianship are likely to be younger and will have qualified more quickly than postgraduate entrants.

Confusion over the comparative worth of some degrees is understandable because of the complexity of higher education in Britain, but the transfer of polytechnics to degree-awarding university status has reduced the complexity and acknowledged that the standards of their awards are equivalent to those of the older universities. In many ways the polytechnic sector led the way with innovative teaching and assessment methods.

Professional education for librarians and information scientists is perhaps just as confusing for many employers, who are confronted with a bewildering range of qualifications. There are first degrees in librarianship and information science, postgraduate diplomas or master's degrees (which are only postgraduate in the chronological sense, since they are not a follow-up of the subject of the first degree). There are master's degrees which are a follow-up of previous professional education, and so are more genuinely 'master's' level, some people would argue. There are research degrees at M.Phil. and Ph.D. level awarded for theses based on research in librarianship. Some of the first degrees in librarianship have a much lower professional content than others, as they are joint honours degrees where the students may spend half their time on another subject such as economics or languages. Some degrees in librarianship have a higher content of 'fringe' subjects than others, where students may spend considerable time and effort on sociology or languages, although being awarded a degree in librarianship. In other schools the 'fringe' subjects have been gradually integrated more closely with librarianship, so it has become possible to look on them as support subjects relevant to user studies, for example, rather than some kind of intellectual ballast needed to turn librarianship into a worthy degree subject. It should be noted that most schools have now included the word 'information' in their degree titles to emphasize the move away from a book-based image and to meet the needs of the growing private sector of employment noted in Chapter 3.

For selectors to assess an applicant's suitability for a job, they need a considerable knowledge of what has been happening in education for librarianship over the past decade. The various courses are accredited by The Library Association enabling successful graduates to apply for acceptance onto the Register of Chartered Librarians by writing a professional development report after an appropriate period of practice. There is, however, much diversification of emphases among the different library schools. Some examples of curriculum development where the pace of change has varied between schools are: teaching the management and technology of library automation; teaching communication skills; the integration of media skills into the course; and teaching library management at a level appropriate to the needs of the young professionals.

Again in teaching and assessment methods there is much diversity between schools, and selectors should be aware of the connections between the skills they are seeking and the educational experiences in these skills which their applicants have had, or not had.

For more senior appointments the whole area of continuing education is relevant, and there are many opportunities open to practising librarians by which they may develop professionally and achieve formal qualifications. The Library Association, for example, has made its regulations for fellowship more hospitable by enabling applicants to present documentary evidence of professional achievement. Librarians can also pursue interests informally. These were investigated by Jones[13] and librarians' preferences listed. In the view of practising librarians the most significant activities for keeping up to date professionally were discussion with colleagues, being active at staff meetings, visiting other libraries, receiving in-service training, reading librarianship literature, attending conferences and workshops, taking part in working parties, and studying for further qualifications. Low down in librarians' preferences were giving papers at conferences, writing articles for publication, holding professional office, and secondment to other libraries.

In the appointment of young professionals to their first post, selectors should also be aware of the problems for young entrants to the profession in gaining work experience. Few libraries retain the pre-library school trainee schemes which were once so common, so it may be that the only work experience the applicant will have had will be a few weeks of field work during the librarianship course. This problem has been recognized by The Library Association in its rules for acceptance onto the Register of Chartered Librarians. Most newly qualified professionals take Route A which is the quickest route and requires at least one year's supervised work experience following a structured training programme approved by The Library Association.

Thus a great deal of the responsibility for work experience moves back into the practitioners' world away from the library schools, and increases the onus on personnel managers to provide the appropriate level of experience for young professionals.

General intelligence/innate abilities

Fraser and Rodger diverge a little in what they recommend selectors to value. Rodger emphasizes more the ability to apply intelligence. How much intelligence is displayed by the applicant in his or her usual mode of working? To test this library employers have devised practical problems or decision-making simulations for the applicants to tackle, in addition to having the traditional selection interview.

Fraser's interpretation of 'innate abilities' seems to be those rather indefinable qualities which stem from a person's education and experience, but go beyond these to give 'a general quickness in the uptake' and 'special aptitudes'. It is generally agreed that western education systems reward academic achievement at the expense of other important skills, so it is useful for selectors to investigate the presence or absence of other skills such as communication, or aesthetic skills (for promotion and display, for example).

Rodger's category of 'special aptitudes' includes mechanical aptitude, manual dexterity, facility in written or verbal expression, facility with figures and creative talent in, say, designing or graphics.

Motivation

Fraser defines this as the way in which the individual applies his or her abilities in practical situations, and to what extent he or she achieves effective results. This is a complex area, and it is helpful to refer back to Chapter 2 on the relevance of motivation theories to library staffing. The importance of assessing applicants' motivation is inestimable, since staff frustration and ineffective results are likely when there is a mismatch between the post and the person. For instance, the person who would be effective answering routine queries, or doing issue-desk work in contact with users, might well be someone whose motivation to work stems mainly from social needs, rather than what Maslow calls identity needs or self-actualization needs. If the person appointed to this job was motivated by self-actualization needs (they wanted to be stretched to the limit of their potential, and be faced with challenge, and responsibility) the results would almost certainly be disappointing.

Another example might be the person who is motivated mainly by security needs. The problems generally arise when innovations take place, say in staffing structures, and the individual becomes a member of an area team, rather than working as a fairly isolated professional in a branch library where there was a secure niche and familiar routines. For these motivated by identity needs and social needs the change would be a source of positive satisfaction, but for the staff member who is mainly concerned with security at work the change may lead to unease and withdrawal symptoms.

Adjustment

Fraser describes adustment as emotional stability, and is concerned with the amount of stress a person at work is capable of standing, particularly in interacting with other people (public or colleagues). As with motivation it is important to achieve a match between the individual's needs and the job requirements. It is probably true to say that there are fewer places for people to 'hide' in libraries than there were in the more tranquil years up to the late 1960s. Libraries are larger, more bureaucratic because of their increasing complexity, and there have been determined efforts to manage them better, through the application of management ideas and techniques. Very often these include an objectives approach to running the library, usually leading to changes in staff deployment because the library plans to move to a more user-oriented stance; traditionally staff were deployed in functional technical duties, rather than in service-oriented jobs. When staff are restructured, for example, into professional teams, there can be serious problems of adjustment for some. Those whose temperament finds it difficult to accept the new ways will devise evasive measures. Subject specialists have been known to seclude themselves in backroom offices, and to resent live readers 'intruding' upon their work with queries and an exchange of views. Team members in public libraries have similarly been observed to have problems in communicating professional ideas to their fellow members, and to revert to non-professional routine work when visiting service points, because they do not know how to cope with their new role of planning projects and letting the non-professionals look after the routine.

By being aware of these problems of adjustment, selectors at the recruitment stage can avert future difficulties by choosing the right people. For staff already on the establishment the problem becomes one of appraisal and training.

Interests

Rodger argues that the questions of importance to the manager compiling a personnel specification are: 'To what extent are a person's interests intellectual? or practical – constructional? physically active? social? artistic?'[14]

Application forms and curricula vitae invariably include a section on 'Interests'. Professional and leisure interests need not necessarily be entirely separate, though they often are. Few categories of workers manage to achieve the consonance of interest between work and leisure that traditionally belongs to writers, musicians, professional sportsmen and academics.

Rodger's view is that selectors should try to match up the demands of the job with the characteristics shown by the category of interests listed by the applicant – artistic, intellectual or other.

Circumstances

The personnel specification provides an opportunity to mention job requirements which may be affected by a person's domestic circumstances. Is mobility an essential part of the job? Are the hours irregular, with evening and weekend duties? Are training opportunities going to occur that would necessitate the job holder being away at weekends or for two- or three-day courses midweek? Is the applicant prepared to move to be within reasonable travelling time of the library?

Since the Sex Discrimination Acts of 1975 and 1986, this is a rather tricky area for interviewers to deal with and it is important therefore that the personnel specification is carefully and clearly expressed. Women applicants must be treated with scrupulous fairness, which is generally interpreted as meaning they should not be excluded because of domestic circumstances, unless it can be shown that men too have been excluded for similar reasons.

5

Recruitment and selection of staff

Assuming the personnel specification effectively lists the attributes required of a person for a particular post then the task of any selector is to discover to what extent these attributes are present.

Sources of information

It is useful to have a view of the information sources available because there is a tendency to think so much of one source, such as the formal interview, as to make insufficient use of others. Figure 5.1 indicates the main sources used in selection.

The diagram illustrates a number of ideas that are central to a discussion of selection. As important as any is the fact that information is obtained throughout the process by both selectors and applicants. Too often selectors will perceive the exercise as one-way only and forget that the applicant is all the time finding out about the post and the library. A study of succession at senior management level[1] has shown that librarians applying for posts at senior levels used a variety of sources prior to interview in order to prepare themselves. They included published sources such as directories, year books, statistical publications, prospectuses, surveys, council reports, local newspapers, professional literature and annual reports. They also contacted individuals known to them who worked in the library advertising the post or who were knowledgeable about it. Visits, usually made on the applicant's own initiative, looking round the library like a user, were also popular. Some librarians provide only brief information about a job and its context and leave the rest to the initiative of the applicants. A number of libraries do, however, provide very attractive packs of information for applicants and potential applicants. Buckinghamshire, for example, produces a folder, 'Information for Applicants', which incorporates an enticing photograph of the cascade at West Wycombe

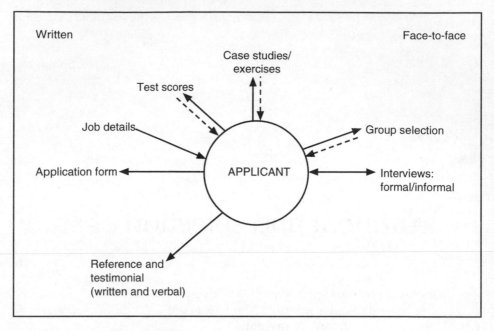

Figure 5.1   The main information sources used in selection

Park and includes a leaflet on Buckinghamshire Countryside Attractions, library publicity as well as an annual report and information about the library and working conditions. As the skills shortage increases it is likely that libraries, especially those in the south-east of England will increase their efforts to recruit staff.

The amount of preparation made by applicants can be a useful guide to their general approach to tasks but there is the danger that applicants may pick up quite erroneous ideas about the job and also that significant information can be missed. Effective management does demand systematic planning, and thought should be given from the beginning to the information provided for the applicants throughout the selection process as well as how to obtain information about the applicants. As Gould emphasizes:

> The organization has to attract them to apply, and throughout the process, particularly when ready to offer a job, has to present itself in such a way that the preferred candidate will be disposed to accept.[2]

The diagram also suggests that information is communicated in two main forms: written and face-to-face. The written information can be read and re-read at leisure and compared. On the one hand the applicant can compare job details for several libraries while the selectors can compare the written applications, references, test scores etc. Case studies and exercises may be completed in written form or can be carried out orally. Group selection methods and the interview are oral exercises and, although written summaries and assessments might be made, the applicants and selectors acquire their information by listening and observing.

In selection two sorts of information are obtained. The most obvious is that which is obtained directly from the applicant, for example in response to a question in an interview or on an application form; and from the selectors' side, the information provided in the job details. The other sort of information is that which is provided indirectly through the process itself, for example the presentation of the information on the application form or at the interview; and from the selectors' side, the way they conduct the interview. Both 'sides' have to be aware whether or not the message they think they have presented is the one received by the intended audience. This is why opportunities should be taken to discover the message that is being received. At the very least, applicants who fail to be successful at interviews and libraries which do not attract quality recruits, ought to become interested in such knowledge. It can be quite painful, but so can any hospital treatment designed to cure an illness beyond the competence of the general practitioner.

Both 'sides' in the selection process will be involved in a matching exercise. The selectors will be trying to match the personnel specification against the applicants and the applicants will be matching the job to their requirements. This may or may not be carried out systematically but it is certain that both sides will have built up a rich, 'holistic' picture of their own situation. The selectors, for example, will be aware of the history of the library's achievements, the management style of the library, and the various individuals with whom the successful applicant will be working. The applicants will be aware of their own domestic situations and their likes and dislikes concerning jobs and people. The richer pictures may contain elements which neither side particularly wants to present to the other.

The selectors and applicants should also avoid treating the present situation as an unchanging one. Both need to look to the future especially when the economic circumstances are such that mobility of staff is restricted and a mistake made is hard to rectify. The library must think very carefully about predictable future developments and the likely changes in the jobs of successful applicants. That is why selection must be seen as something more than describing existing posts and filling them.

Stages in the selection of staff

1 Advertising

Consideration should first be given to making an internal appointment. Where there has been a lack of mobility amongst staff there is likely to be a reasonable field for promotion especially in a large library and internal promotion can be an important motivating factor in such circumstances. Additionally the person's performance and potential will already be known and less training and induction into the procedures and culture of the organization will be required.

Where jobs are advertised externally it is important that information is also circulated internally and our view is that for motivation purposes alone, all internal candidates should be interviewed.

There are a number of standard advertising outlets used by librarians for the recruitment of staff. Certain constraints may be laid down by the parent body such as the advertising of a post internally as a first step or the use of particular publications such as local newspapers. It is unlikely that a search for new outlets will be worth the effort since librarians seeking posts will regularly peruse familiar sources. In Britain such sources include:

> *The Library Association Record Vacancies Supplement*
> *The Guardian*
> *The Times*
> *The Times Literary Supplement*
> *The Times Educational Supplement*
> *The Times Higher Education Supplement*
> *The Daily Telegraph*

Local newspapers are frequently used for non-professional posts. The Job Centres run by the Department of Employment can also be used, and for professional staff, the Professional and Executive Recruitment Service which issues the weekly 'Executive Post/Graduate Post'. There are also specialist recruitment agencies:

> Aslib Professional Recruitment Ltd
> INFOmatch run by The Library Association
> Informed Recruitment Services: a Division of Informed Business Services
> Task Force Pro Libra Ltd

Susan Hill and Alison Jago have described what a good specialist recruitment agency is able to do.[3]

Some organizations make use of advertising agents who normally receive a fee from the medium. They will design advertisements and can also provide response analyses which can be useful for future recruitment.

Specialist staff may need to be recruited through sources such as specialist publications or group contacts.

Search consultants are sometimes used to 'headhunt' senior staff. For executive positions it is claimed that suitable applicants are 'less likely to be reading job advertisements and even less inclined to apply openly to an advertisement, particularly if it is with a competitor organisation'.[4] The consultants will find out as much as they can about the requirements of the client before researching into likely candidates who will normally be approached first by telephone and encouraged to meet the consultants to discuss the position further. Eventually recommended candidates will get together with the client where negotiations can take place.

The first 'message' about the library is passed to the potential applicants by the advertisement and therefore it needs a great deal of thought. In recent years there has been a distinct improvement in advertisements for library and information posts. The objective is to attract those potential applicants the library would wish to attract and discourage those who would be unlikely to make a success of the job. The advertisement should be drafted with that objective in mind and to help to achieve it the librarian ought to be aware of the sort of information the potential applicant would like to have. Use should be made of the job description and personnel specification to provide such information as:

- the name of the organization
- the title of the post (in the professional press titles will be understood; advertisements placed elsewhere need explanations)

P/T Second Senior Assistant Librarian – Balham Library

17.5 hours per week

£7,583–£8,229 p.a. (including Saturday pay)

Balham Library is a bright, modern building with a very busy lending department, currently in need of a Second Senior Assistant to help maintain the high quality service.

You will be a qualified librarian, committed to offering a comprehensive library service to the people of Balham, and your duties will include staffing the information desk and dealing with readers' requests.

If you have energy and enthusiasm and are happy to work two evenings a week until 8 pm, and alternate Saturdays (9 am–5 pm) this could be the part-time post for you.

Application forms available from Leisure & Amenity Services, Personnel Section, Town Hall, London SW18 2PU. Telephone: 081–871 7795.

Please quote ref L/2137

Closing date: 29 November 1991.

Wandsworth
an equal opportunity employer
All applicants are considered on the basis of their suitability for the job irrespective of disablement, race, sex or marital status.

Figure 5.2   Advertisement for a library post

- salary and grade
- main purpose and duties
- the essential qualities being sought
- special conditions such as awkward hours of work and also positive features such as approved training schemes.

Figure 5.2 is an example of an advertisement which does all of these things and gives some flavour of the organization.

There are constraints of space and money but again the message of a penny-pinching organization can be given by very short advertisements or ones which use small type.[5]

Unlike other stages of the selection process, advertising is carried out in public and therefore has an important public relations dimension, giving the library an opportunity to present its image to the profession and beyond. Many librarians make a habit of reading through advertisements whether they are looking for a post or not and their attention can be held by the information and design of a carefully thought-out advertisement.

When a library wants to fill a vacancy quickly library schools can be contacted directly to find suitable candidates who merit support by their schools. In some cases the library may have employed a person as a trainee or as a fieldwork student and systematic appraisal records can be used to suggest persons who would be fairly certain to prove a success in the appointment.

The selection process presents an opportunity to involve staff in a development activity, as a means of maintaining morale, and in order to ensure a good choice is made by those who know most about the job and with whom the person appointed will be working closely.

2   Short-listing

When a number of people apply for a post it is normal to draw up a list of those whom the selectors consider strong contenders. As travel and subsistence costs increase it is likely that short lists will become smaller and, with prospects for promotion generally diminishing, libraries are likely to look more favourably upon internal candidates.

The personnel specification should act as the basis for the short list with the application forms, references and testimonials being measured against it for clues which either qualify or disqualify the applicants for further consideration. Presentation is important. Is it roughly thrown together, badly laid out, full of errors? Does it ramble on inconclusively? Are there unexplained gaps? Application forms should be designed to facilitate this analysis although, as members of larger organizations, libraries are frequently obliged to use less helpful forms.

The basic information should include:

Name, Age, Qualifications, Job history, Experience (main duties and responsibilities), Training, Interests, Health. It is also useful to find out if a current driving licence is held and how much notice is required by the present employer.

There should be adequate space for further information which candidates feel would support their applications.

Many forms require candidates to declare criminal records. The Rehabilitation of Offenders Act 1974 enables the previous offender to 'wipe the slate clean' of their criminal record provided they are not convicted of another offence during a time which runs from the date of conviction. The conviction is then said to have become 'spent' and for the purpose of employment it can be ignored and therefore need not be declared. Custodial sentences of over two-and-a-half years can never become spent. Where a post involves working with children spent convictions must be declared if the post is designated as such.

Application forms are assumed to be part of what the Sex Discrimination Act describes as 'arrangements made for deciding who should be offered employment'. Some questions on application forms could be unlawful if:

(i)   they are asked only of women (or men) and
(ii) it can be shown that the asking of them constitutes 'less favourable treatment'.

In Britain the Equal Opportunities Commission has produced guidelines:

> Questions on application forms should not suggest that the employer wishes to take into account any factors which would, or might, discriminate on grounds of sex or of marriage. Such questions undermine the confidence of applicants that they will be treated fairly and without prejudice, even where there is no intention to discriminate.[6]

The Commission gives examples of questions which might deter some applicants from completing the forms and cause suspicion that the answers might be used in an unlawful manner – questions dealing with families, ages of children, married/single/divorced status, intentions about engagement and/or about having children, intimate personal questions.

Some employers, like Bolton Metro, do collect such information for monitoring purposes. The recommendation in these cases is to detach this information from the completed form. Bolton state boldly: 'This part of the document will be detached before the selection process and the information contained in it WILL NOT be used at selection and it will be treated in the strictest confidence'.

The information also includes that of ethnic origin and the rules that apply to sex discrimination also apply to racial discrimination under the Race Relations Act 1976.

In recent years there has been a growing interest in Biodata as a means of short-listing. Biodata is biographical information which is supplied by candidates and objectively scored by assessors. Using the criteria defined in the personnel specification a pool of biodata items is drawn up which is related to success in the job. There is insufficient research in library and information work to provide a list with high prediction levels, so initially a library may look at biodata provided by successful applicants who have been effective in their posts. Available research suggests biodata items will normally come under the following categories:

> Demographic details (sex, age, family circumstances)
> Education and professional qualifications
> Previous employment history and work experience
> Positions of responsibility outside work
> Leisure interests
> Other information such as career/job motivation [7]

Data would be provided in application forms, designed as biodata question-naires.

The biodata is then weighted according to importance and items combined into groups. The idea is to end up with a single score. Research has shown that biodata has higher validity than interviews and is particularly useful where very large numbers of applications are received. Caution has to be used, particularly with background data, to avoid race and gender discrimination.

A certain amount of doubt exists concerning the value of written references. In a small profession like librarianship deliberately dishonest references are unlikely although it is common for reference writers to highlight strengths rather than weaknesses and this tendency could increase as staff are allowed access to their own personnel files, though the evidence from staff appraisal is that this is not true in the long term.[8] Naturally the personnel management in the library needs to be such that an accurate reference is possible. An effective staff appraisal system will yield helpful information and a participative style ought to ensure that those who know most about the person have a hand in writing the reference. A writer of references needs to be asked about the knowledge, abilities, skills and personal qualities that are considered impor-tant for the particular job, which is precisely what the personnel specification aims to do and if one is not compiled it makes the job of the reference writer more difficult. We have found two questions particularly useful to ask of referees:

> 'How many days sick leave has the applicant had in the last twelve months?'
> 'Would you employ the applicant again?'

Even those who compile personnel specifications do not always use them when obtaining references.

It is common practice to ask for two references and to insist that one is from the applicant's current employer if there is one. In many cases the current employer will be a librarian and it is reasonable to assume that opinion on performance in a job, which has similarities with the one for which the person is applying, is more helpful than a reference from a personal acquaintance.

Many potential applicants will be unhappy about revealing their interests in another job to their current employer and some application forms acknowledge the problem by asking whether applicants object to an approach being made to their current employer. On the other hand it is not unknown for employers to look more favourably on those seeking employment elsewhere if they are valuable members of staff.

In most public sector institutions references for short-listed candidates are requested prior to the interview and are considered alongside other evidence. In the private sector it is common to make appointments subject to satisfactory references and to request them after the interview. Gould is particularly critical of this practice because it 'puts the referee in the invidious position of being able to exercise a veto on the appointment by giving a critical reference or refusing to give one at all'.[9] Our experience has been that almost all written references are good and rarely affect the decision.

Since doubt exists about the value of written references, selectors may choose to obtain verbal references in addition or instead. A telephone conversation with a professional colleague can be quite revealing especially as no permanent record is kept. In fact it is our experience that selectors ask the very questions and provide the very information which they fail to provide when seeking written references.

Testimonials are written without a particular job in mind for use by the person about whom it is written whenever an appropriate occasion arises. They are only of minor value and are rarely asked for by selectors though they may be provided by applicants as additional evidence.

When vacancies become scarcer and the number of applicants is very large selectors tend to search more assiduously for disqualifying data and sometimes this will represent a further refinement of the original specification. For example a narrower age range may be decided upon and any uncertainties about domestic problems or illnesses will be more likely to cause an applicant to be rejected.

3 Informal interviews

Surveys of English public and academic library selection practices other than the traditional interview were carried out in 1978[10] and 1979 and showed that the most popular method was the informal interview and there is no reason to suppose that the situation has changed. It is interesting to note, however, that many institutions issue valuable written guidance to selectors but rarely mention the informal meetings, perhaps because they are not normally perceived to be part of the selection procedure.

For lower-level posts the informal 'interview' will often consist of a tour round the library with a member of staff. The candidate is given a chance to ask questions informally and look around whilst a member of the library staff can make an assessment and feed it back to the selection panel. Candidates may be unaware that an assessment is being made, though good ones will realize that they are being assessed from the moment they arrive. If such an assessment is made it is desirable that the criteria used are directly related to the person specification and are similar to those being used by the selection panel.

For more senior appointments informal meetings are frequently employed. At Manchester Metropolitan University short-listed candidates for two top posts had informal meetings with senior members of the university and a question-and-answer meeting with senior staff who had planned the session beforehand. Informal meetings which include the people with whom the successful candidates will work do help to simulate the situations in which they would find themselves after appointment.

For some people informal discussions are a welcome and relaxing contrast to the formal interview while for others, as one respondent remarked, 'a too detailed preamble to the interview can cause confusion or make candidates ill-at-ease in interview'. In particular this can happen during 'lunch with the candidates' or when candidates are taken round the library together and feel they must be observed asking sensible questions. If the informal sessions are to be used in making the final decisions there has to be some form of feedback to decision-makers by those involved. In most public services the decision will be given on the same day as the final assessment is made so communication has to take place fairly quickly. In the private sector it is common for a longer period of time to elapse between the interview and the final decision.

4   Formal interviews

The favourite, and in many cases the only, face-to-face method used in selection is the formal interview, although studies have frequently found that it is the most unreliable. A study by the Institute of Manpower Studies reasoned that 'the problem is always the role of the interviewer'.[11] In this section suggestions are made which should improve the performance of the interviewer. In librarianship the number of interviewers can range from one to many. In the private sector smaller numbers are the norm with two-level interviews, one with a personnel officer and one with the manager being quite common. In the public sector a panel of interviewers is the usual format.

Again the starting point should be the personnel specification because this spells out what the interviewers should be searching for. The use of an interview form which is directly related to the specification helps to ensure that the interview keeps on relevant lines. The City of Newcastle-upon-Tyne form is a good example (see Figure 5.3).

As far as possible interviewers should want accurate information to be communicated to both 'sides', directly through the information given and indirectly through the process itself and factors that inhibit should be minimized in favour of those that facilitate the flow of relevant information. A helpful framework is provided by R.L. Gorden.[12]

Attention should be paid to a number of factors.

ASSESSMENT SHEET FOR INTERVIEW FOR APPOINTMENT OF ....

Date ....

QUALITIES	SCORING			
Appearance and bearing: smart/scruffy	Marks out of 5			
Disposition: cheerful/surly	Marks out of 20			
Speech: clear/indistinct	Marks out of 20			
Articulation: sense of what he or she says comes across/does not come across	Marks out of 20			
Perceptiveness: quick on the uptake/slow to grasp the point	Marks out of 20			
Attentiveness: listens to questions – keeps to the point/wanders off the point	Marks out of 20			
Intelligence: bright ideas/dull	Marks out of 20			
Suitability: would fit in with the team/square peg	Marks out of 20			
Answer to pre-set question (if applicable)	Marks out of 20			
Relevant experience (if applicable)	Marks out of 10			
Name of Assessor	TOTAL			

131

Figure 5.3   Interview assessment form used by Newcastle-upon-Tyne

(a)   The environment of the interview

Candidates should be properly received. Their names and times of appointment must be known by the first person they will meet whether it be a security officer or a receptionist. If they have to wait a long time tea, coffee or a cool drink could be offered. There should be concern for the place in which candidates wait before being called into the room. It should not be within earshot of the interview room but should be a comfortable area in which it is easy for candidates to compose themselves. Interruptions and outside noise should be avoided in the interview room and seats should preferably be at the same level for interviewers and interviewees. Some interviewers dislike physical barriers between themselves and the interviewees while others prefer to acknowledge the formality of the occasion and also provide a resting place for documents and notes.

(b)   The pattern of the interview

Interviews often follow established lines and, if these norms are followed, interviewees are likely to be more relaxed especially when they become used to the experience. It is a good idea to inform candidates beforehand about the form of the interview, who will be interviewing and what will happen afterwards. There can be practical difficulties if specific times are given to interviewees in advance of the day and there are last-minute withdrawals. To avoid interviewers amusing themselves for half-an-hour whilst waiting for the next candidate it is advisable to give similar attendance times to a few candidates who can be briefed together so long as there is not too big a gap between the briefing and any other activity including the interview. It is usual to begin the interview gently and lead up to more difficult questions, allowing candidates to ask their own questions at the end. A minority believe in making the interview a stressful experience in order, perhaps, to simulate the stresses in the job. We are inclined to agree with Higham[13] that stress interviews are 'anathema to those who take interviews seriously. It is sometimes assumed that by subjecting a candidate to stress – such as rudeness and hostility – in an interview you can somehow get an indication of how he will stand up to stress in the job. There is, of course, no evidence to support this view: the two situations are entirely different, and the causes of stress on the job include many other frustrations besides those in a superior position being deliberately discourteous.'

Interviewers should get together well before the interviews and plan the progress they want to make. This does not mean that the interview will not move spontaneously but it should ensure that it progresses in a logical manner and covers all key points. Susan Hill and Alison Jago[14] refer to a recent survey by the UK employment agency, Reed Employment, which showed that while 4 per cent of candidates said they had been late for interviews, 33 per cent of employers admitted being late. This shows a lack of courtesy and presents a very poor image.

Before the questioning starts candidates should be introduced to the selectors and the plan of the interview should be explained.

(c) Questioning

Obviously the questions should not be unnecessarily complicated or vague. Interviewers may want to use this form of questioning in a deliberate way to test candidates but must always remember they are communicating their own vagueness to candidates. As far as possible the wording of the questions should be decided in advance to ensure that the question is an effective vehicle for discovering whether items in the personnel specification are present or not. 'Closed' questions, requiring no more than yes or no answers, should be avoided because the selectors' object is to hear what the candidate has to say and therefore to ask questions which invite the candidate to do this. Useful approaches include relating questions to experience: 'What experience have you had of dealing with difficult users?'; asking for a discussion of principles or beliefs: 'What have you found to be the best way of dealing with difficult users?'; and introducing hypothetical situations: 'What would you do if a lecturer refused to pay a fine?'

Richard Fear[15] who has written a comprehensive work on interviewing, says that when interviewers are thoroughly trained in his methods they do only 15 or 20 per cent of the talking. He suggests a number of ways of asking open or exploratory questions including the use of 'laundry lists' – listing a number of possible responses and giving a choice to the interviewee. This method can help particularly where an interviewee is having difficulty with a question which requires considerable analysis or in following up a 'clue' provided in previous questioning. For example, the interviewer may want to discover a person's strengths and weaknesses by saying: 'Some librarians like working with readers best, others like working with books and others like classifying and cataloguing. What gives you most satisfaction?' Another way is to offer two views that are more or less opposites and to ask which is held by the interviewee. For example: 'In your last post did you publicize the library as much as you would have liked or, on hindsight, would it have been better to have spent more time on it?'

The opportunity should often be taken to follow up general questions with a request for more detail by the use of probes such as: 'Tell me more about ...' and 'Why does that appeal to you?' However, interviewers should avoid 'grilling' the applicants, which could cause them not to respond freely. Regard must be had to the race relations and sex discrimination laws and questioning should therefore avoid discrimination on ground of race or sex. Questions about personal matters present the most difficulty because 'an employer must be able to satisfy him/herself whether the potential recruit is likely to serve for a reasonable time, come to work with reasonable regularity and meet demands of the job in such matters as mobility, overtime and spending nights away from home'.[16]

The Equal Opportunities Commission offers the following advice:

> No questions should be based upon assumptions regarding women's roles in the home and the family.
> Questions regarding intentions about marriage and having children are, rightly, regarded as impertinent, are resented and should never be asked.

Any questions which are asked to find out whether the individual can meet the needs of the job on hours, overtime, mobility etc. should be asked equally of men and women.

Questions should be about job requirements and not about domestic intentions or arrangements.[17]

There is concern in some organizations that exactly the same questions should be asked of all candidates without variation. Our view follows that of Nottinghamshire County Council: 'Interviews need to be flexible. However, it is important for the interviewing panel to decide upon a core list of questions to ensure that all relevant points are covered. These must be asked of *all* candidates'.[18]

(d) Listening and reponding

Selection interviews are rarely tape-recorded so the only chance to hear what is said is at the interview itself. Careful listening is very important because it also indicates the interviewers' interest in the candidate. Salient points should be noted as soon as possible although it is difficult to make notes without appearing not to be listening. In addition interviewees can be disturbed if notes appear to be taken when information of a highly personal or derogatory nature is imparted. Fear[19] sensibly recommends that interviewers wait until favourable information is given before writing unfavourable information previously given. When interviewing a series of candidates it is easy to confuse one with another. It is a good idea to write a brief description of each person alongside assessment notes to ensure no mistake has been made. What candidates fail to say is as important as what they say. Interviewers should be careful to listen to, and if necessary wait for, all answers and not give a 'halo' to those candidates who start well or have certain outstanding qualities. Nor should one or two early mistakes disqualify a candidate for the rest of the interview. It is well known that interviewers often make decisions after only a short time in the interview.

The response that is made to answers is known to influence interviewees. The interviewer can control the pace of and, through indicating approval or disapproval of responses, affect the course of the interview. At worst this can cause interviewees to withhold information and try to please the interviewers by telling them what they believe the interviewers would like to hear.

Although the primary interest will be on what is said, non-verbal cues will be playing a significant part and the good interviewer will be aware of them. In particular facial expression and body movement are important especially where they conflict with what is being said. There are some difficulties in applying kinesic analysis to selection interviewing because interviewees are often nervous and betray the nervousness under stress. On their part interviewers can ease that stress by responding facially to information given. It is well known that the raising of eyebrows and smiling helps to indicate interest and friendliness.

In spite of its popularity the traditional interview has often been criticized because of its artificial nature and its bias in favour of those who 'interview well' but may not be good at the job. Selectors should, therefore, not ignore the written evidence when coming to their conclusion. A number of librarians have been sufficiently dissatisfied as to devise additional methods which simulate more closely the actual work which the successful applicant will have to perform.

5   Group selection

This method is most applicable when testing what Fraser refers to as 'impact on others'[20] – the ability to get on with others, influence them, and display leadership qualities. The simplest form is to give the group of candidates a topic to discuss and then observe them. Roger Stoakley believes that 'the technique can reveal valuable information on group problem solving, confidence, assertiveness, influencing skills, communication, empathy, leadership and teamwork'.[21] In some cases current topics such as income generation and compulsory competitive tendering are sent to candidates before the selection event. Other topics may be suggested on the day. The observation and analysis should be carried out by a trained assessor.

A second form is that of the case study or command exercise in which candidates take the chair in turn and outline their solutions to a problem, which will have been given to them some time before, and defend it before the other candidates. War Office Selection Boards take this a stage further and require candidates to lead others through a practical difficulty such as crossing a stream.

Each of these group exercises can be presented in written form by individual candidates, can be carried out with the selection panel or with the other candidates or, most realistically, they can be performed with the staff with whom the successful candidate will be working and the case studies can simulate actual problems encountered in the post for which they have applied. Here are a few examples of short exercises used by public libraries which could be either presented in written form or discussed with various groups.

For a medical librarian:

1   Prepare a written report – length at your discretion – justifying starting a current awareness service in a medical library context.
2   Prepare, in note form, a briefing to a senior member of the library staff on the current controversy over the place of the librarian in the medical team – the 'clinical librarian'.
3   Prepare a verbal presentation, as to a medical library management committee, on the value of MEDLARS to a postgraduate medical library with comments on on-line access.

For a team librarian:

You have been appointed Librarian within a team in the County of Exshire consisting of four Librarians and a Leader. Prepare a schedule for a programme of induction and training for yourself to cover the first month of your taking up the appointment. Set out the programme in order of priority giving reasons for your choice of order.

A variation on the case study, reported by one public library in the survey, is the in-tray exercise:

Candidates are given an envelope containing 12–15 'situations' and are asked, immediately prior to the interview, to spend about 15–20 minutes putting these into priority order, making notes on any special points to watch etc. They then bring their answers into the formal interview with them, and are asked to go through their order of priority and to justify their placings, making any special observations etc. (the interviewers adopt a passive role in this).

Assessment of work in groups presents problems but the type of analysis described in Chapter 8 could be used with profit.

6   Tests

One approach to staff selection emphasizes, as we have, careful description of jobs and personnel specifications, another puts its faith in the development of more sophisticated and dependable tests:

There are those who hold the view that subjective methods of assessing human beings will never prove to be adequately reliable and valid and who therefore turn to objective methods such as personality tests and questionnaires, objectively marked biographical questionnaires, interest questionnaires or other devices, in the hope of improving validities.[22]

If tests are to work really well, we should be able to measure how far candidates possess the various attributes required by the personnel specification and, like other methods, they should be good predictors of performance in jobs. The validity of any test is therefore very important and is essentially the extent to which it measures what it purports to measure. Selectors will also be concerned with 'concurrent validity' i.e. how scores correlate with some other measure of the quality being assessed – for example, students' scores on a verbal ability test matching the ratings made already by their tutor. Predictive validity is even more useful as it compares test scores with performance measures on the job taken at a later time. We are not aware of such measures being taken in library and information work. While it is normally not difficult with most methods for candidates to appreciate what the selectors are trying to do (its 'face validity'), some tests appear at first acquaintance not to be related to the job for which the candidate is being tested. In these cases candidates can feel alienated and resentful. As Fletcher points out: 'the main danger is with personality questionnaires which contain items which, when seen out of context, could seem intrusive, offensive or just plain obscure'.[23]

The user of tests should also have confidence in their reliability, which means that the test is consistent in the results it produces. For example a verbal reasoning test that gave wildly differing scores for the same people from one week to the next would be of no value. Fletcher[24] states that a reliability coefficient of 0.75 or above is generally acceptable for ability tests and 0.65 for personality tests.

Most of the popular tests are supplied with information on their reliability and what they purport to measure. The British Psychological Society emphasizes that tests should not be used by untrained people and is therefore concerned that 'there should be adequate control of the distribution of psychological test material'.[25] The two market leaders in occupational testing, ASE, a division of NFER-NELSON, and Saville and Holdsworth, will only supply to trained test administrators registered with them.

Tests chosen should have norms for groups as similar as possible to those you wish to test. Normative information which describes the groups tested and the range of scores is available in the manuals which accompany the tests. There has been a concern about cultural bias in tests, particularly regarding ethnic groups and gender. The British Psychological Society is aware that users could be breaking the law if there is race or sex discrimination and advises them to justify use by proving that the attribute being sought is essential for effective performance in the job and that no other route is available. The Equal Opportunities Commission is critical of test-publishers who 'did not give enough information about sex differences in test performances, the sex composition of norm groups and the interpretation of sex differences in average performance'[26] but do state that 'no body of research or theory now suggests that tests should be used differently for different groups'.

Earlier surveys of English academic and public libraries[27] showed that tests were rarely used. There has, however, been an increase generally in the use of tests by organizations. Shackleton and Newell's[28] survey in 1989 found a considerable increase over five years. Use of tests of ability had increased from 9 to 41 per cent, personality questionnaires from 27 to 37 per cent and assessment centres (where a variety of assessment techniques are employed) from 7 to 25 per cent.

Libraries do make use of tests of attainment such as numeracy, spelling, grammar, and typing often by devising simple tests of their own. For example, Wandsworth gives a test to library assistants requiring them to put cards in numerical (Dewey) order followed by the alphabetical suffix. Others require assistants to do mental arithmetic with fines and giving change.

The effective performance of many jobs is certainly dependent on the employees possessing a number of aptitudes but it is difficult to be precise about them because they can develop with training, experience and achievement.

Greater use is now being made of psychological tests, often referred to as 'psychometric', in the selection of librarians for high-level posts. At Manchester Metropolitan University, for example, personality tests were used as part of the selection procedure for its University Librarian and Head of Reader

Services in 1993. Roger Stoakley states that such tests have been used in Somerset since 1985.[29]

Psychological tests

As Smith and Robertson[30] demonstrate, there are various ways of categorizing psychological tests.

1   Tests of mental ability such as verbal reasoning, numerical ability, spatial ability.

Examples: Verbal   –   National Institute of Industrial Psychology
                             Test 90A/90B
            Numerical   –   Saville and Holdsworth NT2
            Spatial   –   Minnesota Spatial Relations Test

2   Personality tests were originally designed as diagnostic aids in clinical and psychiatric medicine and are probably the most controversial of all. The majority are self-report, asking questions for the candidates to describe themselves in some way and this is related to scores for some known group. The best-known personality test is Cattell's 16 PF. The scores in this test are computed from the analysis of answers to around 200 questions and personality is measured on a ten-point scale for each of the personality factors. Here are some of them:

Low score description	*High score description*
Reserved	Outgoing
Less intelligent	More intelligent
Humble	Asssertive
Shy	Venturesome
Tough-minded	Tender-minded
Trusting	Suspicious
Self-assured	Apprehensive
Group-dependent	Self-sufficient
Relaxed	Tense

We do often refer to 'personality' in everyday speech but it is difficult to pin down its meaning in any precise way. Perhaps Kluckhohn's description[31] is the most apt – in some ways human beings are like all others, in some ways like some others and in some respects like no others. In the past personality was viewed as a characteristic mode which a person consistently chose to deal with the world – 'same old Bill' – but more recently it has been recognized that responses can change with experience and the way people behave will vary with the different situations in which they find themselves. The selector tries to predict how a person will behave in the future and it has to be said that personality tests are of dubious value, although Smith and Robertson[32] believe that they do provide some indication of how a person is likely to behave.

However there is greater doubt about tests which aim to explore the values and psychological states which lie beneath through projective tests. Most of them are visual and subjects are asked to explain pictures which are usually ambiguous. Probably the best-known of these is the Rorschach Ink-blot Test. Kline,[33] a strong critic of the use of personality tests in employment selection, asserts that responses to projective tests 'are believed to show the deepest levels of personality. However, there is, in fact little firm objective evidence that projective tests can reveal anything of the sort. Indeed, there is often little agreement between examiners or the same examiner on different occasions.'

Another type of personality test is the objective personality test which can take any task which discriminates between one person and another and draw inferences from the scores, e.g. handwriting, fidgeting, humour by asking subjects to rate jokes. At the moment we are inclined to support Kline in his objections:

> They are of unproven validity and to use them for selection purpose is unlikely to be useful. Secondly, and more important, I object to their covert and deceitful nature. Different personal qualities are obviously valuable in different occupations. With the old projective and psychometric tests, however, it was obvious, usually, what the test was about. Thus, if an applicant did not choose to reveal himself, he need not. With the objective test there is no such freedom.[34]

3 *Tests of interest and motivation.* Interests are defined as a liking for doing something and are, of course, frequently asked about in interviews. Research, however, has shown a low relationship between interests and job performance.

Examples: Interests − Strong-Campbell Interest Inventory
          Motivation − Thematic Apperception Test

Since all tests can be somewhat threatening it is good practice to inform candidates beforehand and reassure them that the tests are relevant and are only part of the selection procedure. It is also recommended that individuals should be given access to their own results if they wish. This is now made easier and quicker through the use of computers. For instance the PSYASSESS software enables the user to enter raw data from the answer sheets and the system analyses the data and produces a profile and interpretive report on the candidate 'in seconds'. A good example of prior information given to candidates is that provided by Humberside County Council (Figure 5.4).

Until now books on psychological testing have been written by professional psychologists and have tended to be full of professional jargon and detail incomprehensible to non-psychologists. An excellent introduction to testing with information on nineteen tests has been written by Stephanie Jones.[35] It can be used both by managers thinking of using tests and by candidates required to take tests.

COUNTY
PERSONNEL
DEPARTMENT

Appointment of Assistant Chief Officer
of Leisure Services
(Libraries and Museums)

Notes on the Use of Psychometric Assessment Methods

We will be using four psychometric measures as part of the selection process for this appointment. These are:

1. An aptitude test to look at your ability to evaluate the logic of various kinds of argument.

2. An aptitude test measuring your ability to make correct decisions or inferences from numerical or statistical data.

3. A test of productive thinking.

4. A personality questionnaire. This is not a test as there are no right or wrong answers. The questions are concerned with how you typically behave at work and relate to others in a work situation.

The measures we will be using are reputable and we are satisfied that they are relevant to this appointment. They will provide independent, objective and job related information which cannot always be obtained from the interview alone on the degree to which candidates have aptitudes and personality characteristics appropriate to this post.

The results obtained will form one part of the appointment process and decisions will not be made on the basis of these results alone.

Your results will be kept confidential and will not be made available to anyone not involved in the selection decision.

Individual feedback on your psychometric assessment results will be available on request.

HUMBERSIDE
COUNTY COUNCIL

Figure 5.4   Information given to candidates about psychometric testing

6

Staff appraisal

Staff appraisal illustrates very well the nature of management and the reasons why it is a complex activity with a variety of consequences. In a sense management takes place in all organizations otherwise very little would be achieved. Modern management has emphasized the need to be systematic in deciding clearly the objectives of any activity, how it could best be carried out, and how it should be monitored and changed in the light of experience.

Those who employ formal staff appraisal systems have three main reasons for doing so. These reasons are so interconnected that even where only one or two of them are formally recognized the other(s) will be partly present. Randell has distinguished the three main objectives[1] and his ideas are drawn upon in the list below:

1 *Performance reviews*
   To improve the performance of the library and in particular the perform-ance of individual members of staff. This incorporates the discovery of training needs, the motivation of staff, counselling and shaping behaviour by praise or punishment.
2 *Potential reviews*
   To predict the level and type of work the individual will be capable of performing in the future.
3 *Reward reviews*
   To allocate and distribute rewards more fairly.

Like most management techniques, formal appraisal is a systematization of something which already exists less formally. The secret of much successful management lies in formalizing existing practices without destroying the natu-ral strengths of the informal system. Appraising people is a natural and popu-lar activity. Inside and outside places of work people are stating their opinions about others. At work such appraisals are most likely to concentrate on personal strengths and weaknesses and upon job performance.

Trainers are, in fact, often pleasantly surprised by the quality of written appraisals produced by good managers unpractised in the art.

In the early 1970s David Peele[2] was disappointed at finding so few appraisal schemes operating in British libraries and came to the conclusion that many librarians would only involve themselves if forced to do so. In the 1990s the picture is very different. Many more libraries in both private and public sectors are operating schemes with 'innovations which are very much in keeping with the Conservative Government's managerialist philosophy'.[3] In response to a request for personnel management material in preparation for this text a large number of documents were sent describing staff appraisal schemes and it was particularly noticeable how much thought and preparation had been put into the schemes. There are, for example, well-developed schemes in the private sector run by the Chartered Institute of Bankers and the Institute of Mechanical Engineers, and in public libraries by Guille-Allès, Guernsey, Cumbria County, Kensington and Chelsea, the City of Newcastle-upon-Tyne, and the City of Bradford.

The most obvious change has been in the academic sector where David Peele's view has been correct because institutional schemes have been formulated largely because of decisions at a higher level. The starting point was the Jarratt Report of 1985 on efficiency studies in universities in which a recommendation was made that:

> A regular review procedure, handled with sensitivity, would be of benefit to staff and to the university as a whole. In considering the form of a staff appraisal system for a university, three main objectives can be identified:
>
> (a) Recognition of the contribution made by individuals;
> (b) Further assistance for individuals to develop their full potential as quickly as possible;
> (c) Assistance for the university to make the most effective use of its academic staff.[4]

Following Jarratt greater impetus was given by the publication in 1987 of the 23rd Report of Committee 'A',[5] the Committee which recommends national salary scales to the Government:

> Both parties in Committee A are committed to the introduction of an appraisal system directed towards developing staff potential, assisting in the improvement of performance and enhancing career and promotion opportunities, thereby improving the performance of the institution as a whole. It is agreed that it should apply to all categories of academic and academic-related staff at all levels of seniority.

The incentive which perhaps ensured the present 'popularity' of appraisals schemes in universities and the former polytechnics was that increases in pay would be withheld until satisfactory progress had been made on the implementation of appraisal schemes.

There is no lack of information about these schemes. Revill has collected detailed information from eleven former polytechnics and individual schemes have been described together with the thinking behind them.[6]

As a result of her research into appraisal schemes Judith Stewart came to a number of conclusions about the success of schemes[7] and we shall be drawing on these in discussing approaches to appraisal:

1   It must be appreciated that staff appraisal is a very personal and individual experience

Most staff are apprehensive when asked to see their supervisor. In this case a special period has been put aside for the two to meet and talk frankly. Paul Helm, discussing the scheme at the University of Liverpool, expresses a common concern: 'The argument was that since the whole purpose of the scheme was developmental, to enable an individual with the help of his or her head of department, to uncover weaknesses and to endeavour to remove them, no one would speak with the necessary degree of frankness unless he or she could do so in confidence'.[8]

Because the event is so personal most schemes make it clear that records of the interview are confidential to those who really need access. Thus, for example, Robert Gordon Institute of Technology Library states that the 'Record of Career Review Interview form will be treated as confidential; with only you, your reviewer and the Chief Librarian having right of access to it' and the Guidance Notes for The King Edward's Hospital Fund for London state that 'it is of utmost importance that *confidentiality is maintained* by ensuring that appraisal documentation is only seen by those individuals authorised to do so (i.e. Appraiser, Appraisee, Grandparent and the Personnel Officer)'. It is inevitable the people involved in such a personal stressful experience will seek the relief of recounting their experience to friends and colleagues. Equally appraisers may wish to discuss the interview with others. This will be necessary in cases where improvements are needed such as additional training but it should always be made clear to the appraisee that this will have to happen if progress is to be made.

2   The idea and benefits of appraisal need to be sold to staff

When schemes are introduced the aims must be clearly stated and explained. Kensington and Chelsea's cover sheet for the review record provides a suitably bold statement (see Figure 6.1). Graham Luccock has described the doubts staff can have about the true intentions of a scheme:

> Appraisal tends to be regarded with extreme suspicion by staff and trade unions as a means of disciplinary action, either official or unofficial, as well as being a 'big brother' technique of managerial control.[9]

PERFORMANCE REVIEW

To _____ From _____

THE AIMS OF THE SCHEME ARE TO PROVIDE A BASIS FOR:

- Reviewing performance and agreeing objectives
- Improving communication between yourself and your line manager
- Learning and personal development

WHAT DOES THE SCHEME REQUIRE US TO DO?

The scheme requires a six monthly review discussion to:

- Agree learning and development needs
- Clarify your responsibility at work
- Jointly evaluate performance against agreed objectives
- Agree realistic objectives and action plans for the future

Short regular meetings are recommended to monitor progress of what has been agreed.

SOME DO'S AND DON'TS

DO		DON'T
Prepare	↓ ↑	Rush
Listen	↓ ↑	Interrupt
Have an open mind	↓ ↑	Make asssumptions

REMEMBER THAT THIS REVIEW IS ABOUT YOU. BE REALISTIC ABOUT WHAT YOU CAN AND CANNOT ACHIEVE.

Your review discussion will be: on _____ at _____ in _____

The Royal Borough of KENSINGTON and CHELSEA

Figure 6.1 Kensington and Chelsea's cover sheet

Both Judith Stewart[10] and Susan Ruffley[11] discovered negative reactions and anxiety about the introduction of appraisal systems. In both cases there was the suspicion that systems were being introduced because it would be jumping on a management bandwagon. In particular they were seen to be connected with a new businesslike approach being adopted and there were fears that there would be possible misunderstandings and misinterpretation of views expressed during the appraisal interview. The worst approach, Christopher Pollitt reminds us, is 'to introduce an essentially managerialist scheme whilst claiming that it is developmental'.[12]

3 People prefer appraisal schemes with firm structures and frameworks

It has been our experience that participants in meetings like to understand the structure of the meetings. That is why it is desirable to signal progress from time to time to ensure everyone knows what is happening. This is also the case with appraisal. The form which might be used for a preparatory self-appraisal is a good vehicle to use as a basis for the interview. Pennington and O'Neill sum up the requirements quite neatly:

> a consistency of process based on clearly defined public criteria, documentation, joint formulation of reports for subsequent action and an open appeals procedure.[13]

There is, however, difficulty in achieving uniformity of standards. In many areas of staff management we are judging other members of staff so appraisal is not alone in having to deal with this problem. Some variation in standards is inevitable but our own experience in receiving differing reports on the same person from different managers is that it is often the different jobs and therefore the different abilities required that account for the variation. Most managers are remarkably good at judging and, with training and a form of appraisal which provides some structure and guidelines, a reasonable uniformity of standards can be achieved. In cases where there is a definite clash of personalities or philosophies managers have to be encouraged to recognize and admit these difficulties so that a third person can be aware of the problem when assessing performance. Strategies described in Chapter 8 are highly recommended for improving relationships and, in particular, for carrying out effective appraisal interviews.

4 Training for interviewers and for those to be interviewed is of prime importance

Susan Ruffley's conclusions are similar and are reflected in her recommended scheme:

> Before the scheme is introduced the staff will undergo a series of training sessions. These sessions will cover the background and purpose of the scheme as well as the practical skills involved. The aim is that the Library staff realise what

can be achieved through appraisal and learn the necessary techniques. Both the process of interviewing and the completion of the form should be discussed, giving the participants the support and confidence they require.

Some training has already taken place but this needs to be added to and built on. As in the previous training a variety of methods should be employed to train the staff, such as role play and analysis, as well as documentation that can be referred to later. The use of the cascade method to introduce staff appraisal should encourage an understanding of the appraisee's situation and promote a more constructive and positive approach.[14]

5   The appraisal interview is an important occasion

Where appraisal systems are seen to be imposed there is the danger that staff will 'go through the motions' and that the exercise will be a waste of time. A degree of formality in the interview is therefore necessary with no interference by telephone or personal callers. Stewart recommends a neutral room[15] for the interview. The occasion will be considered more serious if both parties are required to prepare before the interview. The Nottingham Trent University scheme, for example, includes a detailed staff preparation form with guidance notes:

In preparing for the Appraisal Meeting, some of the key questions are:

- What am I responsible for and what are my key priorities or objectives?
- What have been my main activities during the past year, and what have been the key successes, problems, or factors affecting my performance?
- What have been my main areas of training and development during the year, and how have these proved useful?
- In what ways could my contribution have been enhanced during the year and what are the things that need to be done to bring this about in the coming year – both personally and organisationally?
- What am I or should I be seeking to achieve in the coming year, what training and development needs will I have in achieving them, and how can these needs best be met?

At least two days before your Appraisal Meeting, you should send a written note to your appraiser of any specific areas that you wish to discuss during the Meeting and (unless you prefer to keep the Form strictly for your own personal use) a copy of the completed Staff Preparation Form.

In some cases there are preliminary interviews followed by final interviews but this can be quite time-consuming.

A helpful summary of a typical scheme (University of Northumbria) is shown in Figure 6.2.

6   The relationship between the appraiser and the appraisee is critical

Most schemes list an improved relationship between supervisors and subordinates as an objective largely through the requirement for managers to talk to their subordinates on matters which are very important to both of them. The

WHAT WILL HAPPEN?

```
┌─────────────────────────────────────────┐
│  APPRAISER arranges Preliminary Meeting with │
│  APPRAISEE and agrees date for Staff        │
│  Development and Appraisal Interview        │
│  FORMS FOR SELF APPRAISAL discussed         │
│  APPRAISEE may wish to use forms to assist in │
│  formulating AGENDA                         │
└─────────────────────────────────────────┘
                    │
┌─────────────────────────────────────────┐
│  PRELIMINARY MEETING Appraiser and          │
│  Appraisee agree agenda for Staff Development and │
│  Appraisal Interview                        │
└─────────────────────────────────────────┘
                    │
┌─────────────────────────────────────────┐
│  APPRAISEE WRITES SELF APPRAISAL            │
│  Prepares for Interview                      │
└─────────────────────────────────────────┘
                    │
┌─────────────────────────────────────────┐
│  APPRAISER prepares and plans for Interview  │
└─────────────────────────────────────────┘
                    │
┌─────────────────────────────────────────┐
│  APPRAISAL INTERVIEW                         │
└─────────────────────────────────────────┘
                    │
┌─────────────────────────────────────────┐
│  APPRAISER and APPRAISEE agree summary       │
│  record of interview.                        │
│  Each should recognise that OUTCOMES will need │
│  to be assessed in terms of DEPARTMENTAL     │
│  PRIORITIES and RESOURCES AVAILABLE          │
└─────────────────────────────────────────┘
                    │
┌─────────────────────────────────────────┐
│  APPRAISER and APPRAISEE sign agreed         │
│  Summary and Professional Development form (B) │
└─────────────────────────────────────────┘
                    │
┌─────────────────────────────────────────┐
│  One copy of SUMMARY RECORD (Form B) is      │
│  retained by                                 │
│  (a) Appraisee                               │
│  (b) Appraiser                               │
└─────────────────────────────────────────┘
                    │
┌─────────────────────────────────────────┐
│  Appraiser, where not Head of Department, notifies │
│  Head of Department on a regular basis of appraisal │
│  interviews completed                        │
└─────────────────────────────────────────┘
                    │
┌─────────────────────────────────────────┐
│  HEAD OF DEPARTMENT notifies Staff           │
│  Development Officer of needs to be met by centrally │
│  provided staff development. Reports back via │
│  monitoring system re who has been appraised and │
│  when                                        │
└─────────────────────────────────────────┘
```

Figure 6.2   Staff appraisal scheme summary – University of Northumbria

appraisal interview, however, cannot be viewed in isolation. Fletcher's researches 'suggest that relatively little is achieved by the appraisal where existing communications are poor, though – paradoxically – this is where the need is greatest and the potential gains highest'.[16]

It is especially difficult for effective appraisal to be carried out openly where a subordinate has little professional regard for the appraiser. The two people may have personal differences which are difficult to change, though the onus is upon the senior person to establish a good working relationship. It is more likely that appraisal is simply highlighting poor management and only considerable effort on the lines recommended in other sections of this book can hope to bring about desirable changes. It is our experience that those managers least willing to operate appraisal schemes tend to be those who are managing staff least well.

The style used by individuals will reflect their management styles which in turn will be influenced by the style prevalent in the organization, which may, of course, vary in different parts of it.

In a library managed on mechanistic lines as described in Chapter 2, a formal appraisal scheme is most likely to be instituted as a useful device for checking that staff are doing what they have been told to do. It may be rejected, however, where controls are already tight enough, or where management fear that their own competence may be called into question.

In an organismic system a scheme might be welcomed if it could be shown to improve staff performance but reservations would be likely concerning the constricting nature of a formal scheme because, in a truly organismic structure, appraisal of each other's performance would be taking place all the time. In fact Stewart found that library staff who 'expressed satisfaction with their present access to senior managers and to staff development opportunities' could see 'little benefit in formalizing the process'.[17] A formal scheme could easily stifle spontaneous action designed to meet problems as they arise. The mechanistic organization would be more likely than an organismic one to accept a method of employing simple trait or numerical ratings, as job performance would be viewed by the latter as a complex matter not amenable to simple ratings. Angiletta states clearly the sort of organismic system he favours:

> one which focuses not on a given event, which gives rise to given documents employing universal and formal language, but on a continuous horizontal relationship between professional colleagues which, while punctuated by time-bound control documentation directed at grades and accountability – a kind of necessary quick dose of vertical power relations – might be best termed 'performance consultation' rather than 'performance evaluation' or 'performance appraisal'.[18]

7   It is vital that discussions are rooted in reality and fact

Our experience has been that appraisees are most concerned about their weaknesses as perceived by the manager even if their overall performance has been appraised as excellent. It is therefore essential in these instances that managers have the correct facts before them on which the judgement has been made. Appraisees will almost always ask for specific events which have led to the criticism. It is also important for the appraiser to be realistic. For example. most schemes are concerned with encouraging staff development but it is counter-productive to offer development when it is known that resources are inadequate.

8 The real benefit of staff appraisal lies in regular and effective follow-up of agreed action plans

In most schemes performance over the past year will be reviewed in the light of the goals set the previous year. The formal appraisal is really a chance for staff to talk to their managers about their work but, of course, appraisal of performance should be going on all the time. Angiletta is attracted by:

> the idea of a dialogue in a series of meetings over time, not necessarily tied to or driven by a salary setting or promotion cycle, which are ad hoc and scheduled, and exist for the purpose of conversing about what the person is doing, where they are going, where they've been, what problems they have encountered, how they might be mediated or remedied, what the fit is between what the person is doing, what the job is, and what the organizational needs are.

9 It is necessary to monitor, evaluate and develop appraisal schemes for their continued success

The starting points will be the objectives of the scheme. Using these as a basis the system should be regularly evaluated. All participants will be able to give their views, for example each year, on the success of the scheme in meeting its objectives and how it might be changed.

Performance reviews

The starting point for an appraisal system should be the desire to improve the performance of the library which requires improvement of the performance of individual members of staff. A number of ideas have already been introduced in this book on participative management and objective approaches designed to encourage staff to participate in decision-making and decide what they and the library wish to achieve in the future. Performance appraisal aims to improve the performance of individuals at work by first of all reviewing their existing performance in the light of previous reviews, if any, deciding on future goals and desirable support, such as training needs, to enable the goals to be reached.

Naturally staff have to be informed of the manager's view of their existing performances in order to be stimulated to improve upon them and in some ways the most important objective of an appraisal system turns out to be the communication of such information to staff. It is surprising how few staff have any accurate knowledge about senior management's view on their performance. Indeed, if they had known, their careers may have developed quite differently, and most importantly they could have improved their performance if only they had been aware of management's views, especially if help had been forthcoming. Our own experience has been that many younger librarians would welcome systematic feedback on their performance and help and advice on improving it.

Appraisal should be viewed in association with the training and development of staff because it helps to identify training needs which have to be met if staff are to improve their performances. If appraisal is to be successful a library must be able to offer training opportunities to staff who are formally appraised. If it cannot do this then appraisal may bring into question many other areas of management for which appraisers are responsible, such as staffing structures, recruitment and deployment of staff and the management information system. There is always a danger that appraisers can be drawn into discussing these wider issues which are claimed by individuals to affect their performances and so to lose the focus of appraisal. Nonetheless appraisee's views should be listened to and subsequent action taken where necessary.

In our opinion too much emphasis has been put on individual performance and insufficient on the context in which the person operates:

> Various commentators have raised the point that few appraisal schemes in existence at present make a conscious effort to take organizational factors into account when assessing performance ... Very few people work in isolation, yet we try to single out each individual and assess his performance as though he were totally responsible for the results.[19]

In assessing performance it would seem natural in a profession like librarianship, in which most people work in groups, that appraisal should start in the work group. Group appraisal implies an objectives approach with objectives agreed by the work group led by the library manager with the support and involvement of senior management. An annual group appraisal system is employed at Manchester Metropolitan University Library. Before each summer vacation the University Librarian and his two deputies (Head of Reader Services and Head of Technical Services) meet the professional staff of each section of the library. The meetings normally last about two hours. The most productive pattern has been to begin with the annual report which is worked through systematically.

The list of objectives agreed at the previous meeting is then reviewed. In practice most of the objectives will have been covered in the annual report and discussion will then centre around those that have not been achieved for one reason or another. It is recognized, for example, that circumstances change and therefore a rigid adherence to objectives determined a year ago would not be in the interests of the library.

The meeting then discusses the list of objectives being proposed for the coming academic year by the section and when these have been agreed they are documented and both the senior managers and the section heads agree on the final version. In practice a number of the objectives develop from the discussion of the annual report at the beginning of the meeting. There is deliberately no attempt to write minutes of the meeting. Only decisions which have been made about the future are documented. Although most of the objectives are to be achieved by the section, the University Librarian and his deputies usually end up with a number of matters they have to address at a more general level, e.g. formulating a method of funding CD Roms, Easter Vacation opening hours, charging for on-line searching. At the end of the exercise the senior managers have as many things to do as the section managers. The meeting ends with a discussion of the estimates.

Where a group appraisal system operates alongside formal appraisal of individuals, the relationships between the two must be thought out carefully. There can be conflict especially where an individual is required by an appraiser to achieve certain objectives which may conflict with group priorities. We have probably all worked with individuals who seemed to develop themselves rather than the service perhaps at the expense of others who 'carry the burdens of the day'. If this conflict is to be avoided, individual appraisal must encourage and reward those who develop in those areas of most use to the library.

Potential reviews

In a period when the numbers of posts are reducing rather than expanding and there is low mobility amongst staff, promotion policies within organizations are likely to be scrutinized more thoroughly than usual. The traditional policy in most libraries has been to advertise internally and externally and for the person who performs 'the best on the day' to obtain the post. Chapter 5 has described some of the difficulties in selecting staff on the basis of interview only and a great advantage in evaluating internal candidates is that their present performance is well known to the selectors. If there is a regular appraisal system information will be even more reliable. With low mobility it is likely in large systems that there will be staff very able to take on posts at a higher level without requiring the basic training and induction needed by external appointees. It must be particularly galling for staff of a library which appoints mainly externally to find many others appointing mainly internally.

Many organizations deliberately set out to identify staff potentially able to work effectively at a higher level and to prepare them for the future. Identification is frequently carried out by means of a potential review. Most libraries shrink from such a positive step partly because internal promotion is not encouraged but also because, as Randell, Packard and Slater observe:

> It is probably the most dangerous in possible psychological effects, for statements about an individual's potential, or lack of it, can be psychologically disturbing. There are also social problems such as identifying 'crown princes': someone may have been labelled as heir-apparent and may start behaving in

that role even though he may not have the capacity for the work for which he is being groomed. There is also the 'self-fulfilling prophecy': making a prediction about a person's potential and publicly announcing it can bring about the prophecy.[20]

Such problems would almost certainly deter most managers from spending time on potential reviews. In addition the difficulty of basing judgements about future performance in general on performance in a different job at a lower level presents even more problems managers could do without. There is some evidence, however, that some librarians favour systematic appraisal as providing a more accurate estimate of their worth for promotion:

> Many of us have been with the Department a long time; many of us have similar experience – so that when we apply for jobs, the interview must be the only deciding factor. Is this enough? Heads of Department reports would provide a constant record of our progress, staff not directly in the management 'eye' would benefit, and interviewers would have more information about each applicant to help in their decision-making. Reports would also help the Staff Officer to write constructive references when a person leaves the Department for a new job.[21]

A noticeable feature of many of the schemes recently adopted in libraries is the emphasis upon staff development. All the schemes we have seen have, at least, a section on staff development and a number in fact gave their schemes such titles as 'Staff Development and Career Review' and 'Professional Development and Review'. Possibly this was done deliberately to provide a more positive image than staff appraisal, even though the schemes also incorporate performance reviews. The initial emphasis in the development section will be upon the person's ambitions and the opportunities that exist rather than potential though it will inevitably be discussed in some way or other.

Although few British librarians operate a systematic potential review system they do frequently involve themselves in discussions with individuals about their future and they do try to help them through their existing jobs. Since internal promotions are becoming more likely with larger organizations and lack of external opportunities it is useful to consider the most useful areas for discussion and help. As librarians move up the hierarchy they inevitably move from professional work towards managerial work and this has to be tackled effectively if the library is to function well. Research has shown that managers' choices increase as they obtain higher-level posts and this also appears to be the case with librarians. If they shy away from managerial tasks because they are more comfortable with professional ones the library is bound to suffer. A survey of librarians moving into senior management posts has shown the following areas of managerial skills to be most important and therefore the ones upon which potential counselling might concentrate:

MANAGEMENT OF STAFF   Motivating. Supervising and allocation of work. Delegation. Working as a team. Counselling. Problem-solving. Selection-interviewing. Training.

PLANNING

Objectives definition. Making best use of resources. Preparing evidence. Financial management. Time management. Confidence building.

BOUNDARY MAINTENANCE

Other chief officers. Authority members. Learning new professional jargon.

COMMUNICATION

Communications. Public speaking. Public relations.[22]

Reward reviews

In the private sector appraisal systems are often used for assembling information to enable organizations to share out rewards. The rewards include bonuses, increments and increased pay. Two factors dominate the criteria to be used. First there is the correct rating for the job and in this respect most public sector employers also have a system of review. Usually this consists of an annual review within which managers can propose a change in grade for a subordinate and individuals can apply for a regrading of their own jobs.

The main reason for regrading will normally be a change in duties since the last time the post was graded and the original job descriptions are no longer accurate. In recent years amalgamations and automation have resulted in changes in duties and responsibilities, though many organizations are reluctant to allow these two reasons to be used as justifications since amalgamations affect so many staff and automation is expected to result in reductions in staffing costs.

Comparisons with other posts in the organization or with posts in other libraries are also used to justify regradings although organizations have been more reluctant to accept such arguments as they have tried to reduce staffing costs.

In practice all these reasons are used by managers, individuals and by the trade union representatives, who act as advisers and often support a case in the event of an appeal.

The second important factor in reward appraisal is the performance of the individual. In the private sector and in libraries in the US, for example, making an extra payment for good performance is common. In the public sector in Britain it is much less common. Some librarians feel that appraisals are not worth carrying out unless the payment of financial rewards is possible in recognition of achievement.

Although pay incentives are unusual in public services it is interesting to note that cash incentives were used in both British universities and polytechnics to persuade academic staff to agree to annual performance appraisals. There is no doubt, however, that performance-related pay has become more acceptable in British industry. An ACAS report on labour flexibility published in 1988 showed that 24 per cent of nearly 600 organizations surveyed had recently introduced performance pay and 19 per cent were planning to do so. As Farmer[23] points out, there is little literature on performance pay for librarians and she is able only to cite American literature. The difficulties of measuring performance in a library, its effect on working relationships and teamwork, are all factors which must be taken into account. As we have already shown, staff appraisal has other objectives and library managers have to ask themselves whether sufficient would be achieved without such payments.

Who does the appraising?

Most personnel management textbooks and, more recently, library management textbooks, list and discuss available methods of appraisal. Hilton[24] has produced a helpful review of the literature, Kroll[25] has discussed methods and there are written accounts of methods used by particular libraries. We have also obtained material from a number of libraries and the emphasis will be upon methods known to be used by them.

In most schemes it is the senior librarians who formally appraise the librarians who work directly for them. In some cases the next person above in the hierarchy ('the grandfather') plays some part. In the British Civil Service, for example, some departments have three layers. The reporting officer reports on performance but promotion markings in those departments which give them may be assigned by either the reporting officer or a countersigning officer, and in some cases there will be a third signatory.

In a few American libraries peer and subordinate appraisal is also carried out. Earlier in this chapter we referred to informal appraisal as a natural and popular activity and it is certainly true that both peers and subordinates can contribute to appraisal in ways which are not possible for those at a more senior level because relationships are different. Anne Turner's reply to a request for information in 'American libraries' aroused so much interest that she wrote an article describing the system used in the Jones Library in Amhurst:

> The principal tool for the evaluation was a General Evaluation Form, which asked library workers to assess their own and others' performances using a numerical rating system. The basic form was in three parts – Technical Performance (eleven criteria), Relation to Public (eight criteria), and Relation to Staff (nine criteria). Additionally, each section had open-ended questions which invited comments, and the whole GEF ended with a final question, 'If I were in charge of this place I'd do something about – '. Workers who were supervisors were also evaluated for, and did evaluations of, Supervisory Skills.
>
> Except for the self-evaluation form all GEFs were filled out anonymously. Supervisors of the workers being evaluated received these forms and made a Composite GEF, which consolidated the ratings and comments of the subject's co-workers. Thus a desk attendant filled GEFs on the other desk attendants and gave them to the circulation manager. The desk attendant also did a GEF on the circulation manager, and gave this to the circulation manager's supervisor (the director). Lastly she filled out a self-evaluation GEF, which she kept to use in her worker/supervisor conference.[26]

At the University of Texas at Austin reports are prepared by subordinates for the supervisor's private use[27] and anonymous peer and subordinate evaluations are made at the Southern Illinois University Carbondale Library.[28] At the University of Tennessee Center for Health Sciences Library two attempts were made to encourage evaluations of library supervisors by subordinates.[29] The experiment was judged unsuccessful when very few subordinates chose to evaluate their supervisors. A letter written by David Weber, Director of Stanford University Libraries, explains why we should be careful not to overvalue subordinate assessments:

> As in student evaluation of faculty, the views of subordinates may be based on narrower concerns than those of the organization. Subordinates are likely to give greater weight to practical matters, assistance with procedures, and departmental personnel issues. They may not see the vital contributions of the supervisor's fundamental planning or goal-setting roles, leadership of task forces and committees, and effectiveness in relations with faculty members and administrators.[30]

Weber's concern is with the interpretation of data collected and not with the method itself, but many British librarians would consider the appraisal schemes described in this section too complex, time-consuming and unnecessary. One does have some sympathy with the British librarians whom David Peele met while researching appraisal in Britain and America who believed their appraisal role was fulfilled if their doors 'were always open' for staff who wished to see them.[31]

The most desirable outcome of appraisal is that staff would appraise their own performances with the help of others. In some schemes self-appraisal is considered to be so important that it is the starting point. In a survey of British academic libraries in 1992[32] it was found that 35 universities and six polytechnic libraries were operating a staff appraisal scheme. This was largely a result of the Jarratt report and the 23rd Report published in 1987 by Committee A of the Universities Academic Salaries Committee. The survey found that the most popular method was one based on self-appraisal. 'The form is completed by the appraisee and then comments are added at the interview following discussions and agreement by both participants.' In recommending a self-appraisal scheme Ruffley believes that 'the use of self-appraisal transfers the sometimes contentious issue of assessment to the individual concerned. The professional status is not impugned and the interview allows constructive guidance to be given'. A great deal is made of the concept of 'ownership' in present-day management and self-appraisal does enable individuals to 'own' their appraisals. A self-assessment used by Staffordshire University Library is shown in Figure 6.3. Where there is no formal appraisal scheme good managers, like good teachers, begin discussion of performance from the position of the subordinate and only later may impose their own assessments, otherwise management views are taken into account and colour subordinates' reactions.

Annual Development Review : Self-Assessment Form

The questions on this form will act as an agenda for your annual development review discussion. You do not need to complete every question, but please complete as many as you think are relevant. The review process will only work successfully if you are prepared to assess your past performance and future development as honestly as possible. To encourage this the form will be destroyed immediately after your discussion.

It will also make the discussion more effective if you let the person who will be involved with your discussion have a copy in advance. This, though, is entirely up to you.

1   List your main activities or duties since your last development discussion.

2   Are there any achievements that you are particularly pleased about in the past year?

3   Which of your activities do you most enjoy and why?

4   Which of your activities do you least enjoy and why?

5   Which of your activities do you think that you do best and why?

6   Which of your activities do you think that you do least well and why?

Figure 6.3   Self-assessment form – Staffordshire University

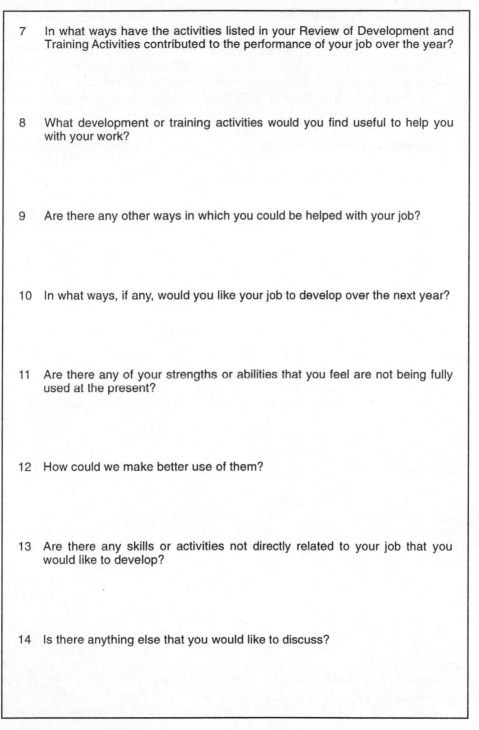

7   In what ways have the activities listed in your Review of Development and Training Activities contributed to the performance of your job over the year?

8   What development or training activities would you find useful to help you with your work?

9   Are there any other ways in which you could be helped with your job?

10   In what ways, if any, would you like your job to develop over the next year?

11   Are there any of your strengths or abilities that you feel are not being fully used at the present?

12   How could we make better use of them?

13   Are there any skills or activities not directly related to your job that you would like to develop?

14   Is there anything else that you would like to discuss?

Figure 6.3   Concluded

Forms of appraisal

The earliest form of appraisal used by libraries appears to have been trait rating. In the US the American Library Association published a standard rating form in its 'Personnel organization and procedure' manual,[33] in which raters were required to score staff on thirty-three traits using a five-point scale, each point being denoted by a phrase or adverb, for example:

THOROUGHNESS

Meticulous in checking. Always sees things through.	Usually thorough. Sometimes skips details under pressure.	Moderately careful. Inclined to take too many short cuts.
	Superficial. Does not follow through if difficulties arise.	Does not complete assignments satisfactorily.

There are many variations on this system both in layout and scoring.

The Institute of Chartered Accountants uses a five-point scale with boxes to be ticked, sometimes referred to as a graphic rating scale. Staff are scored on thirteen performance criteria which are briefly described on the form:

e.g. Dependability – The thoroughness   5   4   3   2   1
demonstrated by the employee in
carrying out work responsibilities
and obligations in a trustworthy,
conscientious, reliable and
punctual manner.

This form of appraisal has a number of advantages. It is relatively easy for the appraisee to fill in the form. A cynic might say that they don't have to think up their own pet phrases because they are already prepared by somebody else. Trait scoring does give the impression, because values are being assigned, that the process is scientific and in some libraries the scores for each trait are aggregated and a total score given for the appraisee. This may leave the appraiser with a comfortable feeling of a job neatly completed but critics would argue that evaluating staff is a more complicated matter and a person does not consist simply of the sum of the traits chosen for an appraisal scheme.

In a few cases a weighted trait system is used in order to give greater rating to those traits which are considered important and it is concern for performance on the job which distinguishes what we believe to be the better trait systems from those which concern themselves too much with personality traits. The reader is invited to assess any trait-rating they experience on the basis of relevance to the job being rated.

Any scoring system faces the problem of standards. As Peele points out: 'The real problem ... comes when we try to answer the question, "What is the standard?" ... the unanswered question – perhaps the unanswerable one – is, "performance compared to what?".'[34] Peele then illustrates the problem by asking how we know what standard to use when rating 'Judgement' on a five-point scale and how to take into account the constraints under which each individual works when rating that person's performance.

In all the new academic schemes we have seen, including all those reproduced in Revill,[35] there is no attempt to score performance. In some public library forms there is the facility to rate staff as satisfactory, below satisfactory or above satisfactory, in key areas. It does appear that organizations are trying to avoid the threat of rating in order to give appraisal a more positive image. Thus a partially 'controlled written report' has become the most popular format. The form itself will contain only a few headings leaving appraisers with freedom to write what they wish. The Manchester Metropolitan University 'Development Form' is typical, containing only four sections (Figure 6.4). Like most of the schemes, however, copious guidance notes are provided with recommendations on how the process should be carried out including completion of the report form.

Many schemes like the Manchester one require both the appraiser and appraisee to sign the appraisal report. Areas of disagreement can be recorded on the form and where there is dissatisfaction with the outcome of the meeting it is normal that an interview can be arranged with the reviewer's immediate manager.

Appraisal interviewing

Earlier in this chapter we referred to the importance of good relationships between appraisers and appraisees. One of the aims of appraisal is frequently to improve this relationship, so communication in the interview itself must be successful to achieve this objective. The questions listed in Figure 6.5 have been used by the authors as an analytical tool for training purposes. Many organizations video-tape role-played interviews or provide training videos themselves. In addition some schemes provide valuable advice to interviewers (Figure 6.6).

Hannabuss has devised 'a simple form by means of which judgements from both people can be identified'.[36] The form is reproduced in Figure 6.7. Appraisers and appraisees can each complete the form after an appraisal and compare perceptions.

Chapter 8 of this book provides guidelines on interpersonal skills relevant to appraisal interviewing including transactional analysis.

1 ACHIEVEMENTS

Please record key achievements of the previous review period making reference to problems encountered, special circumstances and general performance against objectives.

Indicate what is left to be achieved. Also indicate areas in which difficulties were encountered and why. The action needed to meet long-term objectives and others not yet achieved, and to overcome difficulties will form part of the plans for Future Development in part 2.

2 FUTURE DEVELOPMENT

Please detail objectives for the development period ahead. These should refer to Teaching, Research and Scholarly Activity, Management and Administration, and External Activity as appropriate to the post-holder.

3 PROFESSIONAL SUPPORT NEEDS AND ACTIONS AGREED

Please summarise action required to ensure development objectives on the opposite page are achieved. Specify time schedules, individuals involved and the resources needed.

Figure 6.4   Appraisal report – Manchester Metropolitan University

4 CAREER DEVELOPMENT

Please detail particular career and professional interests and any action required to support their development.

5 REVIEWEE'S COMMENTS

Signatures:

Reviewee: . . . .

Reviewer: . . . .

Date of Review:

Figure 6.4 Concluded

Objectives
1   Is the purpose of the appraisal made clear by the appraiser and does it
    appear to be understood and accepted by the appraisee?

Procedure
2   Does the appraiser make clear what pattern it is hoped the interview will
    take?
3   Do the participants appear to understand the points made by each of them?
    Is clarification sought where necessary?
4   Does the appraiser summarize what progress has been made in the inter-
    view from time to time and receive confirmation that the summaries are
    accurate?
5   How far is the discussion a two-way one and how far is it dominated by one
    of the participants? Are they both good listeners?
6   Is sufficient time given for each person to explain his/her position to his/her
    own satisfaction?

Relevance
7   Does the interview keep in step with the purpose of the appraisal or does it
    wander off into irrelevant side-tracks?

Conflict
8   Is disagreement used constructively or does it lead mainly to dissatisfac-
    tion?
9   When one criticizes the other is it made in a constructive way producing
    suggestions along with every criticism?
10 Do participants admit it when they are in the wrong or inadequate in some
    way rather than pretend to be right or adequate all the time?

Non-verbals
11 Are there any contradictions between the verbal and non-verbal behaviour?
    Do the non-verbal behaviours of the two persons help to create an atmos-
    phere of trust and openness?

Action
12 Are the participants clear about action that is required before the next
    appraisal interview and is there a firm commitment to carry it out?

Figure 6.5   Typical questions used to evaluate an appraisal interview

LISTENING

DO

Pay attention

- by looking at the reviewee
- by inclined body language towards him/her
- by minimising distractions

Gather information

- by observing reviewee's body language
- by listening for his/her feelings

Test for understanding

- of facts
- of feelings

Hold your fire

- by suspending judgement
- by not responding too quickly
- by allowing silences

Express understanding

- by reflecting back key phrases
- by showing empathy

DON'T

- Interrupt or show impatience
  - Jump to conclusions
    - Give advice

TRY

- To keep an open mind
- To recognise your own blind spots and prejudices
  - To be responsive more than initiating

Figure 6.6   Reviewer interviewing skills – Napier Polytechnic

INTERVIEW ANALYSIS FORM 1

Name of Appraisee:
Name of Appraiser:

In the questions below appraiser should write an X and
appraisees should write an O.

1   How satisfied are you with the other person's response to you during the
    appraisal interview?
    Very dissatisfied   1   2   3   4   5   6   Very satisfied

2   **For the appraisee only**:
    What is your view of the appraiser during the interview?
    Rigid   1   2   3   4   5   6   Flexible
    Open   1   2   3   4   5   6   Reticent
    Considerate   1   2   3   4   5   6   Inconsiderate
    Indifferent to 1   2   3   4   5   6   Concerned about
    mutual problems   mutual problems

3   **For the appraiser only**:
    What is your view of yourself during the interview?
    Rigid   1   2   3   4   5   6   Flexible
    Open   1   2   3   4   5   6   Reticent
    Considerate   1   2   3   4   5   6   Inconsiderate
    Indifferent to 1   2   3   4   5   6   Concerned about
    mutual problems   mutual problems

4   **For the appraisee only**:
    How satisfied are you with the appraiser's performance during the interview?
    Very dissatisfied   1   2   3   4   5   6   Very satisfied

5   **For the appraiser only**:
    How satisfied are you with your own performance during the interview?
    Very dissatisfied   1   2   3   4   5   6   Very satisfied

6   **For the appraisee only**:
    In your view, was the interview an effective way to achieve your aims?
    Completely   1   2   3   4   5   6   Not at all

7   **For the appraiser only**:
    As 6.

(From Stewart Hannabuss, 'Analysing appraisal interviews', *Scottish Libraries*,
    (30) November/December 1991. pp. 13–15)

Figure 6.7   Appraisal analysis form

7

Staff training and development

Identifying training needs

We have already seen how staff appraisal can be a valuable aid in identifying individual training needs and, as the last chapter showed, the good manager does not view appraisal simply in terms of an annual event but is constantly observing and noting deficiencies. These can be categorized as weaknesses in knowledge, skills and attitudes. A start can also be made by analysing job descriptions and specifications for the knowledge, skills and attitudes required and the deficiencies which exist.

Exit interviews with staff who resign can also reveal deficiencies which training could go a long way to repairing. Where there is a high turnover of staff this is especially important. Exit interviews are normally carried out with those who have voluntarily resigned. They are interchanges 'between the employee who is leaving the organization and a manager or staff person of that organization conducted close to the time that the employee leaves the organization'.[1] It is recommended that it takes place during the last week of employment but not on the last day. There is a problem of confidentiality, especially in small libraries, even if only objective statistical analyses are made public. In many organizations, therefore, personnel officers rather than line managers carry out the interviews. The intention is to find out why staff have resigned. This is not always easy. Our experience has been that staff are often loathe to tell managers the real reasons, therefore skilful and tactful probing needs to be employed. As well as providing valuable information for the improvement of training programmes, interviews could help to improve working conditions and solve staff problems. Some organizations also, or instead, employ 'post-separation surveys' conducted by post or telephone about thirty days after the departure of the employee.

In some libraries, where an effort is being made to take training more seriously, surveys have been made of the whole staff to discover the training

```
┌─────────────────────────────────────────────────────────────────────┐
│                  COUNCIL OF POLYTECHNIC LIBRARIANS                     │
│                  STAFF DEVELOPMENT COMMITTEE                           │
│                                                                       │
│   1    What is your job title?                           Do not use   │
│                                                          this column   │
│                                                                       │
│        . . . . . . . . . . . . . . . . . . . . . . . . . . . . .      │
│                                                                       │
│   2    What is the grade of your post?   3  Is your post Full-time? [ ]   2 [ ]   │
│                                             Part-time? [ ]   3 [ ]   │
│        . . . . . . . . . . . . . . . . . . . .                        │
│                                                                       │
│   4    Which of the following best describes your experience of training in your   │
│        library?                                                       │
│                                                                       │
│      a  my training and development has been excellent      [  ]    4a [  ]   │
│                                                                       │
│      b  my training and development has been good           [  ]    4b [  ]   │
│                                                                       │
│      c  my training and development has been adequate       [  ]    4c [  ]   │
│                                                                       │
│      d  my training and development has been less than adequate  [  ]  4d [  ]  │
│                                                                       │
│      e  my training and development has been poor           [  ]    4e [  ]   │
│                                                                       │
│      f  I have had no training or development               [  ]    4f [  ]   │
│                                                                       │
│   5    List up to three training activities which you have been involved with in the   │
│        past 12 months                                                 │
│                                                                       │
│      a  . . . . . . . . . . . . . . . . . . . . . . . . . . . . . . . . . . . . . . . . . . . .   │
│         . . . . . . . . . . . . . . . . . . . . . . . . . . . . . . . . . . . . . . . . . . . .   │
│                                                                       │
│      b  . . . . . . . . . . . . . . . . . . . . . . . . . . . . . . . . . . . . . . . . . . . .   │
│         . . . . . . . . . . . . . . . . . . . . . . . . . . . . . . . . . . . . . . . . . . . .   │
│                                                                       │
│      c  . . . . . . . . . . . . . . . . . . . . . . . . . . . . . . . . . . . . . . . . . . . .   │
│         . . . . . . . . . . . . . . . . . . . . . . . . . . . . . . . . . . . . . . . . . . . .   │
│                                                                       │
│   6    List up to three areas in which you think that more training would be   │
│        desirable                                                      │
│                                                                       │
│      a  . . . . . . . . . . . . . . . . . . . . . . . . . . . . . . . . . . . . . . . . . . . .   │
│         . . . . . . . . . . . . . . . . . . . . . . . . . . . . . . . . . . . . . . . . . . . .   │
│                                                                       │
│      b  . . . . . . . . . . . . . . . . . . . . . . . . . . . . . . . . . . . . . . . . . . . .   │
│         . . . . . . . . . . . . . . . . . . . . . . . . . . . . . . . . . . . . . . . . . . . .   │
│                                                                       │
│      c  . . . . . . . . . . . . . . . . . . . . . . . . . . . . . . . . . . . . . . . . . . . .   │
│         . . . . . . . . . . . . . . . . . . . . . . . . . . . . . . . . . . . . . . . . . . . .   │
└─────────────────────────────────────────────────────────────────────┘
```

Figure 7.1   Analysis of training and development needs – COPOL

7 If some of your training needs could be met by co-operating with other libraries how interested would you be in attending such events?

very
interested   interested

not very
interested

not interested
at all

[ ]   [ ]   [ ]   [ ]

8 If the following training activities could be organised in conjunction with other libraries how interested would you be in taking part? Please circle the number that best represents your interest

Do not use
this column

very
interested

not interested
at all

a	computer systems in libraries, e.g. Geac, BLCMP	1	2	3	4	8a [ ]
b	microcomputer software applications in libraries	1	2	3	4	8b [ ]
c	interpersonal and communication skills	1	2	3	4	8c [ ]
d	planning a training programme	1	2	3	4	8d [ ]
e	dealing with customers	1	2	3	4	8e [ ]
f	career planning	1	2	3	4	8f [ ]
g	assertiveness training	1	2	3	4	8g [ ]
h	leadership and motivation	1	2	3	4	8h [ ]
i	team building	1	2	3	4	8i [ ]
j	current issues in libraries and information	1	2	3	4	8j [ ]
k	finance and budgeting for libraries	1	2	3	4	8k [ ]
l	introduction to management	1	2	3	4	8l [ ]
m	supervisory skills	1	2	3	4	8m[ ]
n	time management	1	2	3	4	8n [ ]
o	multisite planning	1	2	3	4	8o [ ]
p	libraries as a career	1	2	3	4	8p [ ]

Figure 7.1 Continued

q	marketing libraries	1	2	3	4	8q [ ]
r	industrial relations	1	2	3	4	8r [ ]
s	how to handle the boss	1	2	3	4	8s [ ]
t	staff appraisal	1	2	3	4	8t [ ]
u	exchange of experience seminars	1	2	3	4	8u [ ]
v	other (please specify)	1	2	3	4	8v [ ]

9   If you were able to take part in training activities with other libraries would you be prepared to travel?

nationally (i.e. anywhere)	regionally (e.g. Midlands, North)	locally (e.g. 20 miles)	
[ ]	[ ]	[ ]	9 [ ]

10   Would you be interested in an exchange of jobs, for a limited period, with someone in a similar job in another library?

yes	no	
[ ]	[ ]	10 [ ]

11   If you answered YES to question 10, how long would you prefer such an exchange to be?

one year	six months	one month	one week	other (please specify)	
[ ]	[ ]	[ ]	[ ]	[ ]	11 [ ]

12   Are there any other comments that you would like to make about training in co-operation with other libraries?

. . . .
. . . .
. . . .

THANK YOU FOR TAKING THE TIME TO COMPLETE THIS QUESTIONNAIRE.

WHEN IT IS COMPLETED PLEASE RETURN IT TO THE PERSON RESPON-SIBLE FOR TRAINING IN YOUR LIBRARY SERVICE

Figure 7.1   Concluded

needs which staff feel they have. The example shown in Figure 7.1 is taken from the COPOL survey of 1991. It does, therefore, highlight co-operative training but it did prove useful as an analysis of the perceived needs of staff in each of the libraries participating.

Training needs, however, are not simply a matter of individual benefits, not even the sum total of them. At the general level there are organizational training needs which relate to the general weaknesses in the library which can be remedied, or partly so, by training. As Boydell observes, the weaknesses can only be properly assessed if they are related to the present and future objectives of the organization.[2]

For training to be effective it must be viewed as an essential element in the management cycle and thus the starting point really lies in the changing needs of the communities which libraries serve and the different responses the library is able to make to fulfil those needs by utilizing new skills and technologies. For example, the development of franchising of courses by academic institutions in the UK during the 1990s brought with it a new role for librarians in the validation of these courses. At Manchester Metropolitan University training sessions were held to ensure that staff understood franchising and would be effective members of validation panels.

In public libraries staff structures have been changing partly to enable the library to respond more quickly to community needs (see Chapter 4). Where this has happened the better-managed libraries have recognized that staff cannot be expected to perform differently simply because the structure has been changed and therefore training has been provided. A good example is the training package produced by Leicestershire on 'The effective use of team time'.[3]

Training needs may also be identified through a scrutiny of jobs being poorly performed in the library. If there are written quantitative standards in use for routine jobs it will be known whether these are being met and observations can reveal where qualitative standards are not being reached. In addition there may be complaints from the community served that can be analysed, possibly revealing training needs.

Group needs

The evidence obtained from the analysis of both individual and organizational needs will show that particular groups have their own training needs. This is so likely, and makes training so much easier, that analysis by group should be an essential part of needs identification. Where group members are working closely together it is particularly desirable for them to put forward what they believe to be their training needs as a group. In this way training can much more easily be perceived as being intimately connected with the work, rather than an extra that can be indulged in when there is an excess of funds, which is almost never.

A useful group checklist is produced by The Library Association:[4]

1   Library assistants
2   Senior library assistants
3   Pre-library school trainees
4   Unqualified subject specialists
5   Staff in first professional posts
6   Intermediate professionals
7   Specialists
8   Senior management
9   Clerical staff
10   Manual staff
11   Specialist technical staff
12   Other professions working in libraries.

During the last decade The Library Association's chartering requirements have necessarily concentrated training activities in Britain upon staff wishing to charter. A large majority of these are young professionals in their first posts. A high proportion are able to follow Route A which 'should ensure the new entrant to the profession the best start to a successful and fulfilling career'.[5] Each candidate is required to have a supervisor who is expected to act as a guide and mentor 'not only training them in the duties and responsibilities of the posts and services in which they are employed, but ensuring that they maintain a broad professional perspective'.[6] Training programmes have to be submitted to The Library Association for approval. They can be standard programmes which can be used by an employing organization on a regular basis for a number of candidates or programmes designed for a named individual in a specific post. Since 1992 a proforma has been used requiring supervisors to describe how training will be delivered in areas common to most posts in library and information work. These areas are shown in the checklist Figure 7.2 which can also serve as a checklist for individual libraries analysing training needs.

The responsibility for training

Many libraries have produced written staff development and training policies. Typically they include a statement of aims and objectives, details of responsibilities for training, statements on the various types of training, information on procedures and the records of training which will be kept and the evaluation of training. Figure 7.3 reproduces a policy statement from the library of the University of Nottingham. Excellent examples are those of the University of East London, the University of Hertfordshire, Thames Valley University, Bristol University, and the Institution of Mechanical Engineers.

For training to be successful there must first be senior management support. Undoubtedly the chief librarian will be the most crucial figure but training, like any other organizational activity, will flounder if line managers do not believe in it but have to subscribe to it sufficiently to put up with the incon-

1 *Induction*

    Aims of the host organization.
    How the library/information unit serves these aims.
    Service objectives.

2 *Professional skills*

    Selection of materials.
    Arrangement of materials to facilitate retrieval.
    Maintenance of the stock, physically and in terms of currency.
    Provision of information in response to enquiries.
    Use of computers   (i)   for housekeeping
                           (ii)   for information retrieval
    General administrative procedures.

3 *Management skills*

    Priorities and work organization.
    Problem-solving/decision-making.
    Budgeting and financial management.
    Assessment of training needs.

4 *Analysis and evaluation*

    Evaluation of the service offered.
    Evaluation of managerial practices.
    Evaluation of policy.

5 *Communication*

    Working as part of a team.
    Supervising staff.
    Communicating with users.
    Publicity and promotion.
    Written communications and instructions.
    Committee work.

6 *Training*

    Production of evaluative written work.
    Attendance on short courses.
    Day-to-day training and monitoring.
    Discussion of training received and future development.

7 *Professional involvement/awareness*

    Visiting other types of service.
    Attending professional meetings.
    Discussing general concerns of the profession.
    Meeting other professionals.

Figure 7.2   Checklist of training activities

POLICY STATEMENT
It is the policy of the Library to ensure that positive and continuous support and encouragement are given to all staff in respect of their training and staff development so that they acquire the skills necessary both for the furtherance of their careers and for the delivery of the best possible service to all library users.

AIMS

1   To provide basic training to enable all library staff to carry out their work as effectively and efficiently as possible.

2   To encourage a wide knowledge and understanding of the teaching and research work of the University and other funding bodies and to promote an awareness of the role of the library in support of that work.

3   To ensure that staff are kept up-to-date with technological change and innovation.

4   To encourage awareness of new developments and changing concepts in the library and information world.

5   To encourage all staff to develop good interpersonal and communication skills so that they are able to co-operative effectively with colleagues and to relate well to the great variety of library users.

6   To encourage long-term career development of all staff on all grades.

7   To ensure that all newly qualified librarians gain the skills and experience necessary to achieve the Library Association Chartership.

8   To provide training which ensures compliance with Health and Safety legislation.

9   To promote awareness of the services and the resources available in each of the University's libraries.

10   To encourage exchange visits with the local libraries and information centres.

11   To encourage an awareness of the book trade.

12   To encourage support staff to take advantage of vocational training opportunities.

13   To ensure regular review and evaluation of the above policy.

Figure 7.3   Policy on training and staff development – University of Nottingham

venience of being without staff when off-the-job training is taking place. Because training is one of those management activities which is not automatically in the forefront of the manager's mind (it is not usually an issue which lies on the manager's desk awaiting decisions every day), there is a requirement for a person to be given overall responsibility for the management of training. This person's job is to ensure that the policy is carried out and that the training which does take place is continually evaluated. Ronald Edwards' survey[7] results and guidelines together with the Local Government Training Board's recommendations[8] provide valuable help in producing the training officer's job description. It is especially important for the training officer to be a member of the senior management team and be acknowledged as the link with training personnel of the parent body.

With reductions in staffing over recent years fewer libraries have been able to employ persons whose sole functions are training and development. The more prevalent scenario, particularly in small libraries, is that of a senior manager who has personnel and training responsibilities amongst others.

Whenever a special responsibility is created there is a natural tendency for other staff to leave that specialism to the specialist and neglect it themselves. It cannot be emphasized too strongly that it is not the training officer's job to carry out all the training. The job of the training officer is to operate as a 'fulcrum of training activity' and the 'catalyst for training change and development'[9] and in this role to create a training atmosphere in the library and an acceptance by line managers of their training responsibilities. One way of doing this, used by some libraries, is to form a training group whose purpose is to provide information and ideas on training needs and to support the work of the training officer.

Resources for training

One of the group's main tasks will be to discover training resources in the organization itself. In particular a position statement should be drawn up concerning accommodation, equipment, expertise, and of course, available funds.

1 *Accommodation:* Rooms for large and small groups which allow flexibility of use are desirable. The following measures, adapted from those used by Peter Smith[10] to evaluate accommodation, provide a helpful checklist:

> Thermal – air temperature, air movement, ventilation.
> Visual – natural and artificial lighting.
> Acoustics – reverberation, background noise, sound levels.
> Teaching aids – sockets, access to computer network.
> Room form – size and shape, ease of vision, nature of exit and entry.
> Toilet and washing facilities.
> Eating and drinking facilities.
> Furniture – tables, chairs, writing facilities.

2 *Equipment:* Screens, overhead projectors, equipment for projection from computer screens, computer terminals, laser pointers, video tape recorders and monitors, film and video projectors.

3 *Expertise:* Two main types of expertise are required. The first is knowledge of areas in which training is required. Here the checklist of training activi-

ties (Figure 7.2) can be used and names attached where expertise is available. The second type of expertise relates to the skills required to teach and train and this may be more difficult to discover. Staff may have had teaching experience or they may be known as good instructors but, on the other hand, expertise may be lacking and in that case an important early consideration will be how to train the trainers – it could be harmful to launch a programme only to have it poorly taught.

4 *Funds:* Money available for training in the library budget, or from other funds such as those of specialist training and management departments in the organization.

The mechanistic/organismic paradigm (Figure 2.1) shows how staff training and development claims a larger share of resources in a library managed in an organismic style. A library, therefore, which acts positively in the areas so far discussed in this chapter almost by definition will have organismic characteristics. Staff training and development are intimately affected. Not only will training flourish under certain management styles but training will itself affect that organization and its style of management in the way it is meant to in an organismic library.

Stages of training

As we investigate the various groups and their training needs we can distinguish:

1 Maintenance training, which enables the library to maintain its existing procedures and includes induction training for new entrants to the library system or to particular posts.
2 Basic updating and improvement training in identified areas.
3 Staff development (see pp.196–202).

Even libraries which do little other training involve themselves in induction training. In a sense they have to, otherwise new staff would be unable to perform existing tasks adequately, but many induction programmes are more systematic and recognize that all new staff need a general introduction to the service. It has to be recognized that induction introduces staff to the social and cultural aspects of the organization as much as to the jobs themselves. 'Systematic induction provides the basis for integrating the newcomer into the library as quickly and effectively as possible, and building a foundation for later job training and development. Additionally the positive interest by management in the newcomer can be an important motivator and help to reinforce the enthusiasm with which most newcomers tackle their job.'[11]

Induction of new staff really begins when the person is appointed. The information which is sent out immediately conveys a message to that person. It should therefore be welcoming and contain the basic details the person needs before commencing the job. The practice followed by many manufacturers in their service manuals congratulating purchasers on their judgement in selecting products might well be copied by employers welcoming staff to an institution or authority. It can be quite difficult to do this when it is also felt necessary to ask appointees to declare any previous criminal convictions and to complete medical questionnaires. It is thought best to refer to these requirements briefly in the welcoming letter but to provide the details separately. Basic information will normally include the place and hours of work, where and when to report on the first day and the name of the person to whom they should report, and what they need to bring with them.

On the first day the new employee should be welcomed formally. If possible this should be done by a senior person whatever the position of the employee to indicate immediately that every member of staff is considered important. The London Borough of Richmond-upon-Thames has produced a 'Library Induction Checklist: our key to success at work'. The checklist for Day 1 is reproduced in Figure 7.4.

Many institutions and authorities provide induction packs for new employees which contain a wide range of information about which staff should be aware. Some of these packs are very large and require at least some oral explanation if they are not to be consigned to the top shelf or the waste-bin. The pack given by the City of Edinburgh District Council typically contains leaflets on Health and Safety, Working Conditions, Race Relations, Discipline, Grievance Procedure, Equal Opportunities, Maternity Provisions, Threats or Violence to Employees, Special Leave Provisions, Career Breaks Scheme and Council Aims and Objectives.

The great danger with induction is information overload, usually with the best of intentions, in too short a time. Here, as in many management activities, the manager should try to see things from the point of view of the newcomer.

A study of succession to senior posts in libraries[12] has focused upon the first year or so in a new post. The study revealed the particular needs of new staff and described how they went about this settling-in period. Because there was a distinct lack of systematic induction new staff had to sort things out for themselves. The areas they considered most important are therefore of interest to library managers taking on new staff as well as to new staff themselves.

New staff learn most by working closely with other staff, talking, observing, asking and listening. Encouragement can be given, for example by involving them in joint projects with other staff. The most important persons both inside and outside the library have to be identified and arrangements made for the newcomer to meet them and, where desirable, to visit the places where they work.

A great deal can also be learned through reading reports, statistics, minutes of meetings, circulars, guides, manuals, memos etc. New staff can do this themselves, though important documents can be identified and provided. Within the first year many undertake their own surveys and investigations where they feel they require more information. Throughout this early period they need to be aware that they are making some impact immediately they

Checklist Day 1

Information or task	Date shown	Reviewed Both parties to initial	Satisfactorily learnt Both parties to initial
Referring enquiries, when and to whom.			
Description of staff facilities, staff room, toilets etc.			
Security of personal belongings.			
Briefly introduce to all staff on duty.			
Explain supervisory structure and who will be involved in training.			
Brief resumé of Health and Safety responsibilities, fire and emergency procedures.			
Introduce qualified first aiders.			
Organisational information, e.g. hours of duty, tea breaks, lunch hours, leave, sickness notification, timekeeping.			
Tour of the library drawing attention to general layout, varieties of stock.			
Brief introduction to the community the library serves.			
The importance of good public relations in both manner and appearance.			
Advise on the procedure for referring enquiries to other members of staff.			
Explain basic library terminology e.g. issue, discharge			

Figure 7.4   Extract from library induction checklist – Richmond-upon-Thames

take up the post and should therefore think about and prepare activities carefully. There is not necessarily a 'honeymoon' period during which mistakes will be easily forgiven.

The more senior the post the more likely there will be a considerable amount of choice by the post holder in determining how the time is spent. Most important in the first few months will be talking and listening to key persons in the library and in the organization, assessing strengths and weaknesses and working out a role. At the same time relationships will be built up with superiors, peers and subordinates. It is a great advantage if a superior can take on the role of an approachable aide to whom the new member of staff can turn whenever necessary. Good relationships are formed where an understanding of others' perceptions, beliefs, propensities to act and reaction to various approaches and situations are gained. The most important managerial skills required are discussed in Chapter 8 and once again the role of immediate superiors as approachable aides is crucial for self-development.

Induction training is necessarily conservatively biased and therefore there is a need both for updating and improvement training and for the general development of staff if innovative and positive librarianship is to take place.

Organizing specific training programmes

By looking at a specific training need we can discuss the way training might be organized in an effective way. Imagine, therefore, the following situation. There has been a considerable increase in the number of attempts to remove material from the university library without permission. Culprits are usually caught at the exit from the library when they pass through the security device. The librarian made representations to the directorate and the matter was put to the governors who agreed to an increase in penalties. The secretariat of the university drew up a recommended procedure to be followed at disciplinary hearings which would be attended by alleged offenders. The librarian was anxious to ensure that the library staff knew what to do when users were caught and how to conduct themselves at hearings. The training officer was asked to organize a training programme and the following steps were worked through to meet this training need.

Step 1 – Establish needs
(a) Analyse incidents between library staff and users caught trying to remove material without authorization.
(b) Ascertain the correct disciplinary procedures with the university secretariat including the role of library representative and witnesses.

Step 2 – Determine aim
Write down the aim of the training as clearly as possible. For example the ultimate aim is to ensure that:
(a) The library staff behave correctly and document incidents accurately.

	Method (see diagram p.179)	Responsible staff
Knowledge required of:		
1 Disciplinary rules and regulations	2(a) 2(e)	Secretariat
2 Methods employed by users to remove material without authorization	2(b) 2(c) 2(d)	Circulation librarian
3 Documentation required when reporting incidents	2(a) 2(e)	Secretariat. Deputy librarian
Skills:	2(c)	
4 Communication skills in dealing with users and meetings skills in disciplinary hearings	2(d) 2(e)	Training officer
Attitudes:	2(c)	All trainers
5 Objectivity in dealing with users. Belief in necessity to take action against attempted theft.	2(d) 2(e)	

Figure 7.5   Setting training objectives

(b) The library staff understand disciplinary procedures and perform effectively at disciplinary hearings.

Step 3 – Determine specific objectives
Decide on methods and trainers responsible. See Figure 7.5 for an example.

Training materials

The main methods used in training and development are displayed in Figure 7.6.

If we take training to mean the imparting of specific skills, knowledge and attitudes by direct methods usually involving a trainer, then the common methods are those shown in Figure 7.6 at 1 and 2(a)–(g). In the Disciplinary Procedures example, Step 3 is concerned with methods. The problem is to know what methods are most appropriate and how cost effective they are in terms of time and money. A trainer can best decide whether methods are appropriate by carefully considering the nature of the staff to be trained (their experience, existing knowledge, articulacy, motivation) and then looking at the range of methods available. In some cases there will be published

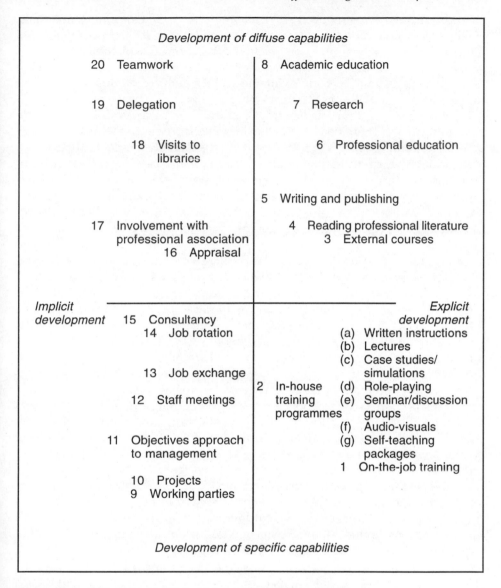

Figure 7.6　The main training and development methods

materials such as case studies, self-teaching packages and videos produced by libraries, commercial organizations and library schools. Examples of videos and training packages appear in the 'Handbook of library training practice'[13] and in The Library Association's 'Survey of Training Materials'[14] which lists non-book training packages used by libraries. In the UK the journal of the Library Association Personnel Training and Education Group, 'Personnel Training and Education' regularly includes articles on methods employed by libraries.

The computer is being utilized increasingly to produce training materials. Computer simulations have demonstrated on-line searching techniques and library housekeeping applications such as circulation control. Interactive video and hypertext are being developed widely in education and will become more important as packages become available and the skills of production are more widely learned and practised.

Another source of training materials is individual libraries and co-operative training groups. There has been a considerable increase in the number of co-operative training groups in the UK during the last few years, partly due to a recognition that co-ordination of activities can offer a better standard of training and a reduction of costs. 'Co-operative training in libraries'[15] describes thirteen of these schemes with detailed accounts of training activities and materials produced or in the planning stage. Again it may be helpful to approach a library school initially to get information on the most active libraries in the area from a training viewpoint. Some schools build up a file of training case studies, induction checklists and outlines of training programmes from libraries all over the country. All have case studies and practical exercises of their own, in addition to those from libraries, so there is a rich but often underused source of materials for use as models, for adaptation to a specific library's needs. The search for such material has been made easier with the publication in 1986 of the *Handbook of library training practice*,[16] which includes many practical examples and outlines good training practice in a range of types of libraries. There are specialist sections on training methods in information sources, automation, conservation, stock management and audiovisual librarianship. All of these show extracts from programmes that have been tried and tested in practice, as well as indicating how to select the most appropriate methods for different kinds of training, from the induction level to the level of training special services staff in community information and interpersonal skills in dealing with different user groups.

In the US Shuman[17] and many others have published collections in library management covering such issues as censorship, interpersonal conflicts, politicking for library managers, and budgeting problems. In the UK Hewitt's pioneering text[18] in the late 1960s was only followed by Oldman and Wills[19] in the late 1970s but more recently Jones' and Jordan's *Case studies in library management*[20] has filled a gap and can be used as a companion to this volume. The problem with such collections is that they tend to be culture-bound, and need careful adaptation from one country to another, or even, some would argue, from one library system to another, when the organizational cultures are very different.

Practical training methods

Lectures and talks

Lectures and talks, whether or not accompanied by audiovisual aids, are normally dominated by the speaker and give minimal opportunity for contributions from the passive audience. Careful consideration therefore should be given to the kind of information conveyed in this way. It is satisfactory for communicating ideas and introducing topics, but is poor at conveying detailed information, unless various take-away handouts are issued by the speaker so that the audience may follow up a general introduction with written guidelines or instructions for action.

An easily followed structure is essential, and it is helpful if the speaker sets this out at the beginning (orally or on a handout or on an overhead projector transparency) and refers to it at various intervals. It is important to decide in advance the key points which you wish to communicate and recapitulate to reinforce them. They may also be reinforced by illustrating with audiovisual aids (audiotape, video cassettes, slides and OHPs are the most common). When these are used make sure in advance that all the equipment works, that it is all plugged in, and that you are knowledgeable about the various controls. This may sound obvious, but it clearly needs to be reiterated, as everyone will know who is a frequent attender at professional or recreational meetings, or who is an *aficionado* of the John Cleese Video Arts Production[21] on the use of, or rather the hazards of, audiovisuals.

Talks which go on for longer than half an hour are not likely to keep the attention of the audience – our attention span is lessening all the time as a result of television conditioning. If you must go on longer than that have a 'buzz group' for neighbouring groups of three trainees to talk to each other about points made, or ask people to write down their views or experience as a relief from just listening. This is often more productive than saying hopefully: 'Are there any questions so far?', which nearly always draws a negative response, unless there is a determined subversive in the group.

The level of language and the tone used (littered with witticisms or sonorously earnest, chatty and informal or sermonlike and portentous) is only partly a product of one's personality. Try to match it to your audience. Check whether they think it does, by sensing their response as the talk proceeds. Look at their faces and talk directly to them, rather than to the ceiling or the back wall or worst of all your own notes. In training, new words and terminology may be necessary, and if you are in doubt as to whether your audience understands these terms, give out a glossary on a sheet of paper (often necessary when talking about computer systems) or explain meanings as you go along.

The most common problems trainers experience here are first, trying to communicate too much detailed information, and second, delivering their talks in a manner which is dull or distracting because of perhaps unconscious mannerisms. To overcome these problems it is advisable to establish how much of the

Please *ring* the score for each feature. High scores for high achievement, e.g. ⑤.

OBJECTIVES
1 Audience made aware of the objectives of the presentation from the start in terms of what members should be able to achieve.

1   2   3   4   5

STRUCTURE
2 Audience clear about how the presentation is meant to proceed and what their role should be.

1   2   3   4   5

3 The presentation clearly followed the logical structure that had been out-lined.

1   2   3   4   5

ARRANGEMENTS
4 Arrangements had clearly been made beforehand giving confidence that the presentation would proceed without foreseeable problems, e.g. seating arrangements, audiovisuals, timing…

1   2   3   4   5

LANGUAGE
5 The language was easily understood by the audience, e.g. non-jargon.

1   2   3   4   5

CONTENT
6 All points discussed were important ones. Less important/marginal ones left to discussion session.

1   2   3   4   5

METHOD
7 Held the interest of the audience the whole time.

1   2   3   4   5

PRESENTATION
8 The presentation had:
   (1) Sufficient variety.

1   2   3   4   5

Figure 7.7   Checklist of features of a good presentation

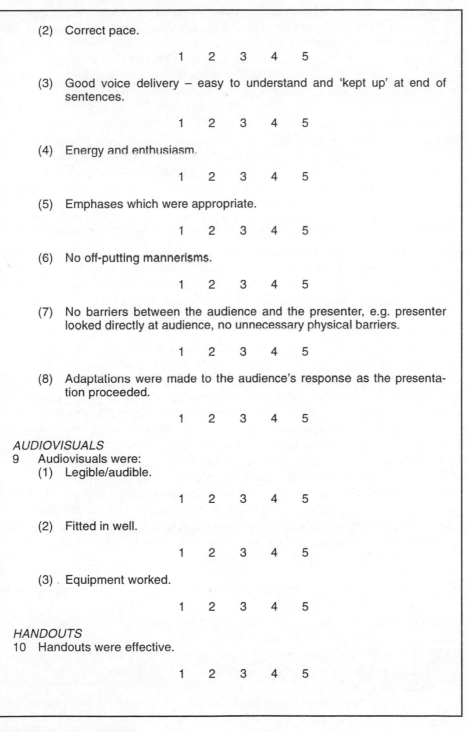

(2) Correct pace.

1   2   3   4   5

(3) Good voice delivery – easy to understand and 'kept up' at end of sentences.

1   2   3   4   5

(4) Energy and enthusiasm.

1   2   3   4   5

(5) Emphases which were appropriate.

1   2   3   4   5

(6) No off-putting mannerisms.

1   2   3   4   5

(7) No barriers between the audience and the presenter, e.g. presenter looked directly at audience, no unnecessary physical barriers.

1   2   3   4   5

(8) Adaptations were made to the audience's response as the presentation proceeded.

1   2   3   4   5

AUDIOVISUALS
9   Audiovisuals were:
    (1) Legible/audible.

1   2   3   4   5

(2) Fitted in well.

1   2   3   4   5

(3) Equipment worked.

1   2   3   4   5

HANDOUTS
10 Handouts were effective.

1   2   3   4   5

Figure 7.7   Concluded

information would be better communicated in typed handouts, or in a looseleaf staff manual for staff to look up later. As for speaking mannerisms, among the most distracting are speaking too fast or too slow, in a monotonous unvarying rhythm, waving hands about all the time, or wearing out the carpet by walking around in small circles while talking. The analysis sheet shown in Figure 7.7 has been used successfully by the authors to obtain feedback from audiences.

Written instructions

The most common forms of written instructions are leaflets, cards, looseleaf manuals, notices containing flow charts or diagrams for a particular section of the library, or a particular process. The trainer is then certain that the important points are not forgotten, and the trainee can check and refer back to the instructions when the trainer is no longer there to explain. Thus they are economical in saving the time of the trainer. Also people learn at different speeds and many staff find it a comfort to be able to remind themselves of procedures at their own speed, and without a trainer asking them whether they understand fully. In the early stages of training it is very hard for trainees to know whether they understand or not, so that may not be a meaningful question unless it is checked by asking them to carry out an activity to demonstrate their understanding.

In preparing written instructions it is important to provide a clear logical structure, and this should be reflected in the layout, headings and subheadings, numbers of pages and sections, and in the use of diagrams (often more appropriate than long paragraphing of prose for explaining, for instance, a staffing structure, or the stages in book processing). At Manchester Metropolitan University Library a house-style manual has been compiled to ensure that all publications are pleasant on the eye and easy to follow. Figure 7.8 shows some of the rules. The more practical examples there are, the better, as many trainees are bemused by abstractions. The form and level of language must be relevant to the trainee group, just as in oral communication. It should be noted that forward-looking organizations inside and outside the library and information profession are making a deliberate effort to communicate in non-sexist and non-racist language. Scan every written communication and script for talks or videos, to check the following points:

1   Use 'he or she' or else the plural, rather than 'he', except when referring to a specific male individual.
2   Use job titles rather than pronouns, e.g. head librarian or children's librarian, rather than the stereotypical 'he' or 'she'.
3   Use the word 'woman' not 'girl'. 'Lady' is best avoided, as is its male equivalent 'Gentleman'. Address people as 'colleagues', but not, please, 'fellow librarians'.
4   Many people for some reason see red when addressed as chairperson, but there seems to be a growing acceptance of the abbreviated 'chair' to avoid the sexist 'chairman'.

Quick Reference
Library Typography and Layout

Library

· Typeface

Times - text and headings.
Helvetica - titles and headings.

use all the same face or change for headings.

· Typesize

Text: 9, 10, 11pt for text.
2pt line spacing.

Headings in text:12, 14 pt.

Titles:
up to 20pt for A5 size
up to 18pt for 1/3 A4
up to 24pt for A4
*(these can only be a rough guide, this very much
depends on the length of the title and the type of
illustration it is used with)*

· Line length

No longer than 10 12 words.
No shorter than five words.

· Paragraphs

No indention.
One line space between paragraphs.
Two line spaces before heading.

· Covers

Try to use short titles.
Do not split titles by illustrations.
Use space to emphasise image and text.
Visually align text and image with the grid and
each other.

· Illustrations

Align illustrations to the grid.
Leave at least two line spaces between the
illustration and the text.

If illustration looks awkward or is floating
in the space put a box key line around it,
and align the box to the grid.

· Abbreviations

There should be no full point between
letters or at the end of abbreviations
eg DTI not D.T.I.

· Alignment

Always align headings across columns.
Always align the lines of each column both
horizontally and vertically.

· Numbers in text

Spell out in full numbers below ten, use
arabic for those over ten, except at the
beginning of the paragraph or sentence
when they should also be spelt out in full.

· Date

Date each publication at the end of the text,
range the date left leaving three line spaces
after the end of the text.

16 June 1994

Figure 7.8   House-style manual

There are other strategies to choose depending where you stand on the sexist/ non-sexist frontier, or 'no-person's land'. Those who favour positive discrimination would use 'she' as a generic term, just as 'he' has been dominant for time immemorial. They would reverse the order some or all of the time, in phrases like Mrs and Mr Smith. They would prefer Ms to Miss or Mrs, to parallel the position of men who have the same 'Mister' whatever their marital state. Those who dislike 'Ms' on aesthetic grounds, or because of its occupational associations (at least for librarians) may simply use their forename and surname without any prefix, and address other people in the same way, as the Quakers have sensibly done for a number of centuries.

An increasing number of journals are changing their rules for contributors, to reduce sexist habits in publications. The US is ahead of the UK on this score, as can be seen from the terms used in the two countries to describe small special libraries. The UK still favours 'one-man band' while the US have rejected that in favour of the 'one-person library'. In general individual rules for avoiding sexism are not as important as changing people's attitudes, so in all communications the aim should be to avoid stereotyping the sexes, for example by implying that all managers are men, that all junior assistants are women, or that because a woman answers a telephone she must be a man's secretary rather than an executive.

Discussion groups

The following four methods all require active participation by trainees. When successful they are extremely effective but when they are poorly managed they can be counter-productive. Research by Jones[22] has helped to provide guidelines for trainers which, if followed, should ensure a positive outcome in most circumstances. Fuller treatment can be found in Part 1 of *Case studies in library management*.[23]

The purpose of discussion groups is to let all members express their views on a problem, so the size should be limited to six to twelve. They may be led by a trainer, or by a group member, or may remain informal and leaderless. Inevitably if the trainer leads, group members will talk less to each other and the trainer will talk for a quite high proportion of the time. Therefore if the objective is for the group to talk more, it is better for the trainer to let the group get on with it, or only join it after the halfway mark.

Discussion groups should be used when the topic lends itself to a variety of opinions and alternative solutions. They should be avoided when there is nothing much to talk about and the topic is straightforward and does not lend itself to a number of different interpretations. It can be useful for developing staff's interpersonal skills in a safe professional context, where most people should have some view to put forward, and are willing to listen to others' views, so as to modify their own starting position. It is particularly appropriate for changing people's attitudes, rather than for imparting knowledge or skills. It is, for instance, widely used, along with role-play, in local authority race awareness courses, which many librarians from the major cities attend.

The factors which tend to make discussion groups go well are, first, the clarity of the objectives. Are group members agreed on the task before them, the problem to be solved, and the outcome that the trainer expects? Second, the group needs to have some structure to get through the task, and that requires a chairperson to review and summarize and mark progress towards goals, and a reporter to keep a record of the group's decisions. The record is better kept in some visible form for all to see, rather than in the notebook of the reporter only – main ideas can be summarized and subheadings and criticisms of ideas on a black or white board, or use flow pens on wall charts. Third, the group will be most satisfactory when everybody takes part and there are no members being carried by the rest. A good chairperson can help by bringing everyone in, or going round the table in turn, but so can other group members by engaging in building and supporting behaviour (see Chapter 8 on interpersonal skills for meetings).

Common problems encountered in discussion groups are domination of the group by the trainer, or by one or two monopolizing individuals, and corresponding retreat into passivity by other group members. This can be alleviated by dividing groups into two, one of the higher contributors and the other of the lower contributors, so that everyone will feel more in their element. To avoid leader dominance the trainer should organize the session so that he or she is not in the group all the time, inhibiting the others, but only comes in at the beginning and end to explain and to hear views and to comment and summarize. Aggressive and obstructive behaviour is uncommon in groups of library and information workers. On the rare occasions when it happens, in our experience, it has had its origin outside the immediate activity, perhaps because people have been compulsorily sent on the training course, or because they have a grudge of some kind against management and wish to get it off their chests before they do anything else. Some people find that the training discussion group is the only opportunity they have for expressing their grievances. In that case it may be worth the trainer taking ten minutes out of the programme for people to let down their hair, before continuing.

Case studies

Case studies are particularly useful in management and interpersonal skills training, because they simulate real-life problems and give trainees a chance to find solutions in a low-risk situation, where they can try out ideas and see what happens, without the possibly disastrous effects which might, if the ideas are half-baked, accrue in real life. The assumption is that this is a learning experience which will develop judgement, and make people into better decision makers. The method is related to discussion groups, in that case studies are usually tackled by a group; though they can be used with individuals as well, who write up their ideas and give them to the tutor or trainer. Thus they give trainees practice in interpersonal negotiations with colleagues, as well as thinking things out for themselves. This is useful for real life where ideas remain pretty futile unless they can be implemented, and that means persuading other people that they are viable and valuable.

It is preferable for trainers to write their own case studies, or to adapt existing ones to their own context. It saves time to use existing cases, but they should be carefully chosen to be relevant to the trainees' level of expertise and experience. It does not go down well to set problems which in real life would be the responsibility of senior management, and impose them on beginning professionals.

The trainer's task is to write or adapt case studies that are credible and do not go 'over-the-top', unless the objective is to entertain rather than instruct. That is not all. Having had copies of the case study reprographed, the trainer must still draw up a programme of instructions on running the case study. For example, the trainer may organize the group into fours or sixes, give them half-an-hour to come up with solutions by discussion, ask for a report at the end (verbal, or overhead projector transparencies or wall posters), and leave time for critical comment on the solutions of the minigroups, and how they compare with classic solutions as set out, say, in management textbooks, or practised in more progressive libraries. In addition to all this, the trainer should work out how the trainees will absorb the case study material. It should ideally be given to them in advance, or sent with the course programme, so that they will come to the discussion with some prior knowledge, and not have to spend the first half hour trying to grasp what the problem is.

If case studies are being written by the trainer, remember that too much detail will confuse and bog down the learners, while too little will mean that they will spend the first session asking for more information. Requests for more information should be approached warily. This is often an excuse for not using the actual information given. One of the reasons why the case study method is so valuable is that it tests people's ability to apply ideas and strategies, and to make use of information sifted from working documents. Reluctance to do this, and slowness in developing these skills, are an unfortunate aftermath of formal teacher-centred education systems. The trainer needs to explain why the method is being used, and equally the trainees should be helped by being given some ideas and theories to apply, in an introduction or handout. Otherwise they will chat around the problem, and come up with rule-of-thumb solutions which make no reference to relevant management or communication ideas.

The most common problems trainers encounter in using the case study method are pragmatism and regression to teacher-centred 'right answer' stances. Trainees may sit around chatting about the problem situation, without any incisive analysis or ability to get to the crux, in the hope that in half an hour they will be told the solution by the trainer. In order to avoid this trainees should work individually or in pairs, writing down ideas, and listing points on what the problem is, and how it may be solved. If no preparation has been done, it may be necessary to issue a handout containing some basic management strategies which could solve the problem. For example, if the case study were about deciding on a formal staff appraisal system, one or two examples of appraisal interview forms used in other libraries (see Chapter 6), plus a ten-point checklist of what appraisal is meant to do from the management literature, would be helpful.

A further problem in using case studies is that people need group skills to work with others in solving a problem. They may be unused to any other kind of work besides individual work, and it may be difficult to gain co-operation to reach a consensus, without individuals feeling mortified because 'their' idea got lost, and a 'worthless' solution was accepted just because a dominant group member kept pushing it rather aggressively. It should be pointed out that people have a choice of behaviour in groups, and can learn to modify their own and indeed other people's by practising the helpful group behaviours (proposing, building, supporting, openness, summarizing, seeking and giving information, and bringing in) and developing strategies for coping with the unhelpful group behaviours (blocking, shutting out, difficulty stating, negative disagreeing, defending/attacking). Case studies are an opportunity for trying out some of these behaviours and learning from the experience.

Role play

Role play is an optional extra to the case study method. Rather than discussing a problem from the outside, the trainees play the roles of the people in the case study and try to reach a solution which takes account of feelings as well as rational analysis. It is used to explain, demonstrate and sensitize, most often in the interpersonal skills areas of staff/user relations, or supervisor/staff counselling and appraisal.

In setting up a role play the trainer must write the scenario, making sure that the incident corresponds to the teaching aim (how to give a counselling interview, how to open up a reference interview), and that it is sufficiently realistic and close to the trainees' experience to be credible to them. A role card may be given to each player, containing details of their position in the library, what they believe to be the circumstances surrounding the incident, and the problem incident itself. The best way to run role plays is to have groups of threes, with two role playing and the third observing their behaviour and commenting at the end of the ten-minute role play. Role reversal is useful, so that each member of the trio has a chance to play both sides of the situation (e.g. from the supervisor's view, and from the junior assistant's view). At the end of the role play it is important to get comments from all the observers, and to draw out general conclusions about what has been learnt, in the hope that learning transfer is encouraged.

The usual problems experienced in using role play are that people worry about having to act, or enter into the role play as if it were just acting, by 'hamming it up'. Emphasize that they are being asked to play themselves, and try to imagine how they would behave in the kind of situation they are given. If trainees are diffident about starting, feeling shy and embarrassed, the trainer may help to break the ice by doing a dummy run with a colleague or one of the extroverted group members. It is also possible to use 'shadows', that is, each trainee has another person backing them up, and they can consult on how to play the role, or take turns to share the same role. In a really tongue-tied group there is the strategy of 'group role play' in which three or four people talk to each other about how the role should be played and only one of them has to play it. A real-life outsider (maybe someone who conducts appraisal interviews in everyday life) may be invited to attend, and give a demonstration of how he or she would have handled the problem in their own job.

Simulations

Zachert[24] provides a valuable guide to simulations in education and training for library management. The book includes detailed examples of the method. A simulation provides enough basic working documents on a library (annual report, readers' guide, estimates, book fund, minutes of library committee, working parties on automation etc.) to provide a realistic background for problem solving. It is a comprehensive form of training, in that it incorporates discussion groups, role play and practical problems or case studies, all within the setting of a simulated library. Zachert provides simulations of American industrial and government libraries. There are also now British simulations of a public library system, *The Bishopsbury Simulation*,[25] and of a polytechnic library system, the Blackford Simulation.[26] Bishopsbury gives examples of how to use the materials in the package to set up exercises as required, but this can be a time-consuming activity. Blackford provides a set of twelve management exercises, with instructions on how to write others as needed. It covers management of audiovisuals, implementing automation, multisite problems among subject librarians, selection, training and appraisal of staff, and drawing up objectives for a somewhat anarchic site library.

Besides these rather elaborate simulations, which are time-consuming to prepare, and therefore only worth using on a sustained training or education programme, one-off simulations of specific library activities or operations, whether manual or computerized, are valuable. The object is to give trainees practice in a risk-free setting, where mistakes do not matter. The method is used for training non-professional staff in, for example, shelving order or filing orders of various kinds. They are given a sequence of documents or books to put in order, or merely a list of class numbers to arrange in correct order, following the library's rules. Only when they have reached about a 90 per cent degree of accuracy are they released to the real-life equivalent. Simulations of automated systems are increasingly used in libraries to train staff in the acceptance and operation of new systems.

Programmed learning

Programmed learning, although suffering a rather bad press in recent years after the original euphoria in the 1960s, is appropriate in library training which deals with fairly clear-cut factual questions, which do not need much discussion. Examples might be using the catalogue or the simpler levels of

A reader comes in and says to the library assistant, 'I want to buy a book called *Games People Play*, but I don't know the author. Can your help?'

Would you look in BBIP   (Turn to page 10)
        or BNB   (Turn to page 11)
   or Bookseller   (Turn to page 12)

Page 10 says:

'Correct. The borrower wants to *buy* the book, so it is important to know whether it is in print. But if very new may not be in BBIP yet, so try Bookseller as second source. Give borrower details needed to buy the book (author, title, publisher, price...)'

Page 11 says:

'Not the easiest way. Borrower wants to *buy* the book, so although you would find details in BNB you would still have to consult BBIP to find out whether in print. So check details in BBIP.'

Page 12 says:

'This would be correct if the book happens to be very recent, but it is easier to try BBIP first, for that contains all books in print apart from recent ones. So find out details from BBIP.'

Figure 7.9   Example of programmed learning

using reference books either to answer reader enquiries or for bibliographical checking.

Its use seems to have been greater in public libraries than in academic or special libraries, and the example (Figure 7.9) from Coventry Public Library gives a typical use of programmed learning for teaching simple enquiry work.

Each of the answers on pages 10, 11 and 12 then refers to page 13, so that the trainer can check that he or she has made a correct note of the details which the reader would need to buy the book.

The advantage of programmed learning is that the trainees can work through it in their own time, but the trainer needs to spend a lot of time compiling the text, unless there is co-operation between libraries. Also the text may get out of date quickly and need frequent revision, unless care is taken to select material that is less likely to lose currency and relevance. The system is quite flexible if used in conjunction with discussion groups with the trainer, rather than leaving the trainees uncertain as to why some answers are right, and why alternative approaches are less valid. They may indeed be equally valid – the trainer should be scrupulous in accepting alternative answers just as good as the ones in the text.

The first disadvantage of programmed learning is that although it appears to be self-sufficient, it usually is not, and trainers need to fit it into a wider context, for example by giving advance instruction, so that the trainees are capable of selecting answers intelligently rather than guessing. The trainer should also find out why trainees chose certain answers, and check that they have in fact learned what was intended (rather than how to use a programmed text, for instance!). Another limitation of programmed learning is that it is said only to teach facts rather than skills and attitudes, but this depends on the way it is used by the trainer who may just check for right or wrong answers or who may follow up the answers with a discussion on ways of solving a problem.

A more sophisticated version of programmed learning is the action maze, which is like a case study but with a list of alternative actions/decisions added at the end. The trainee thinks about the situation, makes a decision, which will lead him or her to another page containing comment on this decision and what it would mean. If it was a bad decision the trainee is given more information to help go back and make a better decision. Zachert gives an example of an action maze in her book of simulations for teaching library management.[27]

Computer-aided learning (CAL)

Computer-aided learning (CAL), the most recent development in programmed learning, developed rapidly in libraries in the 1980s. It is used for two main purposes: user education and staff training (in addition to the taken-for-granted presence in libraries of CAL packages in any subject which the library covers). A CAL package may often be dual function, in that it is designed to teach users how to use the library or its catalogue, but then also proves helpful to teach new staff.

The value of CAL packages is that they are interactive, so that trainees are tested in what they have learned and get immediate feedback on whether they are right or wrong. They can be used independently of a tutor or trainer, by individual learners or small groups around a terminal. The disadvantages are that they are time-consuming to construct, and there is a tendency in some packages for the multiple choice answers to be rather rigid, not allowing for imaginative approaches by the trainee. Thus they have some of the defects of the programmed learning texts of the 1960s and 1970s, which were criticized for rewarding 'tramline thinking' and penalizing 'lateral thinking'.

A typical CAL programme for training in the use of the library was developed at the Australian National University Library[28] in 1984. Its primary purpose was to teach new students how to use the library and its catalogue, and how to research a topic by understanding the uses of dictionaries and encyclopaedias, indexes and abstracts, on-line IR, and audiovisual materials. It was left in the library foyer for eight weeks from the beginning of term, and was designed to be highly user-friendly, to encourage widespread use. Responses to questions required the user to press one keystroke only, and at the end of each frame the user was told what to do next ('go on', 'revise' etc.). The user could control the speed of the programme. Menus were provided to increase user involvement, and enable the user to choose from a wide range of options, such as how to trace a journal article, or how to find audiovisual materials on a topic. User comprehension was tested at intervals by multiple-choice questions, and the answers were scored. At the end of the programme the total score was given with comments such as 'You're a whiz' or 'You haven't been concentrating very well, have you?' From the trainer's point of view the computer has an additional valuable function. It collects statistics of use and rates of success in carrying out the programme, which may lead to modifications and/or wider promotion of the package.

A further development in CAL programmes is the use of interactive video for training purposes. University College, Cardiff, for example, has trained on-line searchers (mainly intermediaries, but some undergraduates have also been instructed) using Philips Laservision videodisc controlled by a purpose-written computer programme. A potentially exciting development has been hypertext. Although its history dates back to the 1940s, it was 1987 before hypertext activity blossomed. 'The basic components of hypertext can be summarized as:

fragments or nodes of text
links
a storage structure which accounts for the other two'.[29]

The author and the users are able to link and navigate from one item to another. Hypermedia extends hypertext to cover other media such as graphics, sound, still pictures, and video. An example of its use is the Hypertour Tourist Information System[30] produced by Gateshead Libraries and Arts to provide customers with information on where to stay, what to see, where to eat and where to shop. Elizabeth Duncan,[31] investigating applications of hypermedia, was aware of its great potential for training but had found little activity by companies. The ideal application of hypermedia would be where a combination of theoretical and practical knowledge is necessary so that text can be supplemented by 'diagrams or digitised still or moving pictures of how a piece of equipment operates'.[32] One can envisage many such applications in library and information work. Elizabeth Duncan is right in her view that systems should be developed as supplementary to the working of the human mind, rather than trying to replace it – a back-up to any form of human explanation.

On-the-job training

On-the-job training, or 'sitting next to Nellie' in folk language, is valuable so long as Nellie is a good communicator and trainer, but being dependent on the Nellies of this world for all training is hazardous unless all Nellies are trained how to train. They need to be given as a minimum a one-day work-shop, during which they write specific objectives for training and practising methods appropriate for attaining each of the objectives covered in this chapter. Finally they would practise working out methods of evaluating the success of training, and would go back to their jobs with a much developed sense of responsibility for 'coaching' their staff on-the-job. See Chapter 8 on Supervision for more details. The dividing line between training and supervision is rightly blurred.

Assessment of competences at work is a major feature in the UK of Scottish and National Vocational Qualifications (S/NVQs). Some Draft Standards for Information and Library Services were produced in 1993[33] and sent out for consultation. The Standards include the work of staff in a range of grades and have been derived from the 'functional map' created for the Library and Information Services Sector. Each 'key function' within the map is broken down into 'key roles' which are further broken down into units of competence which can be tested in a work situation. The purpose is to create standards which have national recognition thus increasing the mobility of information and library staff. It is envisaged that many large-scale employing organizations will become assessment centres whilst smaller organizations will probably use colleges. Qualifications for Information and Library Services Sector are due to be presented to the National Council for Vocational Qualifications by December 1995.

Evaluating training

In many areas of management evaluation is not attempted in any systematic manner, not only because it is difficult but because managers prefer to 'do' rather than spend valuable time evaluating. At its crudest evaluation is the comparison of stated objectives with achievements. As far as training is concerned the achievements, especially in more complex areas such as interpersonal skills, cannot be easily measured or isolated from other influences so that it is difficult to be sure about the value of training. Evaluation is important if the quality of training is to be improved and if it is to be made clear that it is the effect of training that matters most of all.

There are several levels of evaluation each more difficult than the last yet probably more important:

1 *Completion*: The fact that the training took place at all. This can be noted against a checklist of training activities such as those shown in Figures 7.1 and 7.2.
2 *Reaction*: The reactions of trainees to the training experience itself – what they thought about it, how they enjoyed it, what they would retain or leave out if it were offered in future.
3 *Learning*: How well the trainees have learned the knowledge, skills and attitudes the trainers set out to teach them. Other learning may also have taken place, perhaps contrary to the desired objectives.
4 *Job performance*: How well trainees have 'internalized' the training and applied the learning to the job.

5 *The library*: The effect of the training on the functioning of the library – the good or otherwise that has resulted for both the department or unit and the library as a whole in terms, for example, of increased productivity, quality, atmosphere, morale.

Evaluation can take place at various times by various people depending on which of the above are being measured. The first three can be measured during and at the end of the training while the last two need a longer period before a true evaluation is possible. Trainees are dependent upon others who may not have been part of the actual training but whose co-operation and support is vital if organizational improvements are to be effected. Too often trainees attend a course and come back full of enthusiasm, only to find they are unable to use their new knowledge and skills. In such situations the training can prove counter-productive.

Figure 7.10 illustrates the points made in this section by showing how training for dealing with library users might be evaluated.

Time	Level	Evaluator	Method
Mid-training	Reaction Learning	Trainer Trainees	Oral discussion among trainers and with trainees Observation Written tests
End of training	Completion Reaction Learning	Trainer Trainees	Written questionnaire to obtain trainees' opinions Oral discussion among trainers and with trainees Written tests Observation
Period after training	Job performance The library	Line manager	Observation Coaching Analysis of complaints by users, other staff etc.

Figure 7.10 Example of training evaluation

The most popular form of evaluation is the written questionnaire completed at the end of training, preferably following the last session. Some will wish to send it in later but most are prepared to complete the questionnaire on the spot which saves a great deal of time. Williamson, in an excellent piece on the evaluation of training, states that the trainer may expect feedback on:

1 The content of the programme. Was it the right level for the trainees? Was the timescale right?

2 How good was the presentation? What was the quality of the speakers/ trainers?

3 Were the domestic arrangements adequate?

4 Did the course fulfil its own objectives and the personal objectives of those attending?[34]

Our own experience has been that a few questions will provide most of this information and will be happily answered by most participants, e.g.:

1 Did the course meet your expectations? YES/NO

2 What were its strengths?

3 What were its weaknesses?

4 If the course were to be offered again, what changes would you recommend?

5 Any other comments?

Staff development

The training discussed so far in this chapter should improve individual performance in the directions desired by the library manager. If it is well done, staff will also be developed personally – there will be a blending of the learned skills, knowledge and attitudes enabling individuals to make significant, and increasingly self-confident contributions to the library's performance, while feeling a sense of achievement and satisfaction. It is not, however, the explicitly designed activities which alone develop staff as effective members of the organization, but also what Weber refers to as 'the library personnel environment itself'.[35] It includes a whole range of factors which socialize new staff into the existing library ethos, and which may also deter or encourage long-serving staff in taking part in professional and personal development. These factors cover supervisory style, senior management policies and practices in participation, consultation and communication, and the various sectional climates, within which different work groups evolve their own 'in-group' norms of behaviour and communication.

Robert James, for example, writing about the training and management of automation is insistent that 'the most important element in training is the style of management'. At Kingston Polytechnic the 'managerial principle was that people should participate in decisions about areas of work for which they had or would have responsibility'.[36]

For a number of years libraries have been affected by lack of resources during recessions whilst demands on their services have increased. In such situations staff development can easily be viewed as a luxury which cannot be afforded, especially when it takes staff away from their place of work. The alternative view is that staff development is more important when resources are scarce because stagnation is likely when there is lack of mobility both internally through promotion and externally into posts elsewhere. Although the library may stagnate, elements in the world outside do not and well-motivated staff will want to take advantage of these developments to improve services. Advances in information technology are the most obvious examples and to make the best use of them considerable training input is required.

Staff development is sometimes distinguished from 'continuing education'. The former is used in the US to cover the 'systematic development of employees' skills, competences and attitudes in order to enhance organizational effectiveness', whereas continuing education is used to describe 'individual learning experience, often, but not necessarily resulting in increased organizational effectiveness'.[37] There can be conflict between individual and organizational needs, but development as opposed to training generally acknowledges that managers have an obligation to help their staff reach full potential, even if this means they eventually lose them on promotion to another institution.

In recent years there has been a more rigorous assessment of the potential value of development events particularly expensive external events. This is another area where, initially, self-assessment can take place. Applicants can be asked to provide the following information:

What do you hope to gain from this course?
What do you think its value will be to the library?
Is it designed to enable effective learning to take place?
   e.g. Objectives clear?
      Methods appropriate?
      Tutors qualified?
      Good use made of time?
Is it worth the cost?
How will the library manage in your absence?

Jones uses continuing education to mean:

all those activities after the initial qualification in librarianship which contribute to ongoing learning, whether on the job, with the employing library, or provided by outside bodies such as the Library Association and the library schools... through courses, conferences and workshops (which may or may not lead to further qualifications).[38]

Many studies have been carried out in order to discover librarians' motivations for continuing education and, although different terminology is used, the findings are roughly similar and can therefore be employed by trainers wishing to encourage staff to become involved.

Smith and Burgin's research[39] carried out in 1988 and 1989 is consistent with other findings. The main motivation was professional competence – 'the development of proficiencies needed to maintain quality performance, the development of new knowledge and skills, the improvement of on-the-job competence and productivity and concerns with the quality of library service and new developments in the field'. Stone[40] and Neal[41] similarly found that exposure to new ideas and the chance to use the new knowledge on the job were significant motivators.

The second highest motivator was patron service – 'the more effective accommodation of patron needs, the ability to meet patron expectations better, the increased likelihood of providing better patron service, an increase in proficiency with patrons and the improvement in individual service to patrons'.[42]

These motivators have far greater influence than personal concerns such as financial gain, professional advancement and security, though Smith and Burgin found this latter motivator was rated significantly higher by librarians who had been at their present position for seven or more years.

Professional competence and improved patron service are high on the list of reasons given by The Library Association for introducing its 'Framework for Continuing Professional Development' in 1991:

> Evidence from many other occupational groups which have sought to maintain the status of their workforce and ensure high standards of services, is that a formal framework for the continuing professional development of their members is helpful.[43]

Just as appraisals systems have moved towards self-appraisal so The Library Association scheme is based upon individuals taking responsibility for their own lifelong learning. All levels of staff are invited to analyse their present jobs, future roles and personal priorities in order to identify their development needs and to work with employers in meeting those needs. Not only is it anticipated that services will improve but also personal concerns, particularly career development, would benefit. Although it is hoped that funding of libraries will improve in the future, there is reason to believe that 'career planning can become one of the neutralizers of employee frustration and insecurity brought about by limited possibilities of upward mobility caused by severe fiscal policy and current and future cutbacks'.[44]

A feature of staff development is that a great deal of the learning takes place on the job. This is borne out by the research findings of Jones[45] who asked librarians to choose their preferred continuing education activities and found the following were the top ten:

Public librarians
1   Informal discussion with colleagues
2   Taking an active part in staff meetings
3   Giving talks to groups outside the profession
4   Writing staff aids for use in the library
5   Visiting other libraries
6   Receiving in-service training
7   Writing guides, aids for use of readers
8   Reading librarianship literature
9   Attending conferences and meetings
10   Taking part in working parties in your library

Academic librarians
1   Informal discussion with colleagues
2   Taking an active part in staff meetings
3   Visiting other libraries
4   Writing guides, aids for use of readers
5   Writing discussion papers for use in library
6   Reading librarianship literature
7   Studying for further qualifications
8   Attending conferences and meetings
9   { Receiving in-service training
    { Attending short courses

The Library Association scheme encourages employers to create the climate
and appropriate support systems for continuous staff development as a positive contribution to meeting the objectives of the employing organization. Its
guidelines for employers are shown in Figure 7.11. A partnership between the
employer and the employee is a key element in The Library Association's
framework. In drawing up their plans staff are encouraged to discuss their
proposals with employers to obtain their views and agree their role and support. A good organization will already be providing support information in
the staff training and development policy statements referred to earlier in this
chapter. Features of sound practice will include time off and expenses for
attending professional activities, a staff library, a staff development programme
with outside speakers, visits to other libraries and a staff newsletter or journal.
There should also be opportunities for comment on how the library is running
as a whole and the performance of the individual's own section. In Chapter 6
we have already discussed ways in which individual and group appraisal can
meet many of these requirements.

   The practice of visiting other organizations, which was given a high rating
as a continuing education activity in Jones' research, has been developed into
a more formal method of quality improvement referred to as 'benchmarking'.

> Benchmarking has become a hot topic. Many firms are keen to discover every-
> thing they can about the technique because of their need to improve perform-
> ance, while others already using benchmarking wish to keep their successes a
> secret.[46]

The method involves these stages:

1   Identification of areas of own library where there is scope for improve-
    ment.
2   Identification of libraries performing well in those areas.
3   Preparation for visit by a group of staff. The group needs to be clear about
    what it is looking for and how it is to proceed.
4   Investigation as to how new superior practices can be integrated into own
    library.

2. GUIDELINES FOR EMPLOYERS

The purpose of this guideline is to encourage employers to create the climate and appropriate support systems for continuous staff development as a positive contribution to meeting the objectives of the employing organisation.

ACTION   Show commitment to continuing professional development.

Good Practice
- Include a statement of CPD and a strategy for implementation in the relevant organisational documents. Communicate policy and plans to employees.
- Specify the responsibilities of managers, staff and the relevant departments, for CPD activities.
- Establish or utilise appropriate existing systems for career development to help match individual and organisational needs.
- Promote continuing professional development and publicise results through annual reports, newsletters etc.
- Provide encouragement for CPD and recognition of its benefits and achievements in the provision of effective library and information services.

ACTION   Identify needs for continuous staff development.

Good Practice
- Involve employees in identifying development needs of groups of staff and individuals.
- Encourage use of a suitable CPD document. (See personal profile)
- Commit resources to train managers to encourage, appraise. guide and develop staff.
- Make available advice and information on CPD activities to all employees.
- Establish plans for CPD to meet the employing organisation's operating requirements.

ACTION   Implement continuing professional development plans.

Good Practice
- Ensure that adequate resources (financial and human) are available for effective implementation.
- Ensure that sufficient. relevant. cost effective CPD is carried out for each individual. As a guide (based on existing good practice) in each year, a range between 28-42 hours, (the equivalent of 4-6 average working days) of CPD activities is recommended. It should be noted that best practice already exceeds this figure. A proportion of this time will always be own-time learning.
- Collaborate with providers and professional bodies in the provision of relevant CPD programmes.

ACTION   Assess the benefits of continuous professional development in relation to the employing organisation's performance.

Good Practice
- Evaluate. jointly with employees the results and benefits of CPD carried out against defined plans.
- Monitor. review and revise. where necessary. the policies and plans for CPD in the light of experience of its operation.

Figure 7.11 The Library Association's guidelines for employers

200

5   Negotiation for implementation.

John Mortimer claims that two-thirds of 'The Times' 'Top 1000 Companies' claim to use benchmarking. A Benchmarking Centre was set up in Hemel Hempstead as a focal point for companies in the UK. Such a centre has been advocated for libraries by David Cheetham of the University of Northumbria Library which has successfully employed benchmarking to improve its performance.

An important aspect of staff development is how to put into practice what has been learned, especially in a library inert or positively hostile to new ideas or practice. Starting at the very beginning of the young professional's career, it is important to get into the habit of putting one's views across fluently and articulately. This means taking the initiative in speaking to your boss, expressing an interest in a new working party being set up, or circulating a memo or discussion paper to a group of staff, asking for people who have a view to contact you. If no one asks you to write a short report, on returning from a conference or workshop, or from a library visit, write one all the same, and circulate it to whoever should be interested, even if they aren't. If other people do the same, there may be enough material for a monthly staff bulletin, bulked out with news of other visits made by staff or conferences attended, and reviews of new books or journals or audiovisuals of professional interest. Many of these minor initiatives are inhibited, especially among young professionals, by lack of self-confidence, which must often be remedied. Striking a balance between the public and the private image is important, and will eventually lead to a stage where with practice a degree of self-confidence is justified and experienced. Before that happens, however, many people have to go through various immature phases, where they become aware of their own 'masking' and 'miraging' activities, as psychologists call them. They need to practise saying what they really think, especially to older and more senior colleagues, and the next stage is to have evidence to back up one's thoughts. The same could be said for many older more senior people as well. For this kind of self-development, assertiveness training may be useful (see Chapter 8), but so, equally, may be the habit of being well-informed by reading.

The strategy of organizational development (OD) is now often put forward in management circles as the holistic alternative to staff development. The significance is that OD involves an overall review of resources, including staff, in order to develop plans and keep some forward movement in times of financial stringency or cutback. OD tries to look at the library as a whole, by examining the interaction between technologies, organizational structures and people, since efforts to change one of these without the others are frequently doomed to failure. OD strategies involve a large number of staff taking part in intensive working parties or study groups or quality circles. The outcome is sets of recommendations on various aspects of the service, each as specific as possible, and as realistic as it can be, in terms of known resourcing problems. The report and recommendations may be written by the consultants or the library staff themselves with guidance. The latter method is meant to ensure that staff 'own' the recommendations and are therefore more likely to carry them out. Another OD approach is to produce an 'organizational profile', which illustrates problems and successes in areas such as: leadership, motivation, communication, decision-making, goal-setting and monitoring. Staff at different levels are asked to fill in a questionnaire which elicits information on such matters as:

How often are subordinates' views sought, and used?
How often do subordinates talk to supervisors about their work?
What levels of staff feel any responsibility for achieving the library's goals?
How much groupwork/teamwork is there in the various sections?
How are library goals established?
How are decisions made? And at what levels?
How much resistance (covert or overt) is there to library goals?
To what extent is there an informal network resisting formal controls?
At what levels, if at all, does monitoring progress take place?

A recent example of OD is the staff development consultancy carried out at the British Library of Political and Economic Science. The starting point was the belief that staff development programmes were the only way in which the challenge produced by the pace of change in libraries could be met. Although staff development was the focus inevitably the entire organization – objectives, culture, resources, personalities – was under scrutiny, so much so that one has to agree with Christopher Hunt:

> It would appear that a library director, voluntarily submitting his or her organization to such scrutiny and his staff to such possible sedition, is either desperate or foolhardy. There are undoubtedly risks, certainly substantially more labour for the director and other senior staff, but the potential rewards are also considerable.[47]

8

Staff supervision and interpersonal skills training

The Sergean report[1] on job characteristics in the library and information professions revealed that nearly half of those surveyed were responsible for supervising other staff members. However the significance of this is ambiguous. If one asks supervisors what they do, the answer is usually given in terms of the content of their professional work (reference and information work, or technical services for example) without reference to their role as staff supervisors. In his survey of job satisfaction among non-professional library staff Russell[2] found that staff were generally satisfied with the technical expertise of the supervisor but they were dissatisfied with the participation and human relations aspects. Significantly he also found that 'those with non-professional supervisors were more satisfied with the supervision they received than those with supervisors who were professional librarians'. It seems that supervisors are not very clear what supervision entails, or else that they do not see it as an important part of their job. The Curriculum Development Project, however, reinforced the views of practising library managers that they want the library schools to turn out people with 'practical skills in dealing with staff...'[3]

Supervision

The most basic levels of supervision involve planning and allocating the workload so that all the jobs get done efficiently and on time. Logic and accuracy are required if staff are to feel that the tasks are shared out equally, and that there is sufficient time to do them properly. Follow-up is necessary to ensure that quality and quantity of work are being achieved and therefore the supervisor and staff must have some agreed standards for the work. Otherwise there are likely to be mutually irritating exchanges between the supervisor and the staff who have different expectations of what is required.

It follows from setting standards for the work that the supervisor must provide support and training so that staff may reach these standards. This is most often carried out by day-to-day on-the-job training by the supervisor, or by co-workers if the supervisor decides to delegate. Coaching is the most effective on-the-job training and is a recognized management technique for encouraging staff to take more responsibility for their own jobs, and their own learning. Coaching supervisors should try to avoid 'giving orders' and being prescriptive, and instead encourage initiative by giving broader guidance that leaves members of staff with a certain leeway to develop their own judgement and use their intelligence. The objective is to get staff to think more positively about their jobs, to give them more practice in solving problems, and working out answers for themselves. There are a number of difficulties with the coaching approach. It requires skill and sensitivity on the part of the supervisor, to avoid the equal dangers of giving too close supervision and not enough guidance. It demands from the subordinate a more active role than many are used to, or even want. The problem is theoretically explained by McGregor's Theory X and Theory Y. Staff who have been conditioned to a Theory X management style (close supervision, little delegation, authoritarian leadership, communication mainly down the hierarchy) may find it difficult to adapt to a Theory Y management style (expecting staff to set their own goals, be responsible for initiating projects, participating in decision-making, communication up and across as well as down the hierarchy). An example of this gap between Theory X and Theory Y assumptions in a university library centres on who is responsible for staff development and continuing education. Senior management assumes a Theory Y position:

> ...I think we probably have the attitude that, look, these are professional librarians. They are capable, ought to be capable, of being professional, and in that sense we have not structured anything – I suppose, haven't thought we ought to be structuring anything.[4]

Unfortunately, Konn goes on to comment that these attitudes of senior management were not known to lower level staff 'who still considered it the responsibility of senior management to give a positive lead in continuing education matters'. They were still maintaining a Theory X posture, in spite of management beliefs to the contrary, and neither side was aware of the attitudes of the other, which were quite conflicting.

The important question is how to communicate effectively. A first-line supervisor is expected to have adequate expertise and knowledge in the area of work supervised, but equally must be able to interact effectively with subordinates, senior management, and specialists such as training officer, or systems librarian. But people are often raised to supervisory positions on the basis of previous work which does not involve staff supervision, and they can feel very inadequate and insecure. This is a problem also for library school leavers, though many of the schools now provide role plays and group work intended to develop relevant interpersonal skills. Later in this chapter we suggest a framework for interpersonal skills training which could be used either in library schools or as part of an in-service training programme by libraries. It covers the main problems for supervisory staff: leadership style, group skills, assertiveness training, transaction analysis, the management of stress and time management.

Another problem area concerns the content of supervision. What exactly is involved in a supervisory role, beyond knowledge and expertise in the area of work (circulation, or acquisitions, or information services)? The following list provides a basic framework of supervisory activities:

1 Planning and allocating work schedules, including provision for absences such as sickness and annual leave.
2 Helping staff to be effective in their work, by appraisal and training – formal or informal systems and structures.
3 Coaching staff on a day-to-day basis, to develop them in their work, and lead them to habits of taking more responsibility and initiative.
4 Checking that work is completed to agreed standards (quality and quantity), by agreed times, in regular consultation with individuals/teams.
5 Developing teamwork approaches in subordinates, by encouraging two or three to work together on specific activities (either for a fixed period of time, or permanently), talk about their work, and do reports on it, where this is useful, e.g. in monitoring a new service.
6 Giving staff reasons and explanations for doing things in certain ways, and listening to their opinions about the best way of doing things.
7 Treating staff fairly and consistently so that they feel they can come to the supervisor with problems and ideas, whether work-related or personal.
8 Making a point of being aware of staff problems, without necessarily waiting for them to come to you explicitly.
9 Giving staff regular acknowledgement for work done.
10 Handling grievances, taking disciplinary action where necessary. Knowing the legal requirements as well as the institution's own grievance procedures.
11 Having goals for the section or unit you are responsible for, and conveying these goals to your staff, as well as being clear about them yourself.
12 Communicating with senior management, to put your staff's viewpoint, and to channel the section or unit's ideas into the decision-making process.

In a survey of graduate trainees' experiences of on-the-job training, carried out by Jones[5] in 1985, certain characteristics of 'good supervision' and 'poor supervision' emerged as significant for those on the receiving end. Rather more than half the supervisors explained why things were done in a particular way, as well as how to do them. However 47 per cent were not in the habit of giving explanations, and trainees felt that this made their duties more difficult to grasp and rather less interesting. More than half the supervisors did not check whether their juniors understood a task properly, so it was left to the juniors to speak out if they had any difficulties. This could be a problem when in particular they 'did not know enough to ask the right questions'. When awareness of difficulties was established between supervisor and trainee, supervisors were not always good at starting from the junior's viewpoint, as good teachers try to do. They tended simply to repeat instructions, rather than probe where the difficulty lay. Trainees would have preferred them to really listen and understand the problem, which usually looked different at their level.

Feedback on work performance was seen as very important to the motivation of staff. It seems there is a tendency in libraries to give more negative feedback (criticizing when something is not quite right) than positive feedback (acknowledging and giving credit for completed tasks or projects well done). 'There can be few situations more frustrating than that of the employee who makes a great effort to perform well in his job and finds his efforts totally unrecognized.'[6] The best kind of feedback was considered to be regular but informal sessions with the supervisor at the beginning and end of periods of work in different sections or on different duties. These brief but morale-boosting sessions should include some positive reviewing and summarizing of what the trainee had learned, what problems were experienced, and how these could be overcome. They should finish up with looking ahead to the next phase, and what was expected there.

The quality of day-to-day supervision, in the form of coaching, is important to trainees. They like to be given some guidelines on the standards of work expected, both quantity and quality, and apparently this is a vague area in many libraries. It was observed by trainees who had moved around a number of sections in the same library that output and expectations of performance vary considerably even within one library, depending on different supervisors and different work groups with varying degrees of motivation and informal 'group norms' for controlling output and socializing newcomers. When supervisors are not themselves clear about performance standards, this is quickly communicated to their staff, and an often amiable laissez-faire approach becomes the order of the day, to the detriment of service standards ultimately.

The communications skills of supervisors were graphically described in the survey, as were poor communications characteristics. In this respect 'good supervisors' were 'approachable' and also accessible in the sense of making themselves available to talk to their trainees, rather than seeing that as an interruption to their real work. They were prepared to 'listen as well as instruct', were well-informed about their work and able to communicate their expertise without the 'unnecessary use of complex jargon'. The word jargon is used somewhat indiscriminately these days to include any kind of specialist terminology as well as the traditional meaning of 'insider language used to impress or baffle outsiders'. What these trainees objected to was not the use of the appropriate terminology in explaining computers, say, or classification, but a sort of 'status chasing' used by some supervisors in erecting a verbal professional mystique. Preferred communications styles were informal, conveyed enthusiasm rather than cynicism, and were more outgoing and active than withdrawn or passive. Above all 'instructional skills' were seen to be necessary in supervisors, because expertise and personal enthusiasm were to no avail if they could not be passed on by supervisors due to degrees of inarticulacy or incapacity to listen and appreciate the viewpoint of the learner.

An interesting aspect of conveying content, as opposed to style, was that trainees wanted their supervisors to cover problems and difficulties, and how to deal with them, rather than give them talks on an ideal situation (how library operations are supposed to be but rarely are in practice). In many cases trainees had to turn to their peer group for this kind of advice on coping with the realities of library systems. This, however, proved to be no bad thing, since peer group learning emerged in the survey as highly significant in training staff. This is in sympathy with current educational thinking, which argues that teaching someone else to do something is also beneficial for the teacher who has to think things out in order to explain them to others. However the supervisor must be careful to check that peer group learning is conveying helpful attitudes, and not the opposite. It has been known for new members of staff to be socialized by their co-workers into hostile attitudes to users, and sloppy routines which go unchecked by the supervisor, who keeps a low profile in the backroom until summoned by, say, user complaints when the position has got out of hand.

A valuable variation on peer group learning occurs when the supervisor makes a habit of consulting with juniors, to get their ideas, or their responses to her ideas. As one respondent put it:

> I felt happy about the training I received because of the way it was done – i.e. participation and co-operation...The feasibility of new procedures and equipment was discussed in 'brain-storming' sessions, which gave me a lot of experience/confidence.

This indicates that a consultative style is possible even in supervising the most junior levels, and can be much appreciated, especially when as is increasingly the case, juniors may be either graduate trainees, or para-professionals doing City and Guilds or BTEC courses for library assistants.

A final consideration is the encouragement and professional development of the supervisor's staff. Have they been given advice on available courses (part-time and distance learning approaches are now available for library assistants, as well as for professional staff) and opportunities for progress? Has the library's training officer, if there is one, or individual supervisors, if there is no overall co-ordination of staff development, collected a file of prospectuses on courses from the library schools and from local providers of BTEC?

It is probably worth commenting that while many of the above features of good supervision may be considered to be common sense, the survey indicated that such 'common sense' is not all that common among library supervisors. The trainees' rating of their supervisors' effectiveness is shown in the following table:

On the whole very effective   14%
Very effective in parts   20%
Moderately effective   23%
Poor in parts   26%
On the whole quite poor   17%

There seem to be two problems in developing librarians as supervisors. The first is that many staff are not aware of what supervision involves, and that has been covered above. The second problem is that some staff seem to think that supervision is an art one is born with, or not, rather than a set of skills which may be acquired. The rest of this chapter sets out some approaches and strategies which have been used with student librarians and with practising librarians, to develop interpersonal skills. Librarians making use of these approaches should contribute to improving the unsatisfactory situation revealed in Levy and Usherwood's survey[7] of interpersonal skills training in library and information work.

Coping with the difficult member of staff

There are regularly recurring problems in library and information work, which may be grouped under the 'difficult staff member' heading, and which cause many moments of anxiety and feelings of inadequacy among supervisors, especially young and inexperienced ones. The most common signs are poor or variable work performance in terms of quantity or quality or both. These may stem from personal life interfering temporarily or long-term with work performance, and lowering staff motivation. The symptoms include lateness, absenteeism, unreliability, rudeness to colleagues or to the users, irrational judgements leading to erratic and unpredictable work. At some point the supervisor has to do something about it, though many put off the hour of confrontation, hoping it will right itself. In cases of temporary aberration due to domestic problems, love life etc., this may happen, but often postponing 'a little chat' with the problem member of staff leads to an escalation, with complaints pouring in from readers and/or other staff. It should be noted that supervisors may experience problems from higher up as well as from their own subordinates. The 'difficult member of staff' may be the boss, who is constantly 'too busy' to talk to you about work problems, or refuses to delegate professional tasks (not trusting you 'as a recently qualified librarian', may be the excuse), or who makes inconsistent and irrational judgements and expects you to carry them out.

The vital phases for the supervisor are first to recognize the symptoms before they become aggravated, then to try and assign some possible causes and think about these before taking action, to give a 'counselling interview', and plan future monitoring of the person's progress or otherwise. The literature identifies the most common causes as follows:

1   Poor match of abilities/qualifications and the job tasks or degree of responsibility.

2 Motivational problems (see Chapter 2 for sources of job satisfaction among librarians).
3 Work group problems – acceptance or rejection by the group, peer pressure to reject innovation, to take industrial action, for example.
4 Managerial style or organization climate – clash between organic and mechanistic stances of different levels of staff.
5 Working conditions, such as space, heating, lighting, ergonomics of VDUs or other new equipment.
6 Medical problems, which may be divided into physical and mental health problems, the latter often stemming from stress leading to 'fight or flight' symptoms such as 'picking arguments' with colleagues or readers, or drink problems or frequent sickness leave.[8]

The mechanistic approach to counselling difficult staff takes the rational logical view that the supervisor is only concerned with the performance of the person involved and should not get into deep and unproductive discussions about underlying causes, unless these are work-centred. This school of thought provides useful checklists for analysing work-related background to problems, which may indeed lead to a solution in some cases, but may ignore the often complex 'whole person' approach of genuine counselling. Stevens,[9] for example, provides five steps to help problem analysis:

1 *Job analysis.* Is the person's job clearly defined, necessary to the library's goals, with responsibilities clearly set out?
2 *Recruitment skills.* Was the person right for the job, that is, having the right capabilities, experience, qualifications?
3 *Training.* Has the person enough information, guidance and on-the-job coaching to be able to do the job?
4 *Appraisal of performance.* Do supervisor and staff member discuss regularly how the job is done, the problems and successes of the staff members?
5 *Incentives.* What are the rewards of the job for the member of staff, in terms of motivation needs – security, sociability, ego needs, self-actualization etc? Are the needs of the staff member being met?

The more organic approach to the problem staff member advocates training supervisors in basic counselling skills – familiar in such professions as social work and clinical psychiatry, but increasingly being drawn on to help people in occupations other than the 'caring' professions. The most useful strategies which have been used in staff counselling, irrespective of the job content, centre on an understanding of 'styles of helping', and on a framework for conducting the necessary interview with the problem member. DeBoard[10] identifies styles of supervisor behaviour which range along a continuum from problem-centred (basically ignore the personal aspects which may underlie behaviour) to client-centred (basically concentrate on the person as a whole). Another continuum ranges from styles which 'exclude the client' (consist almost entirely of telling or manipulating behaviour) and which 'include the client' (bringing them in to the discussion of what is to be done, and checking their understanding of the situation and of the supervisor's reactions and advice). By knowing of these possible choices of interview behaviour, the supervisor is at least more aware of what is happening during the 'counselling chat', and may avoid the trap of imposing his or her own 'deus ex machina' solution, without involving the other member of staff in arriving at an agreed solution.

A framework for counselling interviews which is widely accepted in the literature and in practice suggests that the supervisor should go through five basic stages, even though in real-life counselling they overlap and merge with one another. The first is 'establishing rapport' which requires, on the part of the supervisor, skills of putting people at their ease, and opening up channels of communication. It is essential to take an 'adult' role rather than a 'threatening parent' role, if there is be a two-way dialogue. The next stage is 'seeing the other person's view of the problems', and indeed getting them to agree that there are problems. This requires listening skills, encouraging the person to talk, and not making early closed judgements. The third stage is 'understanding the problem/agreeing on the problem' which requires going beyond superficial signs to underlying causes. It is helpful at this stage to tackle the problem rather than the person, otherwise the interview may turn into a 'slanging match' (if there is aggression present) or a withdrawal into passivity by the person (if he or she takes refuge in non-assertiveness). The fourth stage is discussing alternative solutions and how and when they may be put into effect. This practical action is the point of all the preceding stages, and no counselling interview should end without specific actions, with time limits, being agreed and understood on both sides. It is important to keep a record of the agreed action, both to monitor future progress and also (if disciplinary procedures become necessary, ultimately leading to the dismissal of the problem staff member) to have a record showing that opportunity was given for improvement, and fair warnings of what was required, within a specified period. The final stage is ending the interview, which requires the supervisor to summarize briefly what has been discussed and what action has been agreed. It is important to fix another interview in a month's time or agreed period, so that both sides have a realistic understanding that the matter is not going to be brushed under the carpet, but must be satisfactorily resolved, with any necessary support forthcoming.

The success or failure of 'crisis counselling' of the kind outlined above depends very much on what general system of appraisal is prevalent in the library, and the reader is referred to Chapter 6 for advice on the alternative approaches. It should also be noted that individual management styles come into play, and it is helpful for a supervisor to be aware of his or her personal style, by considering the questions raised later in this chapter.

Charles Margerison[11] has advocated a similar approach which he calls 'conversation control'. The key is to recognize when to use 'problem-centred' conversation which focuses on asking questions and trying to diagnose the nature and causes of the problem and when to use 'solution-centred' conversation which focuses upon proposals and directions for implementing action. 'A weakness of those who do not have conversation control skills is that they offer solutions when they should assess problems and concentrate on problems when they should be putting forward solutions.' In problem-centred conversation we enquire, diagnose and summarize, whereas solution-centred behaviour is concerned with the giving of proposals, directing and informing. Once we are sure about a problem and we have tested this with the other person through summarizing and reflecting back the problem and received information we have got it right, then we can proceed to solutions.

Margerison offers the following guidelines:

1 Be problem-centred when you are not sure of the facts or the feelings.
2 Be problem-centred when a closer identification of the problem will help with the formulation of a solution.
3 Be solution-centred when you have the facts and the feelings and have sufficient technical competence to make a choice.
4 Be solution-centred when you feel it is time to put forward a proposal.
5 When in doubt be problem-centred.
6 Regularly summarize before you change topic or reach a decision.[12]

Leadership

Useful background reading to this section is given in Chapter 2 on motivation and participative management styles. It is possible, for example, to use the Blake/Mouton grid or the Rensis Likert categories to identify one's own management style in terms of concern for people proportionate to concern for output, or along the authoritarian/consultative/participative continuum. In order to help in this self-analysis, the following statements may be used as a checklist of how you tend to act in typical leadership situations, such as decision-making, discussion meetings, conflict situations and general effort put into work, and how you feel about the emotions involved. To assess your score in terms of the Blake/Mouton analysis of possible managerial styles, follow the instructions at the end of the chapter.

Decisions

1 I place high value on maintaining good relations.
2 I place high value on making decisions that stick.
3 I place high value on getting sound creative decisions that result in understanding and agreement.
4 I accept the decisions of others without strong feelings about whether I agree with them or not – I don't want to get too involved.
5 I search for workable, even though not perfect, decisions.

Convictions

6   I go along with opinions, attitudes and ideas of others, or avoid taking sides.
7   I listen for and seek out ideas, opinions and attitudes different from my own. I have clear convictions but respond to sound ideas by changing my mind.
8   I stand up for my ideas, opinions, attitudes, even though it sometimes results in stepping on others' toes.
9   I prefer to accept opinions, attitudes and ideas of others rather than to push my own.
10 When ideas, opinions, or attitudes different from my own appear, I initiate middle-ground positions.

Conflict

11 When conflict arises, I try to be fair but firm and to get an equitable solution.
12 When conflict arises, I try to cut it off and keep my position.
13 I try to avoid generating conflict, but when it does appear I try to soothe feelings and to keep people together.
14 When conflict arises, I try to identify reasons for it and to resolve underlying causes.
15 When conflict arises, I try to remain neutral or stay out of it.

Emotion

16 When things are not going right, I defend, resist or come back with counter-arguments.
17 By remaining neutral I rarely get stirred up.
18 Under tension I feel unsure which way to turn or shift to avoid further pressure.
19 Because of the disturbance tensions can produce, I react in a warm and friendly way.
20 When aroused, I contain myself though my impatience is visible.

Humour

21 My humour fits the situation and gives a sense of perspective: I keep a sense of humour even under pressure (Ho Ho).
22 My humour aims at maintaining friendly relations; or when strains do arise it shifts attention away from the serious side.
23 My humour is seen by others as rather pointless.
24 My humour is a bit hard hitting.
25 My humour sells myself or a position I am taking up.

Effort

26   I rarely lead but extend help to my staff.
27   I exert vigorous effort and others join in.
28   I seek to maintain a good steady pace.
29   I exert enough effort to get by.
30   I drive myself and my staff.

To relate these leadership characteristics back to Chapter 2, it is worth restat-
ing the basic leadership problem, that is, how to reach a satisfactory compromise between concern for work performance and output, and concern for
people's needs at work in terms of esteem, sociability, security and using their
potential. Examples of how this conflict is dealt with by individual leaders
(who may be charted at representative positions on the Blake/Mouton grid)
are given below.

At one extreme, the 1.1 Blake/Mouton position (see Figure 2.4), is the manager who refuses either to lead or to delegate leadership to others. The approach is often frustrated or cynical, as a result of the manager failing to
influence the organization, and withdrawing from it as far as is practicable.
This kind of manager manages as little as possible, keeps at a safe impersonal
distance, and avoids any face-to-face confrontations. Decisions are rarely taken,
unless there is some kind of crisis, and they are usually based on precedent or
regulations, rather than creative thinking or management techniques, for this
kind of 'manager' is often proud of his or her ignorance of management.

At the other extreme, the 9.9 Blake/Mouton position, is the manager who
tries to involve the entire staff in participative structures and creative approaches, and encourages everybody to undertake positive planning, self-
appraisal and innovative projects. It sounds wonderful in theory, but in practice many staff are not ready for creative responsibility, and feel unhappy and
exposed, so the results may be disappointing in both performance and job
satisfaction. When, however, the right people are in post, or on a work team,
the results can be inspired, with high output and infectious enthusiasm. There
is harmonious integration of tasks and human needs.

The 1.9 managerial style of high concern for people and low concern for
output means that a lot of effort goes into keeping up staff morale, and giving
staff the delegated authority. Direction from the manager is not strong, and
this can be a problem when staff look for initiatives from their boss, and are
told he or she will support whatever initiatives they themselves feel like
putting forward. Another weakness of this style may be that because the
manager likes to be seen as counsellor/confidant, it is difficult to face staff
with their inadequacies, mistakes, failures, and therefore performance tends
to take second place to a cosy togetherness.

The 9.1 managerial style, on the contrary, is based on the view that staff only
perform well when they are given strong direction, clear instructions and firm
guidance and appraisal from above. Power and decision-making is retained
by the manager, and speedy compliance and accountability, rather than crea-

tivity or planning their own work, is expected of subordinates. Performance standards may be reasonably good, but this style of management puts staff on the defensive and tends to reward compliance rather than positive or innovatory thinking. There is a heavy atmosphere of control which may provide security for the average worker, but may stifle the above average.

The use to which the Blake/Mouton grid may be put is training staff to identify their present managerial style, and its implications for their subordinates and for the library as a whole. This self-awareness may then lead to the identification of preferable managerial styles, towards which staff may move gradually. There is the possibility that they may be given greater incentive to modify their style, if, as in certain American organizations, appraisal by subordinates takes place, and managers are made aware of how they are seen by their subordinates. The University of Michigan Leadership Questionnaire (see Figure 8.1) provides an example of how this may be done. Leadership scores are arrived at by using a one-to-five response mode (one point for least favourable, five points for most favourable) and adding up the result for all four leadership factors. The questionnaire can also be used as the basis for a training session for supervisors, who can be asked to rate their own bosses, as well as themselves, according to the four factors. This generates an animated discussion which the trainer can use to build up strategies for the supervisors to take away and try out in the workplace.

Analysis of leadership style using the Blake/Mouton grid includes the management of conflict. Dr Helen Dyson[13] has identified five main ways of responding to conflict and this analysis has been used to help staff to understand their own responses and to think about how appropriate they are.

The categories of response can be shown on a grid similar to that of Blake/Mouton:

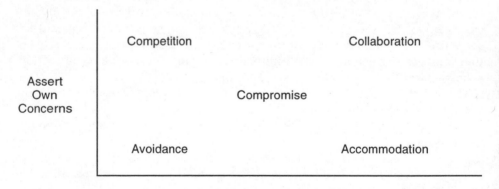

Stated briefly:

Competition is the response you make when you think you are right when giving way means loss of face. It assumes that conflict is inevitable.

1 **SUPPORT** (Enhancing your staff's sense of personal worth at work)

To what extent is your immediate supervisor:

a. Friendly and easy to approach?

b. Willing to listen to your problems?

c. Attentive to what you say?

2 **HELPING STAFF TO WORK TOGETHER**

To what extent does your immediate supervisor:

a. Encourage people who work for him/her to exchange opinions/ideas?

b. Encourage people who work for him/her to work as a team/group?

c. How often does your supervisor hold meetings where you can really discuss things together?

3 **GOAL EMPHASIS** (Enthusiasm for getting things done)

To what extent does your immediate supervisor:

a. Set an example by working hard herself/himself?

b. Keep up high standards of performance?

c. Encourage people to give of their best?

4 **GOAL ATTAINMENT** (Manning, co-ordinating and providing resources so that goals can be attained)

To what extent does your immediate supervisor:

a. Offer new ideas for solving job problems?

b. Encourage you to take action without waiting for detailed review and approval by him/her?

c. Provide supporting resources so that you can plan ahead?

d. Talk to you about improved ways of doing your work?

Scoring
Scoring is carried out by using a one-to-five response mode (one least favourable; five most favourable) for each question and adding up the sum of the parts for each of the four factors.

Figure 8.1 University of Michigan Leadership Questionnaire: the four factors

Collaboration is the response you use to eliminate negative feelings and requires good interpersonal skills. It assumes that conflict is resolvable.

Compromise is an expedient or mutually acceptable solution that partially satisfies both parties but does not really solve the problem. It assumes that each can only gain at the other's expense.

Avoidance assumes that conflict is avoidable but in fact achieves the least of all responses.

Accommodation means that you satisfy the other's needs and neglect your own.

We have used these categories successfully in training sessions. Participants are asked to analyse a case study and to discuss why particular responses were chosen and whether they were appropriate. An important factor in conflict is the norms which exist in an organization: which are the most accepted or socially desirable strategies and what the pressures are upon a person to take one approach rather than another.

Group work

Attending meetings is an inescapable fact of life in library work. Most staff are members of a team or work group which may have regular meetings to review progress, solve problems and plan ahead. In addition staff may be nominated to, or volunteer for, membership of temporary working parties on specific problems or innovations. Also there are informal groups in libraries which organize mainly social events, but sometimes also have a concern with staff development, such as arranging visits to other libraries or to professional meetings. Staff associations may also produce internal bulletins or news sheets, part entertainment, part useful communication. As well as the internal groupings and teams which generate meetings, librarians increasingly find themselves playing a more significant role in their communities, in order to remain in touch with user needs, and to have their say in their parent organization, when funding and future development are in question. Developments in public library service towards a stronger community orientation means that many librarians attend meetings with other agencies, such as Citizens' Advice Bureaux, or WRVS workers, or the numerous other voluntary and statutory agencies which support the variously disadvantaged in their area. Similarly in academic libraries staff are expected to attend board of studies and faculty meetings to ensure that the library's contribution to teaching, learning and research is visible, and relevant to changing needs of the academic community.

The significance of these developments is that staff may expect to attend meetings at more or less regular intervals, and that many may need training in how to get the best out of meetings. This is important in view of the number of hours staff spend in meetings, and the inevitable question that arises: Is there a sufficient return for all this time, or have the meetings proved to be a waste of time, due to unclear aims, poor selection of members, and inadequate briefing, preparation and group process skills?

> Meetings are an important management tool which can be used to pool technical knowledge, create understanding and provide a sense of direction. At their best, meetings can arouse enthusiasm and develop initiative. At their worst, they promote frustration, buck-passing and indifference.[14]

Some people's initial reaction to group work training is that it is all a matter of personality, therefore it is impossible to change people's behaviour in work groups. Research findings show that indeed personality is a significant variable, but that workers can learn to improve their performance in groups and meetings, thus making a more effective contribution to teamwork in their organizations. The influences of personality are observed in people's predispositions towards certain personality styles.

One helpful inventory[15] of personality styles identifies four main categories: the Enthusiastic, which displays a blend of feelings and action; the Imaginative, which shows feelings plus intuition; the Practical, which prefers a combination of doing and thinking; and the Logical, which is marked by intuiting and thinking. The Enthusiastic personality, it is suggested, enjoys new situations, likes change and risk, can be impulsive and is generally open to others' opinions and feelings, as well as having 'gut reactions'. The Imaginative personality on the other hand is more hesitant, working in fits and starts as inspiration strikes. He or she avoids conflict, likes to share ideas but only with a few others, is open to alternatives. The Practical personality likes to use reason and be in control of a situation, by using data, evidence, theories to solve problems and test out theories. The Logical personality takes a basically theoretical position, preferring conceptual models to pragmatic models, is suspicious of the gut reaction, the emotional overtone, preferring analysis and cool planning, based on written papers or notes.

It can be inferred that the Practical and the Logical personalities may clash with the Enthusiastic and Imaginative personalities, since they attach far less importance to analysis and reason and theoretical models, and far less importance to people networks, intuition and creativity, when considering problems and trying to reach solutions. However a more positive way of looking at the influence of personality is to accept that any work group may benefit from a mixture of personality styles which taken together are able to display a range of behaviours from abstract thought to reflective observation and active experimentation to concrete experience. Psychologists are anxious to point out that there is no best or worst style, but that it is helpful to be aware of one's own style in order to become conscious of its advantages and disadvantages in specific situations. It may then be possible to experiment with modifying one's style to fit better with particular circumstances at work, where it has been shown to be something of a hindrance.

Having accepted that personality styles are one element in group behaviour, the next stage is to consider the kinds of behaviour which help or hinder group effectiveness. One of the best known classifications is the Bales 'interaction analysis', which has been widely used in group training in organizations both in industry and in the public service sector and education. Detailed

Behaviour Category	A	B	C	D	E
Proposing					
Building					
Disagreeing					
Bringing in					
Supporting					
Open					
Testing understanding					
Summarizing					
Seeking information					
Giving information					
Defending/ attacking					
Blocking					
Shutting out					

Table 8.1 Group interaction record (derived from Rackham and Morgan)

analysis of the approach is given by Rackham and Morgan,[16] but Table 8.1 shows the basic outline of behaviours, and how profiles of behaviour for individuals in a group meeting may be drawn up. Each column (A,B,C, etc) is filled in for one group member. The number of their contributions in each behaviour category is recorded with a tick, while observing a meeting. At the end of the meeting a behaviour profile is compiled in the form of a histogram, which has a column for each group member, displaying the percentage of different kinds of behaviour which made up their overall contribution. An

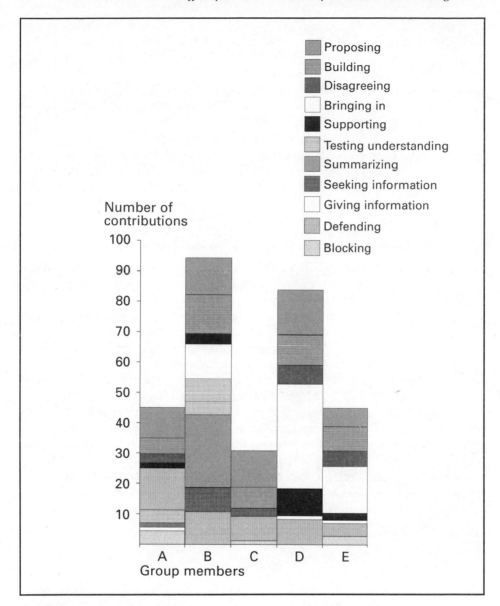

Figure 8.2   Interaction analysis

example is given in Figure 8.2. The assumption is that people thus become more aware of their own behaviour, and may modify it accordingly, for the sake of more effective and positive outcomes to team work, and meetings in particular.

There are a number of important limitations to this training approach, which have become evident to the authors after using it in extensive training sessions with practising librarians. Rae[17] has also provided a useful review of the approach which he has used over a period of eight years. It does not indicate the quality of the contributions, or whether the objectives of the meeting have been clearly understood or finally achieved. Some of the categories of behaviour are not clearly divisible. It is not always easy to record one kind of behaviour which shades off into another. The kinds of behaviour displayed may be partly determined by the nature of the group task, and partly by the context of a meeting (friendliness, cohesiveness of real-life work groups, presence or absence of high status people etc.). Observers need to be trained in how to record behaviour, because they may otherwise be inconsistent in what they record. Some beginning observers record non-verbals (a support nod, or threatening scowl, for example); others do not. Some record lengthy contributions with only one or two ticks; others use a tick for every sentence or short paragraph spoken by an individual. This may lead to confusing results which are not recognizable to the participants as genuine profiles of their respective behaviours. However, when the recording is done reasonably consistently, groups normally are able to identify the resulting histogram as a fairly accurate record of their meeting, given the limitations mentioned above.

To develop group skills from growing awareness of one's own group behaviour patterns, it is necessary to persuade group members to carry out interaction analysis over a series of meetings, and to use the results to make conscious decisions about what kinds of behaviour would benefit the group. What could be tried out by members? More building, more constructive criticism? Less blocking, less difficulty stating? A willed attempt to provide more supportive behaviour, or to bring low contributors into the discussion?

The cumulative effects over a period of time can be considerable. The problem is that the strategy usually only works when a whole group is prepared to give it a try, preferably a group which meets regularly and is motivated to have more effective meetings. It is not so effective if only one or two group members learn the strategy and try to do something without involving the others significantly. However, in a fairly small group, the influence of one or two members practising group skills and trained to 'read' group behaviour may be considerable.

Structure and dynamics of small groups

The components of group activity fall into three main spheres, which interact to provide the overall climate and degree of effectiveness of the group as a whole. The first is the task and technology component, or what the group is supposed to be thinking and doing. Is there a clear set of objectives, agreed by group members, as to the problem to be discussed and the decisions or other outcomes to be arrived at? The second component is the group working arrangements: formality or informality; voting on disagreements or arriving at a consensus through discussion; decision-making or merely consultative; chaired by a senior member of staff or peer group member; arrangements for putting items on the agenda, minute-taking, and circulation of minutes. The third component is the 'affective' element, that is, group members' attitudes and emotions, stemming partly from their personality styles and partly from their feelings about, or vested interest in the items on the agenda.

Criteria for more effective group work are listed below. Members of groups who feel frustrated or dissatisfied with their particular group's behaviours or outputs may use the criteria as a checklist for analysing what is wrong, and trying to improve matters. The group as a whole can learn to become more effective by having a short post-meeting analysis (with or without help of a designated observer), to discuss how far the criteria were met, and how they may improve their next meeting, by paying more attention to criteria not met this time round.

Criteria for effective group meetings

1   The members agree on shared goals, have clear objectives, know what is expected to emerge from the meeting (recommendations or decisions, information giving, agreed standards for some activity taking place on more than one site, e.g. stock editing, A/V).
2   The members work at creating a climate of support and trust, so that there are no barriers to expression of ideas, and members are positively encouraged to contribute. The group develops members.
3   Communication is kept as open as possible, which involves members being prepared to disclose what they really think and feel, and to pay genuine attention to what others think and feel, during the meeting, rather than in the form of cliquey gossip before and after the meeting. Difficulties are brought into the open.
4   Efficient procedures are adhered to for chairing, minutes, agenda.
5   The members are appropriately qualified and prepared to contribute to the theme of the meeting. They have relevant expertise.
6   There is evident leadership (whether formal, from the chair, or informal, from within the members) and thus a sense of direction.
7   The group has positive ways of handling conflict, which often means encouraging constructive criticism, not making easy choices, modifying original ideas by incorporating other people's contributions; it also means moving the meeting on from negative conflict like personality clashes and idées fixes, through the chair with the help of members.
8   The group reviews its achievements, assesses progress at regular intervals through the meeting, rather than rambling inconsequentially. Time management is used to get through the tasks efficiently.
9   The group pays attention to the three essential components of group activity: taking account of the nature of the task, the group's structure and formal working arrangements, and the personality, styles and attitudes of group members.
10   The group recognizes its position in relation to other groups and exercises positive influence on other groups, rather than adopting defensive postures (building a bunker within the organization).

11   The group is cohesive, that is, members use the word 'we', and develop some sense of belonging, achievement or even power, beyond what they experience as individual members of staff. Cohesive groups are most effective, and can be rich learning experiences, provided that they are not deflected to the ideological ends of the members rather than the agreed aims and objectives of the library..

12   The group is rewarding to its members, both in terms of affiliative needs, and task performance needs.

The problems which may arise in groups, to prevent fulfilment of the above criteria, are observable within any workplace meetings. Groups may be un-clear about objectives, confused about the exact purpose of a meeting. Differ-ent levels of staff may have conflicting objectives, overtly or covertly. The meeting may be seen as futile, because it is not given enough power to be taken seriously in the decision-making hierarchy. There may be poor role differentiation, for example a lack of people with expert knowledge, leader-ship skills, or critical acumen, leading to poor quality discussion and incon-clusive 'conclusions'. Intergroup and intragroup conflict may restrict the meet-ing's effectiveness. Finally, there are tasks for which groups are inappropriate, and which are better done by an individual. These include taking operational, routine decisions and implementing decisions. Creative ideas more often come from individuals than from groups, though groups may stimulate creativity and are useful in building and criticizing ideas. 'Brainstorming' is a well-known technique for stimulating creativity – going round everyone in the group and getting them to come out with all the possible ideas or solutions to a problem, irrespective of how practical or feasible they apparently are. When a comprehensive list has been assembled from everybody's spontaneous sug-gestions, and only then, criticism is applied to eliminate the wilder ideas, and build up the possible.

Finally it is important to note that groups need to go through certain stages before they become fully operational, or fully effective. Tuckman's theory of developmental stages identifies the necessary stages of Forming, Storming, Norming and Performing.[18]

During the Forming phase group members suffer anxiety, are dependent on the leader (who may be equally anxious) and try to work out what is accept-able in the situation in which they find themselves. This involves mulling over the nature of the task, trying to agree on what they have to do, but also trying to infer acceptable approaches and methods of tackling the task, which will fit in with everybody else's approaches.

The Storming stage is a rather turbulent one where people begin to recog-nize that there are subgroups who may cause conflict and get in the way of agreement and swift solutions. There may be polarization of opinions or even rebellion against the leader, all of which leads to resistance (often emotional) to getting on with the task.

The third stage, Norming, is essential before there can be concentration on the task. It involves developing some group cohesion, a sense of being a group and the need for mutual support. This enables the group to be more open about their views and to see in practical terms how they can co-operate to produce a solution to the task. Acceptable modes of behaviour and ways of dealing with disagreement and conflict have been worked out.

In the final Performing stage group members use these evolved behavioural norms to solve intragroup conflicts, and work on solutions to the task. They are now able to get on with the task completion, since they have worked out ways of coping with interpersonal problems, and have also become clearer about possible methods of getting a solution to the task side of group work. They have found ways of coping with both the 'process' and the 'product'. Should new members enter the group at this stage, they have certain problems adapting and learning the often unstated norms and nuances of vocabulary and styles and preferred strategies for solving problems. At first they may try to satisfy their own perceived needs in joining the group, but there is nearly always a period of working out group norms, conforming to accepted patterns of behaviour, before the new member can become an effective and accepted contributor.

In practical down-to-earth terms, meetings can only succeed when the following criteria are successfully met. First, the meeting should have a clear purpose which is accepted by its members and by those to whom it reports. Has it the power to make decisions or simply give recommendations or advice? How representative is it of various staff levels and interests? In what ways can it authorize action to ensure that its deliberations are implemented? Second, the members should be carefully selected to include the necessary expertise and specialist knowledge of the topics it will discuss. It should be noted that vertical meetings (members drawn from different levels of staff) will be less informal and possibly more inhibited than horizontal meetings (members drawn from the same level). On the other hand it may contribute more to staff development if members have to learn to be open and express their genuine views (and the views of others whom they represent) in dialogue with more senior staff. Third, members must be sufficiently informed in advance through explanatory agendas, with discussion papers attached, and encouraged to prepare adequately. Decisions made with inadequate information and ill-informed discussion are generally poor quality. It is necessary therefore for the convener to ensure that time is given and members are informed of, and invited to contribute, preparatory papers or lists of discussion points.

Meetings are expensive of time and money, so it is important to keep the agenda to a realistic size which it is possible to cover in the time available. This is of course affected by the ability of the members to come informed and prepared, and not waste time trying to find out about matters during the meeting itself. The chairperson can help to complete the agenda effectively, by starting with a clear statement of what is to be achieved, and noting background papers relevant to particular topics. He or she may need, at regular intervals, to review progress and return wanderers to the point, as well as ensuring that points are understood. When agreement is reached on any issue, it is important to clarify what action will result and to name an individual or group who are to undertake it. It is necessary for the chairperson to keep an accurate record of the outcomes, and check these with the secretary or recorder before minutes of the meeting are finally typed and circulated. Also at the end of a meeting the chairperson should take any follow-up action promptly, by informing those concerned of what they are to do, or by negotiating or asking advice or further information from people not at the meeting.

The job of the chairperson is made difficult in a variety of ways. The most common is perhaps that meetings are seen by quite a high proportion of members as a waste of time, or as unrepresentative of staff views, because the same few people always seem to get their way, usually by monopolizing the discussion. Other problems are that important matters may be ignored, decisions taken may be unclear or inconsistent with previous decisions (in this or a related meeting), and it may not be sorted out who is responsible for acting on the decisions. The chairperson must be prepared to intervene to see that more tongue-tied members are heard, that compromises are negotiated when there is disagreement, and that the right questions are asked before hasty decisions are reached. The problem of reaching a consensus in the absence of formal voting – which is often seen as desirable, especially in academic institutions – is another area where the chairperson needs a strategy. He or she must ensure that all opinions are heard, irrespective of their own known partiality perhaps in favour of a particular solution. By a series of supportive questions the chair should achieve a balanced discussion between different views, even when the proponents of these may be rather inarticulate at putting their own case. It is too easy to write off 'light-weight' members, and earn their hostility to any decisions taken. It is better to try to encourage others to build on what they say, to ensure that everyone is brought in and not ignored. Outbreaks of open hostility between members are another problem, which may be handled best by diversionary tactics before the meeting turns into a gladiatorial arena rather than a decision-making body engaged in rational discourse. The most commonly needed skill is probably the ability to restrain the over-talkative, and draw in the embarrassed and shy, without antagonizing either type. To sum up, an effective meeting will result when the following conditions apply:

(a) a clear aim
(b) good organization
(c) maximum participation
(d) understandable communication
(e) generally accepted standards of behaviour
(f) good morale and mutual regard.[19]

Assertiveness training

Assertiveness training has become best known probably in the context of management training for women, to offset the disadvantages of being in a minority (and perhaps seen as a 'token woman manager') in a male-dominated decision-making network. In such situations a woman may be consciously or unconsciously excluded unless she learns the techniques of self-assertion. However there are wider applications of assertiveness training, which can benefit library staff at all levels who may have difficulty in negotiating with colleagues or users, as a result of habits of either aggressiveness or non-assertion. Levy and Usherwood's survey[20] revealed strong support from library respondents on the desirability of assertiveness training as a basic foundation for academic and public librarians alike.

Assertiveness means being honest and open with yourself and other people about what you think and feel and want to do, in any particular situation. It implies self-confidence, being positive rather than negative, and being able to understand other people's point of view, so as to reach working compromises by negotiation. Non-assertion on the other hand implies failure to express your true thoughts and feelings. You tend to conceal your real reactions to other people's views, and your real needs at work are not made known. Responses to any situation tend to be passive rather than active, negative rather than positive. Another form of non-assertion is a hesitant or apologetic communication style, which has the unfortunate effect of causing little attention to be paid to views which may be quite sound and positive, though delivered in a negative manner. Aggressiveness means expressing your own views, but at the expense of other people. You have no problem standing up for your own opinions and rights, but you are not prepared to give others the same rights you take for yourself.

The implications of these modes of communication in the workplace are considerable. Non-assertive persons are likely to be ignored, rather than getting the attention they hope for by not disagreeing and avoiding any kind of open conflict or argument. They are also likely to suffer a sense of frustration or futility as a result of failing to assert their own needs and real views. In avoiding conflict such staff may then find themselves victims of other people's imposed views, plans and decisions, because they did not make their disagreement known, or put forward alternatives. This can lead to unclear decisions, reluctantly done tasks, and low simmering grievances never brought out into the open. The situation tends to be cumulative. Non-assertive people may be taken advantage of, by taking on more work because they cannot say no. They tend to be consulted less and less, because they never come out and say what they really think, or because their communications are mainly negative. They do not reveal any views or ideas of their own, and they do not disagree with other people's views. Eventually nobody bothers to ask for their views.

Aggressive behaviour at work may be satisfying at the time, since it releases tension for the aggressor, gets the adrenalin flowing and gives a sense of 'I'm winning this game, anyway' or 'Now I've got the bastard'. It has unfortunate after–effects, however. Aggressive outbursts often lead to a certain amount of guilt afterwards, which puts the aggressor in a defensive posture, inappropriate for constructive decisions or solutions to a problem. They leave the person at least temporarily isolated so that the problem, unresolved, requires more time and effort when tempers have cooled. The effect on colleagues of aggressiveness can be either that they are forced to retaliate in kind and there is a general increase in aggressiveness, or that they opt for non-assertion and leave more and more decisions to the aggressive boss. Many aggressive supervisors believe that this is the only way they can get results from their staff. In fact they are likely in the long term to end up with a 'time-serving' staff leaving it all to the boss (since that's what he seems to want), or, in the worst cases, with a staff that channels a good deal of energy into chronic, if small-scale conflicts, following the model of the aggressive boss. Difficult decisions may be delayed or avoided. Fewer initiatives may be taken, and implementing decisions may run into serious problems with a resentful staff.

Assertiveness training centres on a basic 'Bill of Rights', which covers the following principles. People have the right to have their views and opinions listened to, and be taken seriously. They have the right to say no, and have their reasons taken seriously. They have the right to criticize and be criticized, without manipulating or being manipulated. They have the right to ask for information and clarification. They have the right to receive the work/service/goods they were promised, when they took up a job, or purchased goods or services.

The most appropriate training for assertiveness is role-play which can be used to give people practice in assertiveness strategies, as outlined below.

Strategies to develop greater assertiveness

1   Decide what your true views are in any situation, before you go to a meeting, or to a colleague's office to discuss a problem or project.
2   Make a few brief notes in advance which summarize your position, and what you would like the outcome of the meeting to be. Decide on alternatives, or how far you can modify your position without giving up the most important points.
3   Listen properly to other people's points, and acknowledge their arguments, by such devices as reviewing what they have said, or asking, 'Is this what you mean?', or linking their arguments to your own.
4   Make your own views known directly and honestly, even if others are adopting indirect or devious approaches. Show that you know they are being devious, preferably by a humorous acknowledgement of what they are up to. Repeat your views as often as is necessary for a hearing.
5   If eventually your argument or solution is not accepted, try at least to negotiate a modification of the winning argument, so that it incorporates some of your views. This is the assertive way of losing, and is preferable to the aggressive (stalking out of a meeting, or attacking the other solution as

viciously as possible) or the non-assertive mode (subsiding into passivity and the 'Poor me, I always lose' game).

Assertiveness training pays considerable attention to handling conflict and criticism. It is useful to check one's own typical behaviour against the following checklist.

Non-assertive ways of handling conflict include giving in to the other on most occasions, because of deference to the other's status or simply out of a long-term habit of trying to please in order to be liked. It is argued that women are more prone to this traditional kind of behaviour than men. Another approach is to give in to the other, to all appearance, but when their back is turned to bitch or gossip and express the opposite feelings and views to co-workers. A third possibility is that both parties to the argument behave in an insincere accommodating way because they are both being non-assertive. The result is likely to be unhelpful vacillation rather than clear decisions, or if decisions are taken, they are unlikely to last long, because neither side supports them fully.

Assertive ways of handling conflict include stating your requirements openly, and asking the other person to do the same, early on in the negotiation. Assertion involves taking responsibility for your own position and actions, rather than trying to edge it off on to 'the organization', 'this library section' (unless you are genuinely representing other staff with their agreement). It is necessary to check that you have understood the view of the other, by repeating their statements in your own words: 'Is this what you are saying ...?' When you fully understand the other's view you are then in a better position for finding areas of agreement, however small. This is more realistic and positive than going all out for a global solution (either yours or the other person's). When trying to reach an agreed outcome, it is more creative to spend time brainstorming a number of possible solutions, than to cling obsessively to one's initial standpoint. It is even better if the other can be encouraged to produce alternative strategies also. The most helpful and productive negotiations are those in which both parties see the necessity of moving towards each other from their initial positions, but are clear on what they cannot give up, because it is central to their thinking. By the end of a negotiation both sides must be clear what has been agreed, should each state their view of the outcome and say what action they have undertaken to carry out, within a time limit.

Assertive ways of handling criticism begin with an honest assessment, as far as is humanly possible, of how far the criticism is justified, and how far it is derived from your boss's emotional need to put someone down from time to time as a means of showing authority. If the criticism is entirely or mainly unjustified, concentrate on that as a main response. Give precise detail of when you did complete the project, or send off the reply to an enquirer, or deliver your estimates. The point here is to establish the facts, rather than become embroiled in an emotional flurry on the boss's side, and resentment on yours. Practise saying, in the nicest possible way, 'No, it isn't like that...it's like this...' without being either aggressive or non-assertive in style, tone or non-verbals. If the boss is not listening the first time, go through it again, till you have clarified your side of the story.

If, on the other hand, the criticism is only too true, or has an element of truth, acknowledge this, rather than engage in devious and evasive behaviour. The non-assertive response is to stay sullen and silent, or make empty excuses or sweeping denials with little basis in reality. The assertive response is to explain the reasons for the shortcomings, which may well be understandable for a variety of reasons: temporary personal worries; or lack of support from the library-inadequate resources to carry out a job properly; or demoralization at work, perhaps through failure to get a promotion, or through absence of any recognition of previous projects successfully completed. Practise being open about problems at work, rather than trying to deny or conceal them. In that way there is at least a possibility of getting others' ideas, or more resources, to help. End the interview by reaching a new agreement about completing the task or project, provided you get the necessary support. Make an undertaking of a positive kind.

If the criticism is a general 'put-down', rather than a specific complaint about your work, assert yourself by bringing this into the open. Express your feelings at this put-down: 'You've got this wrong, and what you seem to be doing is getting at me without any real justification. That makes me pretty fed-up. What's behind this?' 'Put-downs' may usually be identified because they are rash generalizations and are not linked to any specific piece of work, and because there are strong emotional undertones, suggesting that it is the person who is being criticized, rather than the work. Dealing with aggressive criticism, especially if the person is worked up and in a rage, may involve going away and exercising your right to leave till things cool down. If you do stay and take it, defuse the situation by getting the person to listen to your view, and also to focus on the content rather than the emotions of their own view.

Research in the use of emotions to get one's way at work indicates that women have a particular problem in negotiation, especially in male-managed organizations such as libraries. Women may be expected to behave differently from men, by making more use of 'emotional manipulation'. If they follow this feminine stereotype, they can seriously damage their self-respect and the respect they receive from others. But if a woman tries to avoid this stereotype and 'adopts the more effective techniques used mostly by men, she may be called pushy or aggressive'. Anger, for example, is a more common device for men than for women in getting their way, and may be seen as 'effective' in a man, but 'temper, temper' in a woman.

A fuller discussion of assertiveness for librarians, including many valuable hints on dealing with a variety of situations, is contained in Caputo's *The assertive librarian*.[21]

Transactional analysis

Transactional analysis, like assertiveness training, provides a method of analysing behaviour, especially confrontations between individuals and enables individuals to adapt their behaviour to improve relationships. It has been used to improve personal relationships both in domestic situations and in organizations.[22]

It is based upon the idea that each person has three *ego states* which are separate and distinct sources of behaviour. The parent ego state contains the attitudes and behaviour incorporated from external sources, primarily parents. It is often expressed towards others in prejudicial, critical and nurturing behaviour. Typical parental words are 'right', 'wrong', 'good', 'never', 'disgusting', 'shocking' and 'stupid'. Non-verbal clues include finger-wagging, arm-folding and head-shaking. The child ego state contains all the impulses which come naturally to an infant such as joy, curiosity and enthusiasm. The assumption in transactional analysis is that the most appropriate state will be the adult one which is oriented to current reality and the objective gathering of information. In other words each person speaks and behaves in an adult manner. Ego states are usually depicted as below:

```
    PERSON 1          PERSON 2
        P                 P
        A                 A
        C                 C
```

Each transaction is shown by an arrow. Two adult-to-adult transactions are shown below:

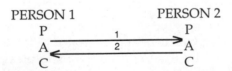

'Crossed' transactions occur when an unexpected response is made, stimulating an inappropriate ego state and usually causing a good deal of ill-feeling. They should normally be avoided, e.g.:

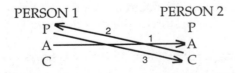

Person 1: 'Do you feel you have made any progress in liaising with Departments this year?'
Person 2: 'Do you think I am a miracle worker?'
Person 1: 'I expect you to answer a question properly when I ask it.'

Strokes are any forms of recognition and can be verbal or non-verbal, positive or negative – a genuine smile would be a positive stroke, whereas a growl would be a negative one.

A *game* is a series of complementary transactions between people which seem straightforward on the surface but where there is an ulterior motive. Typical games in organizations are 'harried' – person plays at being very busy and overburdened and is self-righteous about it – and 'wooden leg' – person always complains of a handicap which prevents achievement yet may reject help because it only emphasizes the handicap.

The 'OK Corral' shows four psychological *life positions* each describing how one feels about oneself and about others. Although in certain circumstances other positions are tenable, it is generally assumed that position 1 is the most desirable.

I'm not OK			I'm OK
You're OK	3	1	You're OK
I'm not OK	4	2	I'm OK
You're not OK			You're not OK

The 'OK Corral'

Managing stress

Stress results from the way people feel about the pressures they perceive themselves to be under. One person may find it difficult to understand how another can be stressed by what appears to be no pressure at all. To understand stress it is therefore necessary to realize that different people have different stress thresholds and all the sources of stress for one particular person are frequently not known by others.

Stress occurs 'when we feel that there are too many pressures or too few resources to deal with them'.[23] 'It is a psychological and physiological response to the perception of a demand or challenge.'[24]

Looker and Gregson[25] see stress as having three sides to it:

1   *The Good*: Excitement, stimulation, creativity, success, achievement, increased productivity.
2   *The Bad*: Boredom, frustration, distress, pressure, poor performance, decreased productivity, failure, headaches, indigestion, colds, unhappy and disharmonious relationships.

3   *The Ugly*: Ulcers, heart attacks, cancer, anxiety, depression, nervous break-
    down, suicide.

The results of stress are therefore not necessarily bad and good managers will
seek to take advantage of the good and to help staff to reduce the bad and
avoid the ugly sides of stress.

Surveys of stress among librarians have produced similar findings. Causes
of stress discovered by Evans[26] and Bunge[27] are summarized in Figure 8.3.
Work overload is a dominant factor caused by increased student numbers in
academic institutions and the demand made upon the library as the amount of
formal teaching decreases. The working environment has become less pleasant through overcrowding and noise. The need for greater accountability has
produced pressure for indicators of performance and the collection of management information not previously required. Although work with users is
generally felt to improve motivation (see Chapter 2), when demands from
users become difficult to satisfy from limited resources there is a build-up of
pressure. 'Work underload' stands out in contrast and can be seen as a response by library assistants to work which makes inadequate use of their
abilities. The position of library assistants is discussed in Chapter 2. Money
worries are also a problem, particularly for library assistants. This evidence
reinforces the points made in Chapter 3 about recruitment incentives in library and information work. With the recession, prospects for advancement
have been affected and the ideas presented in Chapter 2 have therefore become even more relevant if stagnation is not to set in.

One way of relieving stress is to provide more resources to enable staff to
meet demands but there are only limited possibilities in this area. Ideas that
have been put forward in other chapters on motivation, training, staff appraisal and selection of staff are all relevant to the relief of unnecessary stress.
Maggie Forbes, Head of Counselling Services at the University of Hudders-
field, ran a seminar for librarians in 1992 and provided a helpful list of ideas
for coping positively with stress. The similarity between this list and the
objectives of assertiveness training can be clearly seen:

1   Get to know your own limits. Respect them and do not overstretch your-
    self.
2   Find out what works best for you in the way of stress-moderation, i.e.
    talking to someone, practising relaxation, reorganizing your time-table.
3   If you are a worrier or prone to 'hurry-sickness' make sure you compen-
    sate in some way with quiet spaces in your life.
4   Organize and prioritize. Do not waste time and energy being in a muddle.
    Decide what is important to you and leave the rest.
5   If you have a lot on, offload something. Be ready for it to hurt a bit. Admit
    you cannot do and have everything.
6   Stop trying to be perfect – no-one would like you if you were, anyway.
7   Accept the fact that other people will sometimes cause you stress.

Manchester Polytechnic Library (1992)

All Staff	%
1 Work overload	58
2 Patrons	51
3 Money worries	45
4 Prospects	38
5 Working environment	31
6 Poor administration	23
7 Technological change	18
8 Pressure from management	13
9 Work underload	11
10 Satisfaction	8
11 Personality conflicts	0

Professionals	%
1 Work overload	82
2 Patrons	61
3 Working environment	43
4 Poor administration	36
5 Pressure from management	25
6 Prospects	18
7 Technological change	14
8 Money worries	14
9 Satisfaction	4
10 Work underload	0
11 Personality conflicts	0

Non-professionals	%
1 Money worries	83
2 Prospects	61
3 Patrons	39
4 Work underload	22
5 Technological change	17
6 Work overload	17
7 Satisfaction	13
8 Work environment	13
9 Poor administration	9
10 Personality conflicts	0
11 Pressure from management	0

Bunge (1989)	%
1 Patrons	15.0
2 Workload	13.4
3 Supervisors and management	10.5
4 Schedule and work day	7.2
5 Lack of positive feedback	6.9
6 Other staff members	6.9
7 Lack of information and training	6.7
8 Feeling pulled and tugged	4.1
9 Technology and equipment	4.1
10 Physical facilities	4.1
11 Bureaucracy and red tape	3.6

Figure 8.3 Causes of stress in rank order

8   Do not allow yourself to be a victim. Learn to ask for what you want; cope with rejection; say no and stick to it.
9   Decide your goals, ones which are within your grasp and suit you rather than parents, a partner or 'society'.
10 Do not let other people do your thinking – you decide what matters to you.
11 Talk to someone – a partner, a friend, a counsellor.
12 Take exercise to provide an outlet for stress and also keep you in good shape for coping.
13 Have plenty of rest – sleep, breaks in the day, the week, the year.
14 Practise relaxation – whatever kind suits you best:
    breathe deeply
    self-hypnosis
    meditation
    visualization (using your imagination to produce pleasant images)
    self-talk (boost your own confidence, reduce your own fears).
15 Go easy on yourself – like yourself, forgive yourself, allow yourself to fail sometimes. You are human, not a machine; prize your humanity!

There are plenty of tools which enable you to check whether you are suffering from stress. Looker and Gregson[28] have produced a questionnaire with a scoring key, Figure 8.4, and they also highlight the stress problems of workaholics or 'Type A' people (Figure 8.5).

Time management

With library budgets much leaner than they were there is a pressing need for staff to be more productive. Most of this book is devoted to making this possible but if time is not used efficiently productivity will suffer.

The first stage in managing time, as in many areas of management, is self-analysis. This can take two forms. The first is to analyse how your time is spent – this can be carried out over a week or so by keeping a log of your activities. It can either be an open log which records the time spent daily on each task, or it can be structured according to known activities of the job, e.g. planning, meetings, interruptions, telephone, correspondence, reading projects. The log is then analysed according to what you consider to be the key tasks so that you can see whether you are concentrating upon important areas and where time is 'wasted'.

A second self-analysis will concentrate upon the sort of person you are. The self-analysis questionnaire already introduced in this chapter (pp.211–13) will have told you about your management style and this will certainly affect your management of time. You need to decide what your role should be. For example many managers now, in the Japanese style, get out of their offices and talk to their staff about their work and have an open-door policy for staff to come and see them. This is time-consuming and may be considered time-wasting by

SCORING

Score 5 Always
       4 Almost always
       3 Usually
       2 Sometimes
       1 Almost never
       0 Never

ASSESSMENT

Add up your scores and multiply the total by 2

TYPE B	0–39	You are slightly and/or rarely impatient and aggravated. You create hardly any unnecessary stress for yourself and your health is probably unaffected.
MILD TYPE A	40–59	You are fairly and/or occasionally impatient and aggravated. You create some unnecessary stress for yourself and this may affect your health.
MODERATE TYPE A	60–79	You are very and/or often impatient and aggravated. You generate much unnecessary stress for yourself and this may affect your health.
EXTREME TYPE A	80–100	You are extremely and/or usually impatient and aggravated. You generate TOO MUCH unnecessary stress for yourself and this may affect your health.

NOTE: This is a self-assessment of your Type A behaviour. It is only as accurate as you are honest in your answers. Furthermore, Type As are often blind to their own behaviour: for example doing things fast. Type As may not think they are as fast as they actually are.

	NEVER	ALMOST NEVER	SOMETIMES	USUALLY	ALMOST ALWAYS	ALWAYS
Are you on time for appointments?						
Are you competitive in the games you play at home or at work?						
In conversations, do you anticipate what others are going to say (head nod, interrupt, finish sentences for them)?						
Do you feel rushed in the things you do?						
Do you get impatient in queues or traffic jams?						
Do you try to do several things at once and think about what you are going to do next?						
Do you feel you do most things fast (eating, walking, talking, driving)?						
Do you get easily irritated over trivial things?						
If you make a mistake, do you get angry with yourself?						
Do you find fault with and criticize other people?						

From Terry Looker and Olga Gregson, *Stresswise: a practical guide for dealing with stress*, 1989.

Figure 8.4   Stress assessment questionnaire

Your attitude to work

Do you take work home most nights?

Do you frequently think about work problems at home?

Do you voluntarily work long hours?

Do work problems affect your sleeping habits?

Do your family and friends complain that you spend too little time with them?

Do you find it difficult to relax and forget work?

Do you find it difficult to say 'no' to work requests?

Do you find it difficult to delegate?

Is your self-esteem based largely on your work?

Scoring and evaluation

If you answer 'yes' to one of the above questions you may simply be dedicated to your work. However, there is a fine dividing line between dedication and obsessive devotion to work (workaholism) so be on your guard!

If you answer 'yes' to two questions you are obsessive about your work and could easily succumb to workaholism. Beware!

Answering 'yes' to three questions indicates you have an obsessive and compulsive devotion to work. The higher the score the more you are hooked into workaholism. You need to question your priorities for the sake of your marriage, social relationships, health and career. Although it may seem hard for you to believe, you can be damaging the career that you are striving obsessively to enhance.

From Terry Looker and Olga Gregson, *Stresswise: a practical guide for dealing with stress*, 1989.

Figure 8.5   Workaholic checklist

some analysts. You also need to know what works best for you, for example the time of day when you work at your best which is probably when you should concentrate on clearing backlogs of desk work, and how much sleep you need to keep you energetic each day.

All the literature on time management analyses time-wasters – those things which hinder us most in getting work completed on time – and there is a general consensus on the main causes. Helen Gothberg[29,30,31] has studied time management among librarians and her findings are shown in Figure 8.6.

	Special Libraries	State Libraries	Academic Libraries
1	Meetings (scheduled and unscheduled)	Meetings (scheduled and unscheduled)	Attempting too much and estimating time unrealistically
2	Telephone interruptions	Telephone interruptions	Cluttered desk and personal disorganization
3	Drop-in visitors	Attempting too much at once and estimating time unrealistically	Meetings (scheduled and unscheduled)
4	Inadequate, inaccurate, or delayed information	Lack of self-discipline	Lack of, or unclear, communications or instructions
5	Attempting too much at once and estimating time unrealistically	Drop-in visitors	Crises (personal and/or staff)
6	Crises (personal and/or staff)	Inadequate, inaccurate or delayed information	Drop-in visitors
7	Inability to say no	Crises (personal and/or staff)	Inadequate, inaccurate, or delayed information
8	Indecision and procrastination	Inability to say no	Telephone interruptions
9	Lack of self-discipline	Cluttered desk and personal disorganization	Ineffective delegation and involvement in routine and detail
10	Leaving tasks unfinished	Lack of, or unclear, communications or instructions	Lack of self-discipline

From studies by Helen M. Gothberg.

Figure 8.6   Library time-wasters

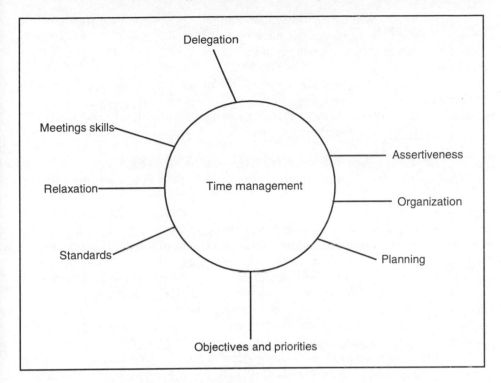

Figure 8.7   Dealing with time-wasters

Managing time is about dealing with these time-wasters and the literature is awash with hints and tips for the manager (as summarized in Figure 8.7). Most of the solutions shown are interconnected and therefore affect each other, so once you have started to manage time systematically using a particular tip many of the others are likely to come into play.

A consideration of objectives and priorities is the most appropriate place to start. 'We must make a conscious effort to use the time available to us to attain our professional and personal goals.'[32] It is therefore necessary to list (writing things down is an important element in time management) our personal, professional, and job objectives and the steps by which we hope to achieve them. Clearly job objectives should reflect the aims and priorities of the organization for which we work.

These objectives and priorities can only be tackled practically each day by systematic planning. A daily list of tasks to be completed is a strong recommendation in all time management literature. Seiwert[32] recommends LEADS:

List activities
Estimate time needed
Allow time for unscheduled tasks
Decide on priorities
Scan scheduled tasks at end of each day.

A successful day will be one in which the priority items have been tackled. Procrastination, the thief of time, must be conquered. Williams[34] recommends four aids to overcoming procrastination:

1   Divide and conquer – breaking down an unpleasant task into smaller tasks.
2   Public commitment to deadlines. 'Once others know that you intend to do a task by a particular time, you will find it much easier not to procrastinate.'
3   Put unpleasantness first by tackling unpleasant tasks first.
4   Congratulations – congratulate yourself each time you stop procrastinating on a task.

Organize your day so that you have periods of 'quiet time' to clear backlogs of important work. There are certain times when you are least likely to be disturbed – early morning, lunchtimes and later in the evenings. Many managers stay late and arrive early to clear their work and this will be a personal decision to make. At busier times ask secretarial staff to make appointments for non-urgent casual visitors and arrange return telephone calls later. At times it may be best to move to another room out of communication to finish important work. Librarians can work in a far corner of a library. When receiving visitors it is a good idea to stand up and remain standing if the visit is judged unimportant. Some people find it difficult to end conversations and need to learn ways of concluding meetings. Standing up, thanking visitors and stressing the next stage should give clues to most people. Managers should also try to keep their desks uncluttered by clearing work quickly and learning to read quickly. One useful tip is to reply to memos by writing on the memos themselves and returning them.

The section on assertiveness in this chapter should be read carefully because the ability to say no is an important factor in reducing work overload. Many people believe they could manage their own time quite well if only the boss would stop imposing upon them.

Delegation, discussed in Chapter 2, is a fundamental strategy in the saving of time. It is not 'allocating duties' or 'work scheduling'. It is about letting somebody else do something you would normally do. It demands giving away some of your authority to enforce action. It gives others freedom of action while you continue to 'carry the can'. It is risky and painful. It can seem unnatural to people who have succeeded so far by doing things well themselves. Delegating will free managers to concentrate on more important issues, but it involves informing, training and supporting subordinates. Remember this when deciding what to delegate, otherwise you could end up saying 'it would have been quicker to do it myself'.

Meetings are thought by many to be the greatest time-wasters, therefore read the section in this chapter on effective group meetings carefully.

Managers should find time to relax both at work and at home. Most people can only concentrate for limited periods and need short relaxation breaks. It is

An overview of the possible styles

1.9 Management Thoughtful attention to needs of staff for satisfying relations with others leads to a comfortable tempo and lack of conflict.		**9.9 Management** Work objectives are achieved through committed people; interdependence through a common stake in organizational goals. (Integration of tasks and human needs.)
	5.5 Management Adequate organizational performance is possible through balancing the necessity to get out work with the maintenance of morale at a satisfactory level.	
1.1 Management Exertion of minimum effort to get required work done is just sufficient to sustain membership of the organization. Conflict with people inevitable.		**9.1 Management** Efficiency in operations of planning, directing and controlling work results from arranging conditions in such a way that human elements interfere to a minimum degree.

HIGH 9 — CONCERN FOR PEOPLE (vertical axis)

LOW 0 — CONCERN FOR PRODUCTION — HIGH 9 (horizontal axis)

Your Selection	Managerial Style		Your Selection	Managerial Style
1	1.9		16	9.1
2	9.1		17	1.1
3	9.9		18	5.5
4	1.1		19	1.9
5	5.5		20	9.9
6	1.1		21	9.9
7	9.9		22	1.9
8	9.1		23	1.1
9	1.9		24	9.1
10	5.5		25	5.5
11	5.5		26	1.9
12	9.1		27	9.9
13	1.9		28	5.5
14	9.9		29	1.1
15	1.1		30	9.1

Table 8.2 Managerial styles

a good idea to do something you enjoy each day to compensate for those activities which you dislike.

Good time management will enable individuals and organizations to reach standards of excellence which are necessary if their aims and objectives are to be achieved.

Assessing one's personal leadership style, using the Blake/Mouton grid

Using the thirty statements on leadership given on pages 211–213, summarize your personal selection in Column II below by entering the numbers of statements 1–30 which you personally identify with. The related management style may be found in Table 8.2, coded in Blake/Mouton terms. For an interpretation of these refer to the Blake/Mouton grid, p.239.

I Element	II Your selection	III Managerial style
DECISIONS		
CONVICTIONS		
CONFLICT		
EMOTION		
HUMOUR		
EFFORT		

Postscript

It has often been difficult for librarians to accept that concepts, which management writers have identified, apply to them and their libraries. This is most apparent where the concept's level of abstraction is high. Theories of motivation or management styles described in the early chapters, for example, are likely to present such problems but the theories should not be dismissed out of hand. Librarians, in general, are unused to analysing the organizations in which they work in any systematic way and in the past have often assumed and accepted that they are unlikely themselves to effect changes in the wider organizations which employ them. As change is now taking place so rapidly, at least in the expectations individuals have of themselves as change agents, librarians have become more interested in organizational analysis though they may still regard themselves as being primarily concerned with the specific job they are undertaking – answering queries, selecting materials, providing services, etc.

Once interest is aroused a variety of reactions is likely from those reading this book for the first time. At the one extreme we have encountered those for whom management theory provides a new enlightenment, which they readily apply to all past and present experiences, almost too enthusiastically. At the other extreme there are those who find it completely irrelevant, and there are those who have had no management experience who initially learn it for examination purposes. Whether the latter later use the theory to understand what is happening to them or their organizations is not clear. Our belief is that the theory is often crude and difficult to apply without modification, but nonetheless it provides a necessary starting point for an understanding of what is happening in the organization.

We hope that the reader will have appreciated how the theory informs the various techniques described in the book, and how this can help to analyse situations and suggest solutions to problems in individual libraries. Some librarians may deny, for example, that they carry out staff appraisal, and may even state their opposition to it, whereas undoubtedly appraisal of some sort is being practised in their library. On the other hand many more librarians are now involved with appraisal systems, often imposed upon them. It would be pleasing to know that greater understanding of the theory and techniques of appraisal has led to improvements in the way it is practised.

Some librarians manage very well without being able to label or analyse what they are doing. They may never have read a management book in their lives but have worked mainly on instinct. Unfortunately instinct is not contagious, but once the underlying reasons for success achieved in an instinctive manner can be articulated they can be passed on to others. Most of what we have written has been derived from the work of people who have tried to apply management ideas to improve the management of libraries and other organizations. We have tried to pass on these ideas to librarians and students of librarianship so that each person does not have to start from scratch and depend simply on his or her instinct.

Others may say that most management is common sense and obvious. The trouble here is that common sense has to be recognized as such and it is those with common sense who are best able to do this for us. This tautology disguises the fact that common sense is generally arrived at through clear thinking and experience. The study of management ideas and their applications to a specific library is quite valuable in helping more people to the higher common sense. It is true that management writing can be circumlocutory and jargon-ridden. We hope that this book has avoided the worst of these faults and will not be used by our readers as an excuse to avoid thinking in management terms.

All librarians have views about what is important in library management and one common to chiefs is that it is the immediate political environment which has to be carefully nurtured if the library is to receive its fair share of resources. At the present time this is more important than ever. However, when this view is held to the exclusion of almost all others the criterion for library activities is whether they will please those who supply the resources. Such a view can stop desirable developments in personnel management. A widely held opinion is that it is not a good idea to reveal too much to influential persons outside the library who may misunderstand and misuse such information. It is therefore thought that the library is best served if flexibility of movement is retained by committing as little as possible to paper and communicating only what it is thought desirable to communicate. Aims and objectives, for example, would not be spelled out, job descriptions and personnel specifications would be vague or non-existent and appraisal would not be recorded. In these circumstances effective personnel management is difficult to achieve, since it is dependent on written records and upon wide communication. Our view is that the political environment has to be taken into account when making decisions but not to the exclusion of other important areas of the environment such as technological, educational and cultural aspects. It also should not be used to exclude professional judgements on the way in which community needs could best be met.

It is noticeable now that many of the management ideas and techniques introduced in the last two editions of this book are being widely practised. The reasons for this change are discussed in Chapter 1. It does mean, for example, that increasingly librarians will be required to write down the objectives for their activities and to justify them; slipshod job descriptions will be less acceptable, and formal staff appraisal will be widely practised. The task now is to carry out these activities with understanding and empathy. The management of staff should be an enjoyable activity for all concerned. It is appropriate that we ended the book with a discussion of staff training in interpersonal skills because the development of individuals able to work effectively with others lies at the heart of good personnel management and it is the means by which the library is able to progress and achieve its aims. Individuals and organizations are complex and an understanding of individuals in organizations is even more complex. The last thing we would want is for the various techniques to be used as blunt instruments imposed upon staff in libraries. Rather we would ask for sensitive personnel management which is flexible enough to recognize and take into account those nuances which make each library different, without jeopardizing the achievement of the objectives sought by each technique.

References

Chapter 1

1 *Borrowed time? The future of public libraries in the United Kingdom*, Bournes Green, Comedia, 1993.
2 Bob Usherwood, 'Public libraries: I have seen the future and...' *Public Library Journal*, **8**(6) November/December 1993, pp.167–172.
3 *Joint Funding Councils' Libraries Review Group: Report*, London, Higher Education Funding Council for England, Scottish Higher Education Funding Council, Higher Education Funding Council for Wales, Department of Education for Northern Ireland, 1993.
4 Liz Orna, 'Information policy issues and challenges for organisations', *Aslib Information*, **20**(3) March 1992, pp.107–110.
5 Alan Fowler, 'Performance management: the MBO of the 90s', *Personnel Management*, **22**(7) July 1990, pp.47–51.
6 UK Office for Library Networking, *Networks, libraries and information: priorities for the UK*, London, British Library Board, 1993.
7 *Joint Funding Councils' Libraries Review Group: Report, op. cit.*
8 UK Office for Library Networking, *op. cit.*
9 *Joint Funding Councils' Libraries Review Group: Report, op. cit.*
10 Sandra Ward, 'Libraries as network information providers', in *Networking and the future of libraries national conference 2–5 April 1992*, Synopses of papers, p.5.
11 Chris Batt, 'The cutting edge', *Public Library Journal*, **8**(4) July/August 1993, pp.112–114.
12 Peter Jordan, 'Intra-institutional relationships', *British Journal of Academic Librarianship*, **7**(2) 1993, pp.101–112.
13 Peter Garwood, 'The impact of the Educational Reform Act on school library service provision and use', *Public Library Journal*, **7**(1) January/February 1992, pp.13–16.

14   *Managing change for school library services: the final report of the Support for Learning Project*, London, British Library, 1992.
15   Peggy Heeks, 'Re-directing school library services', *Public Library Journal*, 7(5) September/October 1992, pp.119–121.
16   David Liddle, 'Back to the future', *Public Library Journal*, 8(6) November/December 1993, pp.177–179.
17   Linda Hopkins, 'The local government review: England, the first tranche', *Public Library Journal*, 8(5) September/October 1993, pp.129–133.
18   *Financing our public library services: four subjects for debate*, London, HMSO, 1988, Cmnd 324.
19   Maggie Ashcroft and Alex Wilson, *Maximising income generation in libraries: proceedings of a seminar held in Stamford, Lincolnshire on 20 February 1991*, Stamford, Capitol Planning Information Ltd, 1991.
20   *Sponsorship in libraries*, Volume 1 Report and survey, Volume 2 Training manual, London, Aslib, 1992.
21   Martina Flynn, 'Developing a commercial information service at the University of Limerick', *Aslib Information*, 20(2) February 1992, pp.68–69.
22   *Competing for quality*, London, HMSO, 1991, Cmnd 1730.
23   Fred Guy, 'Cataloguers face up to CCT threat', *Library Association Record*, 95(6) June 1993, p.366.
24   Karen Tyerman and Nicola Russell, 'Moulding a new generation', *Assistant Librarian*, 85(11) November 1992, pp.162–165.
25   *The quality gurus*, London, Department of Trade and Industry, 1991.
26   *Quality: people management matters*, London, Institute of Personnel Management.
27   Bob Norton and Debbie Ellis, 'Implementing BS 5750', *Aslib Information*, 21(6) June 1993, pp.242–245.
28   R. Collyer, 'BS 5750/ISO 9000', *Proceedings of the 4th International Total Quality Management Conference*, June 1991, pp.179–185.
29   Peter Brophy, Kate Coulling and Maxine Melling, 'Quality management: a university approach', *Aslib Information*, 21(6) June 1993, pp.246–248.
30   Michael Curtis and Others, 'Quality assurance in Kent', *Public Library Journal*, 8(1) January/February 1993, pp.1–4.
31   Frances Slack, 'The library and academic departments', unpublished research report produced for Manchester Metropolitan University Library, 1993.
32   *Joint Funding Councils' Library Review Group: Report, op. cit.*
33   Slack, *op. cit.*
34   Cabinet Office, *The citizen's charter*, London, HMSO, 1991.
35   Library Association, *A charter for public libraries*, London, Library Association, 1993.
36   Debby Raven, 'Library is venue for county charter', *Library Association Record*, 94(4) April 1992, p.225.
37   *Higher quality and choice: the charter for higher education*, London, Department for Education, 1993.

38   Annette Davies and Ian Kirkpatrick, 'To measure service: ask the library user', *Library Association Record*, **96**(2) February 1994, pp.88–89.

39   Peter Lucas, 'Customer consultation and its implications for service delivery', *Public Library Journal*, **8**(2) March/April 1993, pp.53–54.

40   Andrew Stevens, 'Getting to know our customers: the Berkshire user survey', *Library Association Record*, **93**(3) pp.128–132.

41   Tina Jones, 'On-line to customer care', *Aslib Information*, 19(2) February 1991, pp.50–51.

42   John Hinks, 'Customer care in libraries: taken as read', *Library Association Record*, **92**(2) February 1990, pp.109–114.

43   John Pluse, 'Customer focus: the salvation of service organisations', *Public Library Journal*, **6**(1) January/February 1991, pp.1–5.

44   Ian Winkworth, 'Into the house of mirrors: performance measurement in academic libraries', *British Journal of Academic Librarianship*, **8**(1) 1993, pp.17–34.

45   Catherine Cope, 'Performance indicator work in public libraries in the UK', *Public Library Journal*, **5**(4) July/August 1990, pp.95–98.

46   'Performance indicators set', *Library Association Record*, **95**(2) February 1993, p.66.

47   Erich Suter, *The employment law checklist*, London, Institute of Personnel Management, 4th edn, 1990.

48   Rosemary Raddon, *People and work: human and industrial relations in library and information work*, London, Library Association Publishing, 1991.

49   Jon Clark and Roy Lewis, 'Arbitration as an option for unfair dismissal claims', *Personnel Management*, June 1992, pp.36–39.

50   Advisory, Conciliation and Arbitration Services, *Disciplinary practice and procedures in employment*, London, HMSO, 1977.

51   Advisory, Conciliation and Arbitration Services, *ibid*.

52   T. Burns and G.M. Stalker, *The management of innovation*, London, Tavistock, 1961.

53   Olga Aikin, 'Why firms must show a lack of discrimination', *Personnel Management*, August 1992, pp.54–55.

54   Equal Opportunities Commission, *Code of practice: equal opportunity policies, procedures and practices in employment*, London, HMSO, 1985.

55   Institute of Personnel Management, Joint Standing Committee on Discrimination, *Towards fairer selection: a code for non-discrimination*, London, Institute of Personnel Management, 1978.

56   *The law at work*, London, Labour Research Department, 1992, p.26.

57   Olga Aikin. 'In support of motherhood', *Personnel Management*, September 1993, pp.63–64.

58   Ann E.M. Holmes and Richard W. Painter, *Employment law*, London, Blackstone Press, 2nd edn, 1991, p.197.

Chapter 2

1   L.H. Lofquist and R.V. Davis, *Adjustment to work*, New York, Appleton-Century-Crofts, 1969.
2   Dana C. Rooks, *Motivating to-day's library staff: a management guide*, Phoenix and New York, Oryx Press, 1988.
3   F.B. Gilbreth, *Primer of scientific management*, New York, Van Nostrand, 1912.
4   F.W. Taylor, 'The principles of scientific management', in Victor H. Vroom and Edward L. Deci (eds), *Management and motivation*, London, Penguin, 1970, pp.295–301.
5   W. Ashworth, *Organising multi-site libraries*, London, Library Association, 1976, p.1.
6   Norman Roberts, *Personnel in libraries and information units*, London, British Library, 1978, p.24 (British Library R & D Report 5449).
7   Industrial Society, *Introducing new technology into the office*, Leaflet PH/03, London, Industrial Society, 1985.
8   Sheila Ritchie, *Training and management development in librarianship*, Report to the British Library R & D Department, London, Ealing College of Higher Education, 1984, p.108.
9   Ritchie, *ibid.*, p.108.
10 Richard Barlow, *Team librarianship: the advent of public library team structures*, London, Clive Bingley, 1989, p.122.
11 Michael Rose, *Industrial behaviour: theoretical development since Taylor*, London, Penguin, 1981, p.120.
12 Abraham Maslow, *Motivation and personality*, New York, Harper & Row, 1970.
13 E.L. Trist, *Organizational choice*, London, Tavistock Institute of Human Relations, 1963.
14 Noragh Jones and Peter Jordan, 'One year later: a survey of students from the Leeds School of Librarianship', *Research in Librarianship*, **28**(5) January 1975, pp.113–123.
15 Norman Roberts, *op. cit.*
16 Norman Roberts, 'A profession in crisis', *Library Association Record*, **93**(7) July 1991, pp.450–453.
17 Rose, *op. cit.*, p.188.
18 Douglas McGregor, *The human side of enterprise*, New York, McGraw-Hill, 1960.
19 Rensis Likert, *New patterns of management*, New York, McGraw-Hill, 1961.
20 Linda Stewart, *What do UK librarians dislike about their jobs?* Loughborough, CLAIM, 1982.
21 Ritchie, *op. cit.*
22 Barlow, *op. cit.*, p.49.
23 Leicestershire County Libraries and Information Services, *The effective use of team time: a training package*, Leicestershire County Council Libraries and Information Services, 1977.

24　R.R. Blake and J.S. Mouton, *The managerial grid*, Houston, Texas, Gulf Publishing Company, 1964.

25　Blake and Mouton, *ibid.*, p.10.

26　K.M. Plate and E.W. Stone, 'Factors affecting librarians' job satisfaction', *Library Quarterly*, **44**(2) April 1974, pp.97–110.

27　Frederick Herzberg, 'How do you motivate employees?' in Dale S. Beach (ed.), *Managing people at work: readings in personnel*, New York, Macmillan, 1971, p.241.

28　George P. D'Elia, 'The determinants of job satisfaction among beginning librarians', *Library Quarterly*, **49**(3) July 1979, pp.283–302.

29　*Manual for the Minnesota Job Satisfaction Questionnaire*, Minnesota Studies in Vocational Rehabilitation, no.22, Minneapolis, University of Minnesota, 1967.

30　D'Elia, *op. cit.*

31　Norman Russell, 'The job satisfaction of non-professional library staff, unpublished CNAA M. Phil. thesis, Leeds Polytechnic, 1984.

32　Alan Bundy, 'Job satisfaction of subject librarians in British and Australian polytechnics', *Australian College Libraries*, **6**(1) March 1988, pp.24–28.

33　S. Burgess, 'Job satisfaction of reference librarians and cataloguers, *Australian Academic and Research Libraries*, **12** 1982, pp.73–80.

34　A.P.N. Thapisa, 'The motivation syndrome: job satisfaction through the pay nexus', *International Library Review*, **23** 1991, pp.141–158.

35　Julie Banks, 'Motivation and effective management of student assistants in academic libraries', *Journal of library Administration*, **14**(1) 1991, pp.133–154.

36　Thapisa, *op. cit.*, p.153.

37　Leo N. Miletich, 'Pulling together: a 21st century management primer for the befuddled, benumbed and bewildered', *Journal of Library Administration*, **14**(1) 1991, pp.35–49.

38　American Library Association, *Library education and manpower: a statement of policy*, Chicago, American Library Association, 1970.

39　Vietor M. Vroom, *Work and motivation*, New York, Wiley, 1964.

40　Fred Fiedler, *Theory of leadership effectiveness*, New York, McGraw-Hill, 1967.

41　Edgar M. Schein, *Organisational psychology*, Englewood Cliffs, NJ, Prentice Hall, 2nd edn, 1970, p.70.

42　Schein, *ibid.*

43　Plate and Stone, *op. cit.*

44　K.W. Howard, 'A comprehensive expectancy motivation model: implications for adult education and training', *Adult Education Quarterly*, 39(4) Summer 1989, pp.199–210.

45　Mary Crowder and Kate Pupynin, *The motivation to train: a review of the literature and the development of a comprehensive theoretical model of training motivation*, Minds at work, 1993.

46　A. Touraine, *Sociologie de l'action*, Paris, du Seuil, 1965.

47　B.G. Dutton, 'Staff management and staff participation', in Ross Shimmon (ed.), *A reader in library management*, London, Bingley, 1976, pp.132–133.

48   Dutton, *ibid.*, p.140.
49   Ashworth, *op. cit.*
50   Malcolm Tunley, *Library structures and staffing systems*, London, Library Association, 1979, p.25.
51   Ken Jones, *Conflict and change in library organizations*, London, Library Association, 1984, p.146.
52   Jones, *ibid.*, p.147.
53   Rooks, *op. cit.*, pp.14–16.
54   H. Roy Kaplan and Curt Tausky, 'Humanism in organizations: a critical appraisal', *Public Administration Review*, **37**(2) March/April 1977, pp.171–180.
55   Jones, *op. cit.*, p.91.
56   Stewart, *op. cit.*
57   Clare Nankivell, 'Class of '88', British Library Research and Development Department, unpublished.
58   Stewart, *op. cit.*, p.16.
59   Tania Konn and Norman Roberts, 'Academic librarians and continuing education', *Journal of Librarianship*, **16**(4) October 1984, p.267.
60   Richard Proctor, 'Fighting professional stagnation: staff development in practice', in John Hall (ed.) *Fighting professional stagnation*, Leeds, Leeds Polytechnic School of Librarianship, 1982, pp.53–73.
61   Proctor, *ibid.*, p.61.
62   Dutton, *op. cit.*
63   Ed Walley, 'Public library purpose', unpublished paper, Leeds Polytechnic School of Librarianship, c. 1980.
64   Carl Rogers, *On becoming a person*, London, Constable, 1961.
65   Geert Hofstede, *Culture's consequences: international differences in work-related values*, London, Sage, 1980.
66   Rooks, *op. cit.*, pp.4–16.
67   P. Grady Morein *et al.*, 'The Academic Library Development Program', *College and Research Libraries*, **31**(1) January 1977, pp.37–45.
68   W.J. Vaughan and J.D. Dunn, 'A study of job satisfaction in six university libraries', *College and Research Libraries*, **35**(3) May 1974, pp.163–177.
69   Stewart, *op. cit.*, p.15.
70   Konn and Roberts, *op. cit.*, p.273.
71   Angela Bowey, 'Perceptions and attitudes to change: a pilot study', *Personnel Review*, **9**(1) 1980, pp.35–42.
72   Library Association, *Equal opportunities in the library profession*, London, 1992.
73   Sheila Ritchie, 'Women in library management', in Anthony Vaughan (ed.), *Studies in library management*, Vol. 7, London, Bingley, 1982, pp.13–36.
74   Russell, *op. cit.*, p.102.
75   Library Association, *Free and equal access: the Library Association and equal opportunities*, London, October 1992.

Chapter 3

1 Library and Information Services Council (LISC), *Basic professional education for library and information work: a discussion paper*, London, Office of Arts and Libraries, 1984.

2 Library and Information Services Council (LISC), *Continuing professional education for library and information work: a discussion paper*, London, Office of Arts and Libraries, 1984.

3 Library and Information Services Council (LISC), *Training for library and information work: a discussion paper*, London, Office of Arts and Libraries, 1984.

4 Library and Information Services Council (LISC), *Library and information work in a changing environment*, London, HMSO, 1982.

5 Nick Moore, *The library and information workforce: its structure and nature*, London, Acumen, 1984.

6 Blaise Cronin, *The transition years: new initiatives in the education and training of professional information workers*, London, Aslib, 1983.

7 Janet Shuter, 'Let's hear it from the silent majority! – or what's wrong with library manpower planning apart from the word manpower', *Information and Library Manager*, 2 September 1985, pp.31–41.

8 Library Association, Futures Working Party, *Final Report*, London, 1985.

9 Library Association, Futures Working Party, *ibid.*, p.3.

10 Library and Information Services Council, *Basic professional education, op. cit.*, p.8.

11 Felicity Bray and Christopher Turner, *Monitoring the library and information workforce*, London, British Library Research and Development Department, 1991 (British Library Research Paper 97).

12 *Equal opportunities in the library profession*, Library Association, 1992 p.26.

13 *Ibid.*, p.vi.

14 Brenda White Associates, *Education and recruitment of junior professionals: a study in the library and information profession*, London, British Library Research and Development Department, 1989 (British Library Research Paper 63).

15 *Ibid.*, p.75.

16 Mike Freeman and G.L. Lee, *Perfect fit?: investigating the alleged mismatch between LIS schools' output and the needs of H E LIS sector as employers in England and Wales*, London, British Library Research and Development Department, 1993 (Report 6106).

17 Clare Nankivell, 'Class of '88', British Library Research and Development Department, unpublished.

18 Brenda White Associates, *op. cit.*, p.76.

19 Nankivell, *op. cit.*

20 Nankivell, *op. cit.*, p.42.

21 Mike Freeman, 'Education and training for librarianship and information services in the UK: a broad overview of some trends and issues', *New Library World*, **94**(1108) 1993, pp.12–14.

22   Edward Dudley *et al.*, *Curriculum change for the nineties*, Boston Spa, British Library Publications Section, 1983.

23   Clare Nankivell, *op. cit.*, p.18

24   Brenda White Associates. *op. cit.*, *p.81*.

25   Blaise Cronin, 'Post-industrial society: some manpower issues for the library/information profession', *Journal of Information Science*, **7** 1983, pp.1–14.

26   Donald Davinson and Norman Roberts, 'Curricula in SLIS', unpublished report to the British Research and Development Department, 1984.

27   Donald Davinson and Norman Roberts, 'The overlooked factor: the resource issue', *Education for Information*, **3** 1985, pp.29–37.

28   Donald Davinson and Norman Roberts, 'Developments in information education and their implications for SLIS in the UK', *Journal of Documentation*, **42**(1) March 1986, pp.1–10.

29   Davinson and Roberts (1986), *ibid.*, p.8.

30   Andrew Mayo, 'Linking manpower planning and management development', *Industrial and Commercial Training*, **22**(3) 1990.

31   Herbert Schur, *The education and training of information specialists in the 1970s*, Sheffield, University of Sheffield Postgraduate School of Librarianship and Information Science, 1972, p.96.

32   David Bell, 'Why manpower planning is back in vogue', *Personnel Management*, **21** July 1989, pp.40–43.

33   Mary Auckland, 'Surviving the skills shortage: is there a problem?' *Information and Library Manager*, **9**(2) 1990, pp.4–7.

34   Patricia A. Kreitz, 'Recruitment and retention in your own backyard', *College and Research Library News*, **53**(4) April 1992, pp.237–240.

35   Beryl Morris, 'Surviving the skills shortage: exploring the options', *Information and Library Manager*, **9**(2) 1990, pp.11–22.

36   Julie Bobay, 'Job-sharing: a survey of the literature and a plan for academic libraries', *Journal of Library Administration*, **9**(2) 1988, pp.59–69.

37   Morris, *op. cit.*

38   LAMSAC, *The staffing of public libraries: a report of the research undertaken by the Local Authorities Management Services and Computer Committee for the Department of Education and Science*, London, HMSO, 1976, 3 vols.

39   Library Association, Colleges of Further and Higher Education Group, *Guidelines for College and Polytechnic Libraries*, London, 4th edn., 1991.

40   Sylvia Webb, *Creating an information service*, London, Aslib, 2nd edn. 1988, pp.91–92.

41   D.V. Arnold, *The management of the information department*, London, Deutsch, 1976, p.90.

42   Margaret Slater, *Ratio of staff to users in special libraries*, London, Aslib, 1981.

43   Bray and Turner, *op. cit.*, p.21.

44   Nankivell, *op. cit.*, p.34

45   Slater, *ibid.*, p.112.

Chapter 4

1   Philip Plumbley, *Recruitment and selection*, London, Institute of Personnel Management, 5th edn, 1991, p.11.
2   B.G. Dutton, 'Staff management and staff participation', in Ross Shimmon (ed.) *A reader in library management*, London, Bingley, 1976, pp.129–145.
3   Don Mason, *Information management*, London, Peter Perigrinus, 1978, ch. 6.
4   L. Rothenberg, 'A job-task index for evaluating professional staff utilization in libraries', *Library Quarterly*, **41** October 1971, pp.320–328.
5   Mason, *op. cit.*
6   From notes supplied by Newport Public Libraries.
7   Plumbley, *op. cit.*, p.7.
8   Alec Rodger, *The seven-point plan*, London, National Institute of Industrial Psychology, 3rd edn, 1970.
9   John Munro Fraser, *Employment interviewing*, London, Macdonald and Evans, 5th edn, 1978.
10 R. Sergean, J.R. McKay and C.M. Corkill, *The Sheffield Manpower project: a survey of staffing requirements for librarianship and information work*, Sheffield, University of Sheffield Postgraduate School of Librarianship and Information Science, 1976.
11 Clare Nankivell, 'Class of '88', British Library Research and Development Department, unpublished.
12 Robert Spicer, *How to know your rights at work*. Plymouth, How To Books, 1991, p.92.
13 Noragh Jones, *Continuing education for librarians*, Leeds, Leeds Polytechnic School of Librarianship, 1977.
14 Rodgers, *op. cit.*, p.13.

Chapter 5

1   Peter John Jordan, 'Succession at senior management level in libraries', M. Phil. thesis, 1986, University of Bradford.
2   G. Raymond Gould, 'Finding the right candidate Part 2', *Records Management Journal*, **2**(1) Summer 1990, pp.61–67.
3   Susan Hill and Alison Jago, 'Recruitment and selection of staff', in Ann Lawes (ed.) *Management skills for the information manager*, Aldershot, Ashgate, 1993.
4   Greg Fish, 'Staff recruitment and education', *The Australian Accountant*, **55**(7) August 1985, pp.45–46.
5   Helen Osborn, Borough Librarian of Newport, has provided some interesting notes on research she has carried out and we have used some of her findings.
6   Equal Opportunities Commission, *Fair and efficient selection: guidance on equal opportunities policies in recruitment and selection procedures*, Manchester, 1986.

7   Marie Strebler, *Biodata in selection: issues in practice*, Brighton, Institute of Manpower Studies, 1991.

8   James Walker, Clive Fletcher and Leith Taylor, 'Performance appraisal: an open or shut case?' *Personnel Review,* **6**(1) Winter 1977, pp.38–42.

9   Gould, *op. cit.*

10   Peter John Jordan, 'Staff selection in public libraries', *Library Management News*, 9 August 1979, pp.27–32.

11   Stephen Bevan, 'Staff selection: art or science?' *The Accountant's Magazine*, **93** June 1989, pp.33, 34.

12   Raymond L. Gorden, *Interviewing: strategy, techniques, and tactics*, Homewood, Illinois, Dorsey Press, 1969.

13   T.M. Higham, 'Choosing the method of recruitment', in Bernard Ungerson (ed.), *Recruitment handbook, op. cit.*, p.37.

14   Hill and Jago, *op. cit.*

15   Richard A. Fear, *The evaluation interview*, New York, McGraw-Hill, 4th edn, 1984.

16   Equal Opportunities Commission, *op. cit.*, p.28.

17   *Ibid.*

18   Nottinghamshire County Council, Leisure Services, *Personnel procedures handbook*, Nottingham, 1992.

19   Fear, *ibid.*

20   John Munro Fraser, *Introduction to personnel management*, London, Nelson, 1971.

21   Roger Stoakley, 'The selection and appointment of professional staff', *Public Library Journal*, **5**(5) September/October 1990, pp.115–117.

22   Ungerson (ed.), *Recruitment handbook, op. cit.*

23   Clive Fletcher, 'Psychological testing', *Personnel Management*, 21 December 1989 (Factsheet 24).

24   *Ibid.*

25   British Psychological Society, *Psychological testing: guidance for the user*, Leicester, 1989.

26   Equal Opportunities Commission. *Avoiding sex bias in selection testing*, Manchester, Equal Opportunities Commission, 1988.

27   Jordan, *op. cit.*

28   Viv Shackleton and Sue Newell, 'Management selection: a comparative survey of methods used in top British and French companies', *Journal of Occupational Psychology*, **64**(99), pp.23–36.

29   Stoakley, *op. cit.*

30   Mike Smith and Ivan T. Robertson, *The theory and practice of systematic staff selection*, London, Macmillan, 1986.

31   Clyde Kluckhohn and Henry Murray, *Personality in nature, society and culture*, New York, Knopf, 2nd edn, 1953.

32   Smith and Robertson, *op. cit.*

33   Paul Kline, 'Personality threats', *New Society*, **24**(552) 3 May 1973, pp.241–242.

34   *Ibid.*

35 Stephanie Jones. *Psychological testing for managers*, London, Piatkus, 1993.

Chapter 6

1 Gerry Randell, Peter Packard and John Slater, *Staff appraisal: a first step to effective leadership*, London, Institute of Personnel Management, 3rd edn, 1984.

2 David Peele, 'Some aspects of staff evaluation in the UK and the USA', *Library Association Record*, **74**(4) April 1972, pp.69–71.

3 Christopher Pollitt, 'Models of staff appraisal: some political implications', *Higher Education Review*, **20**(2) Spring 1988, pp.7–16.

4 Committee of Vice-Chancellors and Principals, *Report of the steering committee for efficiency studies in universities*, London, 1985.

5 Committee of Vice-Chancellors and Principals, *Twenty-Third Report of Committee A*, London, 1987.

6 Don Revill (ed.), *Working papers on staff development and appraisal*, Brighton, Council of Polytechnic Librarians, 1992.

7 Judith Stewart, 'Performance management, staff appraisal', notes supplied with lecture given at Manchester Metropolitan University, April 1993.

8 Paul Helm, 'Bringing in staff appraisal: the experience of one university', *Higher Education Management*, **1**(2) July 1989, p.193.

9 Graham Luccock, 'Public Library Training 11', in Ray Prytherch (ed.), *Staff training in libraries*, Aldershot, Gower, 1986, pp.27–40.

10 Judith Stewart, 'Library staff reactions to staff appraisal', *Copol Newsletter*, 57 January 1992, pp.36–39.

11 S.C. Ruffley, 'Staff appraisal, its introduction and role in an academic library', M.A. thesis, 1991, Manchester Polytechnic.

12 Christopher Pollitt, *op. cit.*

13 Gus Pennington and Mike O'Neill, 'Appraisal in higher education: mapping the terrain', *Programmed Learning and Educational Technology*, **25**(2) May 1988, p.165.

14 S.C. Ruffley, *op. cit.*

15 Judith Stewart, *op. cit*, p.37.

16 Clive Fletcher, 'Management/subordinate communications and leadership style: a field study of their relationships to perceived outcome of appraisal interviews', *Personnel Review* **7**(1) Winter 1978, pp.59–62.

17 Judith Stewart, *op. cit.*, p.37.

18 Anthony M. Angiletta, 'On performance consultation with bibliographers: a non-rational and non-Machiavellian perspective', *Acquisitions Librarian*, (6) 1991, pp.123–130.

19 Kenneth J. Pratt, *Effective staff appraisal*, Wokingham, Van Nostrand Reinhold, 1985, p.32.

20 Gerry Randell, Peter Packard and John Slater, *op. cit.*

21 *Camden Newsletter*, **58** August/September 1976, p.1.

22   Peter John Jordan, 'Succession at senior management level in libraries', M.Phil. thesis, 1986, University of Bradford.
23   Jane C. Farmer, 'Performance related pay for librarians: an overview', *Personnel Training and Education*, **9**(2) 1992, pp.53–57.
24   Robert Hilton, 'Performance evaluation of library personnel', *Special Libraries*, **69**(11) November 1978, pp.429–434.
25   H. Rebecca Kroll, 'Beyond evaluation: performance appraisal as a planning and motivational tool in libraries', *Journal of Academic Librarianship*, **9**(1) March 1985, pp.21–32.
26   Anne M. Turner. 'Why *do* department heads take longer coffee breaks? A public library evaluates itself', *American Libraries*, **9**(4) April 1978, pp.213–215.
27   'Action exchange', *American Libraries*, **8**(8) September 1977, p.42.
28   Roland Person, 'Library faculty evaluation: an idea whose time continues to come', *Journal of Academic Librarianship*, **15**(3) July 1979, pp.142–147.
29   Jess A. Martin, 'Staff evaluation of supervisors', *Special Libraries*, **70**(1) January 1979, pp.26–29.
30   'Action exchange', *op. cit.*
31   David Peele, *op. cit.*
32   S.C. Ruffley, *op. cit.*
33   American Library Association, Subcommittee on personnel organization and procedure of the ALA board on personnel administration, *Personnel organization and procedure: a manual suggested for use in public libraries*, Chicago, 1952.
34   David Peele, *op. cit.*
35   Don Revill (ed.), *op. cit.*
36   Stewart Hannabuss, 'Analysing appraisal interviews', *Scottish Libraries*, (30) November/December 1991, pp.13–15.

Chapter 7

1   Carol S. Jacobs, 'The use of the exit interview as a personnel tool and its applicability to libraries', *Journal of Library Administration*, **14**(4) 1991, pp.69–86.
2   T.H. Boydell, *A guide to the identification of training needs*, London, British Association for Commercial and Industrial Education, 1973.
3   Leicestershire Libraries and Information Services, *The effective use of team time*, Leicester, 1977.
4   Library Association, *Training in libraries*, London, 1977.
5   Library Association, *Routes to Associateship: regulations and notes of guidance*, London, 1991.
6   Library Association, *op. cit.*
7   Ronald J. Edwards, *In-service training in British libraries: its development and present practice*, London, Library Association, 1976.

8   Local Government Training Board, *Training and development of training officers*. London, 1974.

9   Edwards, *op. cit.*, p.149.

10 Peter Smith, *The design of learning spaces*, London, Council for Educational Technology for the United Kingdom, 1974.

11 P. Robertson, 'Systematic induction', in Library Association, *Guidelines for training in libraries*, London, 1980, p.A2.

12 Peter John Jordan, 'Succession at senior management level in libraries', M. Phil. thesis, 1986, University of Bradford.

13 Ray Prytherch (ed.), *Handbook of library training practice*, Aldershot, Gower, 1986.

14 Library Association, *Survey of training materials*, London, 1988.

15 A. Macdougall and Ray Prytherch (eds), *Cooperative training in libraries*, Aldershot, Gower, 1989.

16 Prytherch, *op. cit.*

17 Bruce Shuman, *The River Bend casebook*, Phoenix, Oryx Press, 1981.

18 Roy Hewitt, *Library management case studies*, London, Crosby Lockwood, 1969.

19 Gordon Wills and Christine Oldman (eds), *Developing the librarian as a manager*, Bradford, MCB Books, 1975.

20 Noragh Jones and Peter Jordan, *Case studies in library management*, London, Clive Bingley, 1988.

21 *Can we please have that the right way round?* London, Video Arts, 1977, VHS videocassette.

22 Noragh Jones, 'The use of simulation in the teaching of library management', Ph.D. thesis, 1985, University of Bradford.

23 Jones and Jordan, *op. cit.*

24 Martha Jane Zachert, *Simulation teaching of library administration*, New York, Bowker, 1975.

25 L.C. Guy *et al.*, *The Bishopsbury simulation*, London, Ealing College of Higher Education, 1981.

26 Jones, *op. cit.*

27 Zachert, *op. cit.*

28 Mary Anne Neilson and Margot Bremner, 'CAL in Australian National University Library', *Infuse*, **9**(2) April 1985, pp.12–14.

29 Patricia Baird and Lizzie Davenport, 'Hypertext: has it come out of the research closet?' *Aslib Information*, **19**(10) October 1991, pp.342–343.

30 Ian Hunter, 'The Hypertour Tourist Information System: an application of Hypercard', *Aslib Information*, **19**(10) October 1991, pp.350–352.

31 Elizabeth Duncan, 'Hypermedia–a business update', *Aslib Information*, **19**(10) October 1991, pp.348–349.

32 Duncan, *op. cit.*

33 Information and Library Services Lead Body, *Information and library services draft standards*, London, 1993.

34 Michael G. Williamson, 'The evaluation of training' in Ray Prytherch (ed.) *Handbook of library training practice*, pp.226–262.

35   David C. Weber, 'The dynamics of the library environment for professional staff growth', *College and Research Libraries*, **35**(4) July 1974, pp.259–267.

36   Robert James, 'Training and management of automation', *Training and Education*, **4**(3) 1987, pp.3–7.

37   J.J. Groark, 'Staff development for academic librarians: the art of the possible', *Bookmark*, **38**(3) Spring 1979, pp.143–147.

38   Noragh Jones, 'Continuing education for librarians', *Journal of Librarianship*, **10**(1) January 1978, pp.39–55.

39   Duncan Smith and Robert Burgin, 'The motivations of professional and paraprofessional librarians for participating in continuing education programs', *Library and Information Science Research*, **13**(4) 1991, pp.405–429.

40   Elizabeth W. Stone, *Factors related to the professional development of librarians*, Metuchen, Scarecrow Press, 1969.

41   James G. Neal, 'Continuing education: attitudes and experiences of the academic librarian', *College and Research Libraries*, **41**(2) 1980, pp.128–133.

42   Smith and Burgin, *op. cit.*, p.409.

43   Library Association, *The framework for continuing professional development*, London, 1992.

44   Peter E. September, 'Career planning as a personnel function: its importance in academic libraries', *Journal of Library Administration*, **14**(4) 1991, pp.51–68.

45   Jones, *op. cit.*

46   John Mortimer, 'Measuring up to the mark', *The Engineer*, **276**(7145/6) 22 April 1993, p.34.

47   Christopher J. Hunt, 'Library staff development consultancy: a means to achieve a better library', *Personnel Training and Education*, **8**(1) 1991, pp.3–7.

Chapter 8

1   R. Sergean, J.R. Mckay and C.M. Corkill, *The Sheffield Manpower Project: a survey of staffing requirements in librarianship and information work*, Sheffield, University of Sheffield Postgraduate School of Librarianship and Information Science, 1976.

2   Norman Russell, 'Library supervisors could do better!', *Library Work*, (3) January 1989, pp.6–9.

3   Edward Dudley *et al.*, *Curriculum change for the nineties*, Boston Spa, British Library Publications Section, 1983.

4   Tania Konn and Norman Roberts, 'Academic librarians and continuing education', *Journal of Librarianship*, **16**(4) October 1984, pp.262–280.

5   Noragh Jones, 'On-the-job training: the trainees' view', *Training and Education*, **3**(1) 1986, pp.12–19.

6   Russell, *op. cit.*, p.9.

7   Philippa Levy and Bob Usherwood, *People skills: interpersonal skills train-ing for library and information work*, London, British Library, 1992 (Library and Information Research Report 88).

8   See, for example, Valerie Stewart and Andrew Stewart, *Managing the poor performer*, Aldershot, Gower, 1982.

9   R.E. Stevens (ed.), *Supervision of employees in libraries*, Illinois, University of Illinois Graduate School of Library Science, 1978.

10 R. DeBoard, *Counselling people at work*, Aldershot, Gower, 1982.

11 Charles J. Margerison, 'Interpersonal skills – some new approaches', *Jour-nal of European Industrial Training*, **12**(6) 1988, pp.12–16.

12 Margerison, *ibid.*, p.16.

13 Based on a handout prepared by Helen Dyson and used on continuing education courses organized by The Library Association.

14 Marie L. Thorne and Rennie Fritchie, *Interpersonal skills for women manag-ers*, Bristol Polytechnic/Manpower Services Commission, 1985.

15 Leeds University Counselling and Career Development Unit, 'Personality style inventory', duplicated handout, c.1985.

16 Neal Rackham and Tony Morgan, *Behaviour analysis in training*, New York, McGraw-Hill, 1977.

17 Leslie Rae, 'Interpersonal skills training eight years on', *Industrial and Commercial Training*, **16**(1) January/February 1984, pp.6–9.

18 B.W. Tuckman, 'Developmental sequence in small groups', *Psychological Bulletin*, **63** 1965, pp.384–399.

19 Thorne and Fritchie, *op. cit.*, p.21.

20 Levy and Usherwood, *op. cit.*

21 Janette S. Caputo, *The assertive librarian*, Phoenix, Oryx Press, 1984.

22 Dave Barker, *TA and training: the theory and use of transactional analysis in organizations*, Farnborough, Gower, 1980.

23 J.E. Hodges, 'Stress in the library', *Library Association Record*, **92**(10) Octo-ber 1990, p.751.

24 C. Bunge, 'Stress in the library', *Library Journal*, **112**(15) 15 September 1987, pp.47–51.

25 Terry Looker and Olga Gregson, *Stresswise: a practical guide for dealing with stress*, Hodder and Stoughton, 1989.

26 Jacky Evans, 'Manchester Polytechnic Library: a report discussing the management and control of stress within the organisation and its people', December 1991, B.A. Information and Library Management project at Manchester Polytechnic.

27 Bunge, *op. cit.*

28 Looker and Gregson, *op. cit.*

29 Helen M. Gothberg, 'Time management in academic libraries', *College and Research Libraries*, **49**(2) March 1988, pp.131–140.

30 Helen M. Gothberg. 'Time management in special libraries', *Special Librar-ies*, Spring 1991, pp.119–130.

31 Helen M. Gothberg. 'Time management in state libraries', *Special Libraries*, Fall 1991, pp.257–266.

32   Lothar J. Seiwert, *Managing your time*, London, Kogan Page, 1989, p.10.
33   Seiwert, *ibid.*, p.28.
34   Graham L. Williams, *Getting results with time management*, Sheffield, Library and Learning Resources Sheffield City Polytechnic, 1988.

Index

Assessment and Development Centres

Iain Ballantyne and Nigel Povah

The dramatic growth of assessment and development centres as a people development method in recent years has generated an increased demand for guidance on how to design and run them. This new book, by two of the UK's leading specialists in the field, will go a long way towards meeting that need.

It looks at the entire process, from the underlying concepts to the most effective methods of validation – not forgetting the organizational politics involved. The main objectives of the book are

- to establish a thorough understanding of the principles and practice of assessment centres
- to provide sufficient knowledge to enable practitioners to run some events for themselves
- to help readers to recognize where they may need to call on outside expertise
- to equip readers to ask pertinent questions of any prospective advisers.

Assessment and Development Centres represents a practical approach which is sure of a warm welcome from HR professionals.

Contents

1995   200 pages   0 566 07484 2

Gower

Coaching and Mentoring

Nigel MacLennan

The coaching/mentoring approach is probably the most effective way of helping others to achieve optimum performance in the workplace. Dr MacLennan's latest book covers the entire subject from basic skills to designing and implementing a tailor-made coaching and mentoring system. He starts by explaining the nature of achievement and the factors that determine it, and then introduces a seven-stage model that will enable managers and supervisors to encourage their people to develop their skills. He examines the problems commonly encountered and shows how to overcome them or, in some cases, turn them to positive account.

The book is interactive throughout, using cartoons, humour, self-assessment questions, case studies and illustrations to reinforce the text. A particularly valuable feature is a set of checklists that together summarize the key elements involved.

Coaching and Mentoring is, quite simply, a comprehensive manual of the best methods known today of helping people to succeed.

Contents

Preface • Understanding achievement • An introduction • The requirements •The key skills • Advanced development skills • Advanced assessment and analysis skills • Teams and organizations • For people problems • Identifying and overcoming barriers to achievement • The barriers to • Coaching and mentoring systems • The final issues •Coaching and mentoring for the most common skills • Personal skills • Management skills • Functional skills • Holistic skills • Appendix • References and Bibliography • Index.

1995   320 pages   0 566 07562 8

Gower

Copyright Theft

John Gurnsey

Copyright was developed to protect the printed word. In the late twentieth century can it and does it realistically serve to protect authors of audio, video and electronic products that are the vehicles of information supply in our multi-media age?

Systematic copyright theft forms part of a multi-billion dollar international industry, which is able to thrive partly because it is easy to overlook what is known to be theft when the original material remains intact. But what was a 'cottage industry' 30 years ago has now become much more sophisticated, so that pirate books printed in Taiwan flood the markets of West Africa, and audio tapes printed in the Far East appear in Saudi Arabia, Australasia and even Europe. The threat to publishers is alarming, and increasing. The burgeoning of the electronic information industry today makes copyright theft an urgent issue.

John Gurnsey has reviewed all forms of copyright theft, from commercial to domestic, gathering the experiences of a wide range of organizations across book and electronic publishing. Book, electronic, database, audio, video, games and multimedia publishing are all considered along with the question of whether existing laws can effectively serve such a rapidly changing industry.

Copyright law is an extremely complex area: this book is about the abuse of it, rather than the law itself. In helping publishing companies understand more about copyright theft, it might help them to avoid it in at least some of its forms.

1995   208 pages   0 566 07631 4

Gower

Current Awareness, Current Techniques

Feona Hamilton

Anyone running, or involved in providing, a library and information service needs to keep users of that service up to date with developments in their special areas of interest. A current awareness service will do just this, with the added bonus of providing useful publicity for the library or information department at the same time.

This book shows how to set up a current awareness service step by step – where to find the sources, how to interview potential recipients, how to analyse interview results, and how to disseminate the resulting information. A section of case studies giving examples of current awareness service provision in different sectors, and a directory of sources for current awareness are also included.

This is a guidebook for librarians and information managers wishing to provide an excellent CAS which will satisfy the needs of its recipients, and lead to an enhanced reputation for the providers.

Contents

1995   200 pages   0 566 07626 8

Gower

Essential Health and Safety for Managers
A Guide to Good Practice in the European Union

Ron Akass

Managers are employed for their professional expertise, which may not include familiarity with workplace health and safety. Nevertheless, the avalanche of health and safety regulations introduced as a consequence of the Single Market is exposing managers to a real risk of contravening them, which can have serious personal consequences.

This book, written for all managers of people, shows how health and safety can become intuitive, an everyday part of the workplace routine that is an integral part of the job, and not an appendage to it.

- Part One covers the fundamentals of health and safety, including the Health and Safety at Work Act 1974 (HASAWA) which remains the UK's primary health and safety legislation, notwithstanding the EC-driven regulations.
- Part Two describes legislation made under HASAWA before 1993 which is applicable to most businesses. In this part there are chapters dealing with key health and safety matters – fire, accident reporting and COSHH – as well as a composite chapter covering a number of regulations, which are simply explained.
- Part Three deals with the six sets of regulations enacted under the aegis of HASAWA to give effect to EC Directives. These regulations already apply although there are transition periods in which to achieve full compliance for three of the six. Each regulation is covered in detail in a separate chapter.

At the end of each chapter, 'Management action checklists' contain questions which enable the reader to review the principal requirements of the regulations or subject covered.

1994   284 pages   0 566 07332 3

Gower

A Handbook for Training Strategy

Martyn Sloman

The traditional approach to training in the organization is no longer effective. That is the central theme of Martyn Sloman's challenging book. A new model is required that will reflect the complexity of organizational life, changes in the HR function and the need to involve line management. This Handbook introduces such a model and describes the practical implications not only for human resource professionals and training managers but also for line managers.

Martyn Sloman writes as an experienced training manager and his book is concerned above all with implementation. Thus his text is supported by numerous questionnaires, survey instruments and specimen documents. It also contains the findings of an illuminating survey of best training practice carried out among UK National Training Award winners.

The book is destined to make a significant impact on the current debate about how to improve organizational performance. With its thought-provoking argument and practical guidance it will be welcomed by everyone with an interest in the business of training and development.

Contents

Introduction • Part I: A New Role for Training • Introduction to Part I • The context • Models for training • Appendix to Part I: A survey of best training practice • Part II: The New Processes • Introduction to Part II • Training and the organization • Training and the individual • Performance appraisal • Design and delivery • Effective information systems • Part III: Managing the Training Function • Introduction to Part III • The role of the training function • The task of the trainer • Appendices: The UK training environment • National trends • Government policy • Competency-based qualifications • Index.

1994   240 pages   0 566 07393 5

Gower

Harrod's Librarians' Glossary
9,000 terms used in information management, library science, publishing, the book trades and archive management
Eighth Edition

Compiled by Ray Prytherch

This is the latest edition of a standard reference source, first published in 1938. The new subtitle reflects the changing emphases of the information world: technological developments and electronic formats have so altered the range of skills required by information professionals that some fundamental changes had become necessary.

The Glossary explains and defines terms and concepts, identifies techniques and organizations, and summarizes the activities of associations, major libraries, Governmental and other bodies in the broad field of information management – library and information science, authorship, publishing, archive management, printing, binding, conservation, and the book trade.

Harrod's is international in coverage, and is unique in depth and currency, and in the convenience of the single-volume format. The new volume contains revised entries for over 600 organizations, over 1,400 other new entries, and about 50,000 words of new text.

For the first time, an International Advisory Board was formed to improve specialist coverage in areas such as records management, conservation and preservation, networking and computer terminology, and to provide greater depth to the international perspective; the Board includes participants from the United States, Australia and Japan.

Addresses are now given for most associations and institutions, consortia, cooperatives, networks and major libraries; another new feature is the inclusion of references to recent books and articles.

1995   720 pages   0 566 07533 4

Gower

A New Manual of Classification

Rita Marcella and Robert Newton

This new manual builds upon the work of its predecessor *Sayer's Manual of Classification for Librarians 5th Edition*. In the tradition of *Sayer's* it provides a clear and comprehensible overview of classification theory, policy and practice, and a description of the major general classification schemes. Much valuable material has been drawn from the earlier editions whilst rigorously updating throughout to ensure that overall coverage is as current as possible. Particularly valuable are discussions on the use of classification in a variety of environments, and the impact of new technology on classification.

Now that classification is taught and studied in very different ways and levels in library and information schools, a book which surveys, summarises and comments on the enormous body of work that exists on classification, will be useful to lecturers, students and professional librarians alike.

Contents

Preface • Part One: Principles and Systems • Rationale: why classification? • The theory of classification • General classification systems • Special classification schemes and alternatives • Indexes, thesauri and classification • Part Two: The Management and Application of Classification • The functions of classification in the library • Classification policy and administration • Part Three: Information Technology and Classification • An introduction to classification and the computer • Classification and the OPAC • Automatic classification • Further reading • Index.

1994   304 pages   0 566 07547 4

Gower

The Practice of Empowerment
Making the Most of Human Competence

Dennis C Kinlaw

Organizations are downsizing, re-engineering and restructuring at an ever-increasing rate. The challenge now is to find better and better ways of harnessing the mental resources of the people who remain.

Dr Kinlaw, one of America's leading authorities on management development, sees empowerment as a way of improving organizational performance by making the most competent people the most influential most of the time, and his book provides a comprehensive and detailed model for achieving this objective. Drawing on examples and case studies from successful companies, Dr Kinlaw describes a practical, step-by-step process for introducing or extending empowerment in an organization or any part of an organization, and shows how to use feedback, team development and learning to good effect.

For managers considering, or involved in, empowerment programmes, and for concerned HR and training professionals, this new book represents an important resource for improving organizational performance.

Contents

1995   208 pages   0 566 07570 9

Gower

Records Management Handbook
Second Edition

Ira A Penn, Gail B Pennix and Jim Coulson

Records Management Handbook is a complete guide to the practice of records and information management. Written from a multi-media perspective and with a comprehensive systems design orientation, the authors present proven management strategies for developing, implementing and operating a "21st century" records management programme. Where most available titles are biased toward dealing with inactive records, this book gives a balanced treatment for all phases of the record's life cycle, from creation or receipt through to ultimate disposition.

The *Records Management Handbook* is a practical reference for use by records managers, analysts, and other information management professionals, which will aid decision-making, improve job performance, stimulate ideas, help avoid legal problems, minimize risk and error, save time and reduce expense.

Special features of the second edition include:
- new chapters on record media, active records systems and records disposition
- new information on management strategies and programme implementation
- revised guidance and material on records appraisal and record inventorying
- expanded and increased information on retention scheduling, records storage and electronic forms.

1994   320 pages   0 566 07510 5

Gower

Structured Employment Interviewing

Paul J Taylor and Michael P O'Driscoll

Research shows that structured interviews are markedly superior to the traditional approach found in so many organizations. They produce selection and promotion decisions that are fairer and more consistent, and as a predictor of future job performance they have much greater validity.

This book describes and illustrates the two main approaches to structured interviewing: the behaviour description interview and the situational interview. It explains

- how to plan the interview
- how to develop suitable questions
- how to conduct the interview
- how to evaluate candidates

The text is supported by specimen forms, job analyses and interview questions. Also included are complete structured interview guides covering three different jobs.

For personnel professionals – and indeed all managers anxious to improve the quality of decision-making in this key area – *Structured Employment Interviewing* represents an invaluable resource.

Contents

Preface • The traditional interview approach • The structured interview approach • Preparing for the behavioural description interview • Conducting the behavioural description interview • The situational interview • Implementing a structured interview approach • Appendices • Glossary of Terms • Bibliography • Index.

1995   160 pages   0 566 07589 X

Gower